The Forerunner of All Things

The Forerunner of All Things

Buddhaghosa on Mind, Intention, and Agency

MARIA HEIM

OXFORD
UNIVERSITY PRESS

OXFORD
UNIVERSITY PRESS

Oxford University Press is a department of the University of Oxford.
It furthers the University's objective of excellence in research, scholarship,
and education by publishing worldwide.

Oxford New York
Auckland Cape Town Dar es Salaam Hong Kong Karachi
Kuala Lumpur Madrid Melbourne Mexico City Nairobi
New Delhi Shanghai Taipei Toronto

With offices in
Argentina Austria Brazil Chile Czech Republic France Greece
Guatemala Hungary Italy Japan Poland Portugal Singapore
South Korea Switzerland Thailand Turkey Ukraine Vietnam

Oxford is a registered trademark of Oxford University Press
in the UK and certain other countries.

Published in the United States of America by
Oxford University Press
198 Madison Avenue, New York, NY 10016

Library of Congress Cataloging-in-Publication Data
Heim, Maria, 1969–
The forerunner of all things : Buddhaghosa on mind, intention, and agency / Maria Heim.
pages cm
Includes bibliographical references and index.
ISBN 978–0–19–933104–8 (pbk. : alk. paper)—ISBN 978–0–19–933103–1
(cloth : alk. paper)
1. Karma. 2. Theravada Buddhism—Doctrines. 3. Buddhaghosa. I. Title.
BQ4435.H45 2013
294.3'422—dc23
2013008728

1 3 5 7 9 8 6 4 2
Printed in the United States of America
on acid-free paper

For Steve

Mind is the forerunner of all things. Mind is chief, and they are mind-made. If one speaks or acts with a wicked mind, suffering follows even as the cartwheel follows the hoof of an ox.

Mind is the forerunner of all things. Mind is chief, and they are mind-made. If one speaks or acts with a pure mind, happiness follows even as one's shadow stays near.

—DHAMMAPADA 1,2

Contents

Acknowledgments

ONE OF MY favorite passages in the Pāli canon has Ānanda declaring that "half" the good life is friendship with good people, companionship with good people, and closeness with good people, only to be corrected by the Buddha to the effect that these constitute not half, but the *whole* of the good life (S.v.2). The passage is speaking of the religious life, but I have found that the Buddha's affirmation of friendship with wise and helpful teachers is true for the intellectual life as well. My gratitude for such intellectual friendship must go first to Charlie Hallisey for his sage advice over many years, his care for my intellectual development, his perceptive reading of draft chapters, and his sharing with me his Harvard course on Buddhaghosa and Buddhist commentaries.

This project progressed only through the thoughtful guidance of many friends and colleagues who participated in the various forums in which parts of it were presented, including a workshop at Amherst College, "Contours of the Moral Person"; the Five College Buddhist Studies Faculty Seminar; the Harvard Divinity School lecture series and conference, "Moral Worlds and Religious Subjectivities"; and insightful audiences at Indiana University and University of Pennsylvania. More specifically, I am very grateful to Beatrice Chrystall, Sarah LeVine, Steven Collins, Lilian Handlin, Jock Reeder, Janet Gyatso, Georges Dreyfus, and Jonathan Schofer for reading parts or all of the manuscript, in several cases more than once. I am also very grateful for conversations with Aaron Stalnaker and David Wills. Toward the end of the project, I benefited from discussions with Buddhist scholars and neuroscientists at a workshop in Telluride (John Dunne, Thupten Jinpa, Richard Davidson, and others) and at the Mind and Life Summer Research Institutes. Many thanks also to Jay Garfield for the time and meticulous care he put into the project reading drafts and helping me shepherd it through its final stages.

The book could not have been written without the generous material support from the John Simon Guggenheim Memorial Foundation and two sabbatical leaves from Amherst College. I am grateful for the support of the Religion Department at Amherst (Diane Dix, Andrew Dole, Robert Doran, Tariq Jaffer, Susan Niditch, David Wills, and for a time, Jamal Elias) for the amicable environment to work on the project. And I thank Paola Zamperini for offering her comments on the manuscript and for her own distinctive form of Buddhist companionship.

Finally, I am always grateful to Steve for enduring this project with good humor and consistently intelligent advice on how to make it better, and to my little sons, Soren and Zack, just for being there. It is to Steve that it is dedicated.

Abbreviations for Pāli Texts

A	*Aṅguttaranikāya*
As	*Atthasālinī (Dhammasaṅgaṇī-aṭṭhakathā)*
Dhp	*Dhammapada*
Dhp-a	*Dhammapada-aṭṭhakathā*
D	*Dīghanikāya*
Dhs	*Dhammasaṅgaṇī*
Ja	*Jātaka-aṭṭhavaṇṇanā*
Khp	*Khuddakapāṭha*
Kv	*Kathāvatthu*
Kv-a	*Kathāvatthu-aṭṭhakathā*
Mil	*Milindapañho*
Mp	*Manorathapūraṇī (Aṅguttaranikāya-aṭṭhakathā)*
Mp-ṭ	*Sāratthamañjūsā (ṭīkā on Mp)*
Nett	*Nettipakaraṇa*
Paṭis	*Paṭisambhidāmagga*
Paṭis-a	*Paṭisambhidāmagga-aṭṭhakathā*
Pj I	*Paramatthajotikā I (Khuddakapāṭha-aṭṭhakathā)*
Ps	*Papañcasūdanī (Majjhimanikāya-aṭṭhakathā)*
Pv-a	*Paramatthadīpanī (Petavatthu-aṭṭhakathā)*
S	*Saṃyuttanikāya*
Sp	*Samantapāsādikā (Vinaya-aṭṭhakathā)*
Spk	*Sāratthappakāsinī (Saṃyuttanikāya-aṭṭhakathā)*
Sv	*Sumaṅgalavilāsinī (Dīghanikāya-aṭṭhakathā)*
Vibh	*Vibhaṅga*
Vibh-a	*Sammohavinodanī (Vibhaṅga-aṭṭhakathā)*
Vism	*Visuddhimagga*
Vism-mhṭ	*Visuddhimagga-mahāṭīkā*
Yam	*Yamakapakaraṇa*

The Forerunner of All Things

Introduction

THIS BOOK OFFERS a philosophical exploration of intention and motivation—about what prompts us to do what we do. I offer this exploration by investigating the ideas of the Buddha and his fifth-century CE commentator, Buddhaghosa, both of whom were, like me, fascinated with what intentions are, and why and under what circumstances we are inclined to attribute them to ourselves and others. In a narrow sense, I focus on Buddhist canonical and commentarial assertions that identify intention as the central internal component of action, but in a much broader sense, I explore the moral phenomenology and underlying anthropology in which early Buddhist theories of mind, action, and morality were advanced and understood. I argue that Buddhist ideas can contribute to many modern discussions of intention because they suggest highly sophisticated yet very different paradigms than we currently have for how we might think about them.

My motivation in working on these questions stems from a dissatisfaction with the dominant working understanding of moral agency current today. This conception assumes an agent who acts according to beliefs, desires, and reasons, but whose psychological depths are seldom alluded to, much less explored. This agent is largely conceived of as free, rational, and autonomous; evaluating the morality of her actions is largely a matter of evaluating her choices. Ethics is envisioned as a project of identifying the right sorts of reasons and deliberations that should prompt her choices or, in more virtue-oriented approaches, establishing the virtues or qualities of character (themselves often arrived at via rational deliberation) that should inform moral choice. Insofar as intention is paired with choice, we are left with a notion of moral agency located in the movement of the sovereign will.

This dominant conception of the moral agent has traceable historical underpinnings in the modern West that have been well documented.[1] What is surprising is how such a psychologically thin conception of the moral agent comes to be imported into Buddhist understandings of agency. This is surprising not so much for the anachronism it displays as for the way it conceals a substantial body of psychological resources that would offer an important counter to it. Buddhist texts, in fact, provide some of the most complex investigations of moral psychology available in human intellectual history, more intricate and far-reaching perhaps than many models of the mind and agency available in contemporary cognitive science. The moral phenomenology advanced in early Buddhist sources suggests a complicated moral agency that may better account for the lived and subjective experience of moral action.

We might also register some surprise at how little work has been done on the textual resources in Buddhist studies that would alter the dominant vision and, more narrowly, on the textual tradition we refer to as the Theravāda. The importance of intention's role in action (karma) in Buddhist thought has been something of a truism in many modern textbook renderings of Buddhist ethics, yet little work has been done to see what this might have meant in the canonical sources, not to speak of how it was interpreted at the commentarial level. Texts that richly describe moral phenomenology, chiefly the Abhidhamma literature, have been largely sidelined in current Theravāda studies despite their enormous importance to many Buddhists past and present. Additionally, despite being a monumental figure in the intellectual history of the Theravāda, Buddhaghosa (and the commentarial tradition he represents) has been widely neglected, though he offers very pertinent and probing explorations of human experience. And finally, modern scholarship remains in the early stages of learning how to read the different genres and layers of Buddhist literature that would help us to learn from them. This book offers an initial attempt to advance our understanding of Theravāda on many of these fronts.

Learning How to Read

Scholars of Buddhism interested in tracing the development of moral thought in ancient India have frequently noted, often with considerable

1. Murdoch, *The Sovereignty of Good*; Rosenthal, *The Era of Choice*; Schneewind, *The Invention of Autonomy*.

admiration and approval, the Buddha's assertion in the *Aṅguttara*: "it is intention (*cetanā*) that I call action (*kamma*); intending, one acts by body, speech, and mind" (A.iii.415). This focus on intention is said to have challenged and transformed Indic thinking about karma in radically new ways.[2] No longer is karma simply a matter of ritual action (as Brahmanical tradition is said to have regarded it); it becomes a moral idea. This move, according to one scholar, "ethicised the universe," offering a revolutionary shift toward defining karma in moral terms and then locating morality in internal processes of motivation and intention within the individual.[3] There is less clarity about what the Buddha meant by *intention* and why he makes this claim than there is enthusiasm for this program of ethicization. How subsequent Buddhist thinkers understood this connection of karma to intention has attracted less attention than it deserves, as has the motivation for this link.

If we are to understand how the link between karma and intention was understood by the tradition, we will need to attend closely to the discursive contexts in which it found meaning. Our explorations of the defining of karma as intention are intertwined with the discourses, be they psychological, narrative, rhetorical, legal, or philosophical, in which this central idea (and similar claims) are invoked. To know what it means to say that karma is the chief component of intention, we must know more about the texts in which this formula occurs. We must learn how to read the different genres of Buddhist thought.

Pierre Hadot—to whom I am indebted for many of the ideas that animate this section—has suggested that "one cannot read an ancient author the way one does a contemporary author."[4] We cannot understand meaning without appreciating "the rules, the forms, the models of discourse" of

---

2. Although *karma* is the Sanskrit version of the Pāli *kamma*, and I generally use Pāli terminology throughout this study, *karma* has entered the English lexicon to such an extent that I use it here without italicization or translation. Karma means, at bottom, action, particularly action that is both the result of previous conditions and brings about future effects for the agent.

3. Gombrich, *How Buddhism Began*, 51–52.

4. Hadot, *Philosophy as a Way of Life*, 61. My section heading borrows from Hadot (pp. 101–9), though it is used somewhat differently. Hadot is writing about historical phenomena specific to Greco-Roman antiquity and the demands that diverse philosophical writings from this world make on their readers (which will, of course, be very different from the demands ancient Buddhist texts make on us). What is helpful here is how explicit Hadot is about our modern ignorance in knowing how to read ancient texts, even as he suggests valuable ways to learn to read them.

a text. In studying ancient thinkers, Hadot argues, we must take account of "all the constraints that weighed upon them," which included "literary genres, rhetorical rules, dogmatic imperatives, and traditional modes of reasoning."[5] It is only through learning to interpret *how* texts make meaning that we can determine *what* they mean. This book is as much an exercise in learning how to read different kinds of Theravāda literature as it is a quest to understand intentional action, for the latter cannot occur apart from explicit attention to the former.

One way to learn how to read Buddhist canonical texts is to learn how other thinkers in the tradition have read them, and here we have enormous resources at our disposal in the commentarial traditions. My approach differs significantly from many modern treatments of Theravāda texts in that I do not go directly to the canonical sources—"Buddha's words"—without the guidance of the fifth-century figure Bhadanta Buddhaghosācariya, chief commentator in the Pāli tradition and one of the greatest minds in the history of Buddhism. In this, I follow more traditional Buddhist ways of encountering scripture that presume the need for a teacher in gaining access to what the Buddha said and meant. Buddhaghosa is my guide in learning how to think about and learn from Buddha's words. He provides not only an exposition of word and meaning but also a disciplinary practice of learning how to read these texts in ways that modern scholars are only beginning to understand. As I have begun to learn how to allow Buddhaghosa to train my thinking about what is important, which problems need to be solved, and the kinds of strategies one can deploy in resolving them, some of my initial questions about intentional action have changed and, I think, become more interesting. This book offers not merely suggestive answers to questions about action and intention, but new ways of asking questions about them.

Yet even as Buddhaghosa has helped me learn to read both canonical and commentarial texts, the contours of his own systematic thinking have gradually come to occupy central stage in my engagement with philosophical ideas about intention. In this sense, my approach is a departure from interpretative paradigms that read him in a secondary fashion, solely as an expositor of more primary and important texts, and more or less confined to and interpreted within the historical tradition we call Buddhism. For me, Buddhaghosa has become a thinker with whom I can engage

---

5. See ibid., 7 (Davidson's "Introduction").

philosophically about a range of issues relating to intention and moral agency. Though seldom practiced in South Asian or Buddhist studies, this is a very ordinary way of reading great thinkers in the Western traditions, in which Aristotle, Kant, or Marx can be read as interlocutors with whom modern scholars can engage our contemporary concerns. I read Buddhaghosa as a thinker who can help me understand and discuss moral agency in new and complex ways.

Such an approach entails striving to meet, as Hadot puts it, "two equally urgent contrary requirements" (67). The first is the requirement to aim for the ideal of objectivity and impartiality, which entails a rigorous "exercise of self-detachment," required to avoid distortion and anachronism. This involves, as suggested earlier, learning to read ancient texts by interpreting them within the discursive contexts through which they make meaning, as well as situating them within the social, historical, and material conditions from which they emerged. It entails care and attention to the form and content of a work in which, to the degree possible, we can come to discern the intention or sense of the author. At the same time, Hadot argues that this striving for objectivity makes possible an equally important movement in which the interpreter is "in a certain sense implicated in the interpretation":

> If one tries to understand a text properly, I believe that afterward one can be brought, almost spontaneously, to discover its human meaning, that is, to situate it in relation to the general problem of humanity, of the human, even if it is not edifying at all. Thus one can basically do as the Stoics did concerning their representations. First, begin with adequate and objective judgment: this is what is said. Then, eventually, make a judgment of value: this has a given significance for my life. This time, one can speak of a return to subjectivity, a subjectivity that, incidentally, attempts to elevate itself to a universal perspective.[6]

---

6. Hadot, *The Present Alone Is Our Happiness*, 68. Drawing on Gadamer, Sheldon Pollock's discussion of the "philologist's meaning"—the indelible meaning brought to a text by the reader—is a valuable articulation of similar ideas, though he sees the hermeneutic stage of *applicatio* as less a two-part process than Hadot: "Discovering the meaning of such texts by understanding and interpreting them and discovering how to apply them in a particular legal or spiritual instance, or even thinking about a work of art in relation to one's own life, are not separate actions but a single process" (Pollock, "Future Philology?" 958; Gadamer, *Truth and Method*, 335–36).

Hadot argues that working for the objective meaning of the text, its truth, becomes a condition for another movement toward discovering subjective meaning in it, of how it might speak to *me* and *my* concerns about being human. (Importantly, the subjective here leads outside self, to the human in a more general sense.) This latter sense, what Hadot calls the "actual sense" of a text, is premised on the idea that explorations of the past can have a "personal, formative and existential sense." This sense is not identical to the author's meaning:

> In fact, the meaning intended by the ancient author is never actual. It is ancient, and that is all there is to it. But it can take on an actual significance for us to the extent that it can appear to us as, for example, the source of certain actual ideas, or especially because it can inspire an actual attitude in us, an inner act, or a spiritual exercise.[7]

When a text becomes the "source of certain actual ideas," which may not have been anticipated by the author yet are made possible by the text, we are poised to explore new truths and understandings.

This set of ideas about how to read has guided my treatment of Buddhaghosa. Toward the first requirement, the pages that follow attempt the careful, critical work required to explore, without anachronism, what both Buddha (as recalled in the canonical texts) and Buddhaghosa meant and what they were doing. On the basis of this groundwork, there is an additional layer of potential actual meaning as Buddhaghosa prompts us to think about moral intention and agency in new ways that can speak to our own contemporary problems.

Buddhaghosa

Who was Buddhaghosa and what did he do with the Buddha's words? Buddhaghosa is, of course, linked to a commentarial tradition much older than himself, and insofar as his work is based on earlier exegesis (much of which likely stretches back to the Buddha's day and was transmitted in all three councils), it is not entirely creative or original. Buddhaghosa was the principal translator into Pāli of the ancient Sinhala commentaries. But his process of edition and translation was taken by the tradition to indicate

7. Hadot, *The Present Alone Is Our Happiness*, 68.

authorship in an important way; in the postscripts attached to each of the commentaries, Buddhaghosa is said to have "made" (*kata*) the commentaries just as he "made" his own work, the *Visuddhimagga*. Buddhaghosa is thus both the recipient of an ancient tradition and the crafter of a new version of it that rendered the original version obsolete, for his work supplanted the Sinhala versions that are now lost to us. The Sinhala commentaries were said to be in disarray when he came to them; Buddhaghosa brought them to order in service of a vision of a systematic whole, the scope and breadth of which scholars are still attempting to discern.

In his own account of what he is doing, Buddhaghosa claims not to "advertise his own standpoint" and only very rarely suggests that he is offering his own preference in putting forth an interpretation.[8] There is a certain self-effacement in his style that both reflects and promotes a conservative approach to, and rhetoric about, knowledge. Buddhaghosa's commitment to the authenticity of the tradition is suggested by his emphasis on locating himself merely as the latest in a chain of teachers that goes back to the Buddha. Yet even as he engages in a certain rhetorical erasure of his own originality, he makes evident his creative genius, nowhere more apparent perhaps than in his own work, the *Visuddhimagga*, which the subsequent Pāli tradition rightly celebrates. His success in this project of conveying authenticity through his own skills in interpretation establishes his role as the voice of orthodoxy—a status reflected in his monastic name, Buddhaghosa, the "voice of the Buddha."

The *Mahāvaṃsa*'s account of Buddhaghosa emphasizes his monumental importance to the subsequent Pāli tradition.[9] In its account, composed some 700 years after his lifetime, Buddhaghosa is said to have been from India, born into a Brahman family, and celebrated for his mastery of Vedic texts, grammar, and the arts of disputation. In India, he became interested in Buddhist systems of thought and ordained as a monk to study them

8. Vism 25; Ñāṇamoli, *The Path of Purification*, xvii, xxxii. On Buddhaghosa's role as a critical editor, see Endo, "Buddhaghosa's Role as Commentator: Faithful Translator or Critical Editor?" and "Some Observations on the 'Introductory Sections' of the Pāli Commentaries."

9. Ñāṇamoli, *The Path of Purification*, provides a translation of the relevant passage from the *Mahāvaṃsa* on pp. xxxiv–xxxv. Ñāṇamoli also gives a précis of the 15th-century Burmese work story of Buddhaghosa, the *Buddhaghosuppatti*, pp. xxxvi–xxxix. The *Buddhaghosuppatti* is edited and translated by James Gray. On Buddhaghosa and his work, see also Malalasekera, *The Pāli Literature of Ceylon*, ch. 5; Law, *The Life and Work of Buddhaghosa*; Finot, "The Legend of Buddhaghosa"; and Collins, "On the Very Idea of the Pāli Canon," 98–99. For another traditional source on Buddhaghosa (as well as other Buddhist authors), see the 14th-century *Saddhammasaṅgaha* (JPTS, 1890).

out of intellectual curiosity before becoming persuaded of their truth and thereafter a committed Buddhist. He was sent by his teacher to Sri Lanka to learn the Sinhala commentaries because the commentaries in India had fallen to pieces. He was instructed to translate them into the learned and translocal language of Pāli, or the "language of the Magadhans," as the text refers to it. When he arrived at Anuradhapura, his mastery of the Dhamma and skill in articulating it were tested by the monks of the Mahāvihāra before they were willing to give him the texts. (The Mahāvihāra, the "Great Monastery," was an important center, sectarian affiliation, and textual lineage within the tradition we now call the Theravāda.)[10] They asked him to provide an exposition of two verses, whereupon Buddhaghosa demonstrated his skill and knowledge of the Buddha's teachings by his composition of the *Visuddhimagga*, a brilliant explication and summary of the two verses but also the Dhamma as a whole.[11] That Buddhaghosa could expand at such length—the English translation of this text is over 850 pages—with an eye for both precision in treating details and systematizing a larger theory, convinced the Sri Lankan scholars that he could translate the commentaries. The text then asserts that the teachers of the Mahāvihāra honored him as "Metteyya" (the future Buddha) and accepted his commentaries as "if they were the canonical texts themselves" (*pāliṃ viya*). These extraordinary claims put his work on par with the Buddha's teachings.

Subsequent Mahāvihāra tradition holds that all of the main commentaries or *aṭṭhakathās* were composed or compiled by Buddhaghosa. This is an enormous corpus of work that includes commentaries on the five Nikāyas, two commentaries on the Vinaya, and commentaries on the seven books of

---

10. As Peter Skilling has pointed out, the widespread use of the term Theravāda is a modern development and does not serve us well if conceived of as a historical identity that premodern Buddhists in South and Southeast Asia used to describe themselves. However, given its ubiquity in contemporary usage, it is a difficult term to do entirely without. See Peter Skilling, "Theravāda in History" and "Scriptural Authenticity and the *śrāvaka* Schools: An Essay towards an Indian Perspective."

11. As B. C. Law notes, Buddhaghosa himself says that the *Visuddhimagga* is an exposition of just one verse (S.i.13), which reads: "when a wise man, established in morality (*sīla*), develops mind (*citta*) and wisdom (*paññā*), then that monk, ardent and intelligent, disentangles the tangle" (Vism 1 and 711; see Law, *The Life and Work of Buddhaghosa*, 3, 15–18). This verse indicates a path of practice that Buddhaghosa uses to inform the structure of the *Visuddhimagga*: morality (*sīla*), cultivation of mind (taken to refer to *samādhi*), and wisdom (*paññā*), which are the trainings that disentangle the tangles of our condition of craving and suffering in *saṃsāra*.

the Abhidhamma.[12] Most of these texts bear a shared postscript at the end that says that they were made by Buddhaghosa. This postscript may have been appended by the Mahāvihāra monastic authorities as their "sign of approval," as suggested by Bhikkhu Ñāṇamoli.[13]

Modern scholars have read the history of authorship of these commentaries quite differently and have been skeptical that all of these commentaries were, in fact, authored by Buddhaghosa. Many scholars call into question the idea that Buddhaghosa was the author of the commentaries on the *Jātaka* and the *Dhammapada*, and his authorship of the *Atthasālinī* is doubted because in its beginning the author describes himself as having been instructed by Buddhaghosa to compose it.[14] The two Vinaya commentaries have also been ascribed to other authors, and modern scholars suggest that only the commentaries on the first four Nikāyas were composed by Buddhaghosa. Some scholars suggest that Buddhaghosa should be seen as the head of a team of scholars who translated the very large body of material ascribed to him by the traditional sources, a not unlikely scenario.

As important as this historical critical approach has been for our understanding of the *production* of these texts, it is less useful for understanding the *reception* of them and how the attribution of authorship worked in the Pāli world. It has clearly been important for the Mahāvihāra tradition to see Buddhaghosa as the translator of a large body of commentary and to read these many works as, in some important sense, his; as we have seen, attaching commentaries on all branches of canonical texts to his name and authority is in evidence in the postscripts of the texts themselves, as well as much later texts such as the *Mahāvaṃsa*. Considering what authorship meant in the reading and reception of texts can aid us to see that the proper name Buddhaghosa has more than one signification, only one of

---

12. These are commentaries on the first four *nikāyas*, and the *Paramatthajotikā* on the *Khuddakapāṭha* and *Suttanipātha*, and the *Dhammapadaṭṭhakathā*; the Vinaya commentaries called *Samantapāsādikā* and the *Kaṅkhāvitaraṇī*, and the Abhidhamma commentaries: the *Atthasālinī* on the *Dhammasaṅganī*, the *Sammohavinodanī* on the *Vibhaṅga*, and the *Pañcapakaraṇaṭṭhakathā* on the other five books.

13. Ñāṇamoli, *The Path of Purification*, xxix.

14. Cousins, "Good or Skilful? *Kusala* in Canon and Commentary," 159, n. 14; von Hinüber, *A Handbook of Pāli Literature*, 151. There is also the suggestion that the *Visuddhimagga* and the *Atthasālinī* have at least one clear point of disagreement (Endo, "Buddhaghosa's Role as a Commentator," 24). Scholars have argued that the style of the *Dhammapadaṭṭhakathā* and *Jātakatthavaṇṇanā* is so different from the other commentaries that they must have a different author. See Malalasekera, *The Pāli Literature of Ceylon*; Law, *The Life and Work of Buddhaghosa*; and Mori, "Recent Japanese Studies of the Pāli Commentarial Literature," for discussions of Buddhaghosa's authorship of the various commentaries.

them the flesh-and-blood individual we imagine who actually sat down, translated, and edited some or all of these texts. The name Buddhaghosa also designates the authorship of a systematic corpus of material recognized and celebrated by the Mahāvihāra scholars. The name Buddhaghosa has a role, a *function*, as Michel Foucault puts it, that endows a certain status and authenticity to these texts. Foucault suggests that the author's name characterizes "the mode of being" of a text and "manifests the appearance of a certain discursive set and indicates the status in this discourse within a society and a culture."[15] We have already seen how, in one quite explicit articulation of this function, the name Buddhaghosa is said to be, literally, the voice of the Buddha; it is also linked to Metteyya and to texts that should be received as if they were canonical.

In addition to making powerful claims through designating these texts the work of Buddhaghosa, the author function signals that they can or should be classified and read together. According to Foucault, the author function is a "complex operation" that "constructs a certain rational being we call 'author' "; this construction is a projection "of the operations that we force texts to undergo, the connections that we make, the traits that we establish as pertinent, the continuities that we recognize, or the exclusions that we practice."[16] When modern historians suggest that the *Jātaka* and *Dhammapada* commentaries cannot be Buddhaghosa's because they differ substantially in style from the Nikāya commentaries, they are projecting a set of choices about authorship along stylistic considerations—fashioning a set of choices and projections that premodern Sinhalese and Burmese authorities did not make. For the premodern scholars, in contrast, a wide range of stylistically heterogeneous texts are classified together under the same status and authority. Modern scholars may not be wrong in their choices and assumptions; my point is only that there are different operations at work in constructing the authorship of these texts, and *these operations have entailments for how we might read them.*

When we read the whole body of commentaries attributed to Buddhaghosa as Buddhaghosa's, we read them differently than if we see them as authored by different, unknown authors. Foucault says that the author function provides "a certain unity of writing" and can serve as a basis through which "to neutralize the contradictions that may emerge

15. Foucault, "What Is an Author?" 107.

16. Ibid., 110.

in a series of texts."[17] On this note, and again to rely on the *Mahāvaṃsa*'s explicit instructions on how to read, we can observe that the *Mahāvaṃsa* attributes to the Mahāvihāra authorities a robust insistence on consistency: they tested Buddhaghosa's mastery of the Dhamma by requiring him to reproduce the *Visuddhimagga* after the first, and then the second, versions were lost. His ability to reproduce verbatim the same text each time was taken as the required evidence of his peerless command of the teachings and how to communicate them. We, of course, do not have to accept these claims at face value or to read the texts doubting that internal contradictions are possible; we need not suppress inconsistencies or attempt to enforce a homogeneity that is not in evidence in this large body of material. Rather, the point of recognizing the claims implicit in attributing these texts to Buddhaghosa is to open up certain ways of reading them and to do so in a way that is conscious of the choices we make.

Not only does considering the reception of the texts offer one way—but certainly not the only way—to read them but also evidence internal to the texts suggests the hand of an author who wrote or edited these commentaries with an eye to how they work within a larger whole. Buddhaghosa, whom we might refer to in this context as the "implied author,"[18] has much to say about the interpretative choices he is making in particular commentaries and often directs his readers to other commentaries or to the *Visuddhimagga* to read further on a topic or to look to places where he employs a different approach. There is a sense that emerges from the texts themselves of what G. P. Malalasekera has referred to as a "synthetic unity."[19] In addition, there are large passages that are quoted more or less verbatim in several different commentaries, appearing in Sutta, Vinaya, and Abhidhamma commentaries. These may suggest a single authorial or editorial hand for at least certain blocks of commentary that traveled widely within and across these collections.

While focused on Buddhaghosa, on occasion I turn also to other commentators, especially when I am seeking further views or explications

17. Ibid., 111.

18. Steven Collins uses the language of "implied author" when referring to "the implied single authorial voice" of the *Visuddhimagga* ("Remarks on the *Visuddhimagga*," 503). I suggest, and evidence will follow, that such a voice is apparent across many of the works attributed to him. See also Collins's introduction to Wijayaratna, *Buddhist Monastic Life*, on following the tradition's reading of the sources in a synchronic fashion, which can guide us to read them this way also (xii–xix).

19. Malalasekera, *The Pāli Literature of Ceylon*, 94.

of what Buddhaghosa has said. Dhammapāla, who lived perhaps a century after Buddhaghosa, wrote subcommentaries (*ṭīkās*) on many of the *aṭṭhakathās* and on the *Visuddhimagga* and some commentaries on books in the *Khuddhakanikāya*, adding a layer of learning and insight to the root texts, as well as to what Buddhaghosa is up to.[20] These practices of continual elaboration then lent themselves to a quite different process, one of contraction, when students need manageable handbooks like the *Visuddhimagga* itself, to rein in the expansion of meaning of the Dhamma. Buddhadatta, perhaps a contemporary of Buddhaghosa, wrote manuals or handbooks on the Vinaya and the Abhidhamma that attempt to condense the enormity of doctrine in helpful summaries. Another important handbook is Anuruddha's *Abhidhammatthasaṅgaha*, which dates from perhaps the 10th century. Due to its clarity and mastery of Abhidhamma and its relative brevity, this text has become the standard primer for Abhidhamma students and the place where many scholars turn before (or in lieu of) going to the canonical Abhidhamma texts.[21]

Before I go on to describe how we can shape our questions about intentional action, it is necessary to articulate my strategy for navigating the enormous body of work just described. The different contexts and genres in which the formula linking karma and *cetanā* is invoked include the entire early Pāli literature, that is, Suttanta, Abhidhamma, Vinaya, and narratives. At the canonical level alone, this body of material constitutes, depending on how they are counted, some 30-odd books, some of them multivolume works. The commentaries attributed to Buddhaghosa roughly double this corpus, not to speak of the additional layers of subcommentary and handbook. Even if undaunted by the sheer volume (and I certainly make no claims to fully control it), the most intrepid scholar must be unsettled by the inherently expansive nature of this material.

It is expansive in two senses. First, the writing of commentaries and the processes of exposition are considered by the tradition to be a process that can go on indefinitely, and it often seems that it has—the body of commentarial material one can look at on any particular passage is often considerable. The texts are also highly intertextual within these layers—sermons refer to other sermons, Buddhaghosa invokes other passages in his commentary—and following the web of connections for even one passage can be consuming (though usually highly rewarding).

20. See ibid., ch. 6, on Dhammapāla and Buddhadatta.

21. Nārada and Bodhi, *A Comprehensive Manual of Abhidhamma*, 1.

There is a second sense in which the material is expansive. Buddhaghosa shows us how to read texts in a manner so as not to close off and settle meaning, but rather to open and expand it. This is a hermeneutic principle that echoes the nature of the Dhamma itself, which, we are told, is endless. Even the Buddha, when reflecting on the depths of the Dhamma subsequent to his awakening, grew exhausted and, for all his omniscience, could not reach the end of it or discern its borders. We can learn from Buddhaghosa how to see the ways meaning can be expanded upon, how a single passage may lead in many directions, and how the process of exposition is itself a creative engagement with the endless possibilities of the teachings and with the endless possibilities of human experience that the teachings explore.

To illustrate how Buddhaghosa opens up a text, one can begin to notice and trace his systematic efforts to contextualize what the Buddha said. His creating context and setting can be, it sometimes appears, an endless task. Why did the Buddha give this sermon? To whom? Why did that person, in particular, need to hear it? Is there a distant karmic backstory from a previous life that explains the present moment? Or is it sufficient to describe the immediate circumstances of the present teaching, which may include particulars of the audience's biography, psychology, religious status, and relationships with others? What might count as the immediate circumstances to which Buddhaghosa anchors a teaching sometimes surprises us with their narrative scope and attention to detail. These efforts at contextualizing are always important for understanding the meaning Buddhaghosa sees in the text and cannot be set aside. Buddhaghosa also provides exposition of the words of a teaching, a commentarial service that raises possibilities as much as it defines, provides editorial functions, and attends to the letter and spirit of the text. In any of these services, Buddhaghosa may appear to digress to other topics and bring up other texts that elaborate them, though what might appear to us to be a digression can always be accounted for in view of Buddhaghosa's particular horizon of meaning if we look closely enough, and it must be regarded as at least potentially important for us.

To begin to follow some of Buddhaghosa's leads (and often one simply cannot follow all of them to all the places they go if one wishes to finish one passage and take up another) is to find oneself in a heady and exhilarating world of possibility. Charles Hallisey has evoked Paul Ricoeur's idea of the surplus of meaning in reference to Buddhaghosa's interpretive style.[22] Ricoeur argues, in ways similar to Hadot's ideas about the "actual sense," that the meaning of a text is "to be conceived in a dynamic way as a direction of thought opened up by the text."[23]

> The sense of a text is not behind the text, but in front of it. It is not something hidden, but something disclosed. What has to be understood is not the initial situation of discourse, but what points towards a possible world, thanks to the non-ostensive reference of the text.[24]

For Ricoeur, the process of understanding a text is a dynamic event in which a reader encounters "new modes of being," a new capacity for knowing oneself.[25] Meaning is neither determined by authorial intention nor projected onto the text by the reader. Rather, interpretation is an active and dialogical receiving of new possibilities for thought.

Buddhaghosa, we may suggest, treats the Buddha's words in a similar vein. His encounter with them discloses particular avenues of possibility but by no means exhausts them, as he frequently makes clear. His toolbox of hermeneutical instruments is equipped for opening up different meanings of a text: its phrasing (*byañjana*) and sense (*attha*), the ways it was received by the audience to whom the sermon was originally delivered, how it might be received in the future, what other texts should be engaged to interpret this one, the many possibilities for confusion, and the possibilities for correct understanding. He frequently indicates that much more could be said on a particular passage but that he is constrained by the specific purposes at hand to attempt to go further. For Buddhaghosa, Buddha's words—the Dhamma—is an endless and dynamic encounter, checked only by (again, borrowing from Ricoeur) the "finitude of human knowledge."

---

22. This section is greatly indebted to Charles Hallisey, in personal communication and his course on Buddhist Commentaries (Spring 2009, Harvard Divinity School).

23. Ricoeur, *Interpretation Theory*, 92.

24. Ibid., 87. See also Gadamer: "all reading involves application, so that a person reading a text is himself part of the meaning he apprehends. He belongs to the text he is reading. The line of meaning that the text manifests to him as he reads it always and necessarily breaks off in an open indeterminancy" (Gadamer, *Truth and Method*, 335).

25. Ibid., 94.

We will trace this interpretative stance—which informs my own reading of canon and commentary—in Buddhaghosa's work. As exhilarating as this is, there are practical challenges: how might I ever hope to read enough of this huge corpus of texts to claim some understanding? And if every detail counts, how might I ever write a book that can be finished? And perhaps most importantly, how does my own finitude of understanding circumscribe the possibilities I can see in a text? While these challenges will be pulling on us throughout, and I will attend to the latter one in the next section, my strategy at least for navigating the largeness of the material before me is twofold: my lens centers on matters of intentional agency (which are often embedded in moral psychology and always depict a distinctive anthropology), and it focuses on discerning those properties of discursive form or genre that are important for interpreting ideas about intentional agency.

Genre and Approach

We can interrogate the complicated phenomenon of intentional agency in different contexts for very different purposes, as we know from how intention in our own modern intellectual context is treated. In our own milieu, intention is understood variously, depending on the discipline or field in which it is investigated: different questions and theories about intention evolve in the context of law than in philosophical circles or in neuroscience, for example. Folk or narrative accounts of intention do yet a different kind of work with the idea of intention. Similarly, in the Pāli sources, questions about moral agency and culpability take on a different cast when treated in the context of monastic law than they do in lists and commentaries describing moral phenomenology, which in turn have different concerns than narrative thinking about agency and morality. What these different methods of teaching are trying to *do*, whether it is teaching restraint in a monastic context or advancing an analytic account of human experience in the Abhidhamma context, cannot be separated from what they are trying to *say*. We cannot grasp content without attention to method.

Buddhaghosa has much to say about what the three branches of the *Tipiṭaka*—that is, the Suttanta, the Vinaya, and the Abhidhamma—are doing, and his commentary treats them in a methodologically disciplined fashion that respects their distinctive approaches. The disclosure of meaning is guided by the formalities of each genre. He considers their different methods of instruction, to what sort of people they are geared, their distinct purposes, and the different ways they are profound. Often, as we will see, he allowed the range of possible readings of a given passage to be determined by these considerations.[26] In addition to his following closely the tradition's divisions of Suttanta, Vinaya, and Abhidhamma, Buddhaghosa sometimes suggested that narrative, what he called "*jātaka*," was a distinctive method of teaching or way of knowing (*pariyāya*) alongside the traditional branches.[27] Of course, the narrative collections are usually considered part of the Suttanta, gathered together with other miscellaneous books, but Buddhaghosa thought that narrative is distinct enough as a method of teaching that it could sometimes be referred to in this way. In the organization of my chapters, I have followed Buddhaghosa in his sensitivity to context and genre and in his treatment of these four ways of knowing.

Buddhaghosa's hermeneutical devices show us what the Buddha's teachings mean and how they make meaning. But he is also codifying and creating distinctive models of discourse of his own, of which he is highly self-conscious. Because he is often very explicit about the rules and conventions of interpretation, he can help us to see certain inner structures and logics of the canonical sources and his own writings that are indispensable to our understanding of the ideas.

In addition to learning from Buddhaghosa about the rules of discourse in the intellectual world he is creating, it is important to describe some of the choices and ideas at work in my dialogic engagement with the sources. One obvious way to chart these choices and ideas is in the process of translation, of finding the English terms to describe the Pāli concepts as we attempt to make them intelligible to us. The study of Buddhist moral psychology requires some knowledge of Western religious, psychological, and philosophical systems to articulate with any precision the complexity of the Buddhist categories. At the same time, I am keenly alert to the very uneasy fit between Buddhist categories and those of the Western traditions and particularly attentive to the very many ways in which the Buddhist ideas cannot be readily mapped onto Western categories. I think, too, that it is in the very ways that the categories do not fit that we can learn most

26. For example, he has much to say in a large passage quoted in several places on the different methods and styles of the three baskets, and these guide his readings of particular passages (Sv.i.17–22; As 19–24; Sp 17–24).

27. Sv.iii.883; As 63.

from them, but we cannot know how precisely this is so unless we have a reasonably adequate account of both intellectual histories.

The interpretative process involves more than choices about translation but also an explicit awareness and engagement with contemporary currents of ideas on topics that are in some cases similar to, but not fully overlapping, the ancient Buddhist concerns. We live in a moment when questions of agency are being scrutinized in very complex ways in many disciplines. Traditional philosophical treatments of intention and action continue to develop, even as challenges to them are mounted from other disciplines. Cognitive scientists are bringing rich and fascinating empirical evidence to our understandings of human agency that has called into question both folk and philosophical accounts of it. Agency is also increasingly examined in light of social and institutional power, both in the concrete ways that forms of power and ideology have shaped human lives in the past and in some of the startling ways that modern institutions both make possible and inhibit human agency in radically new ways. These conversations pull on me as I read Buddhist texts. Modern worries about agency shape my readings of them in ways that constrain my interpretations, even as they make possible new evolutions for Buddhist ideas. I read with many problems and questions in mind about how agency and human nature have been understood and contested in my historical situation, and these questions animate and shape the particular ways I explore what the Buddha and Buddhaghosa can teach us.

Questions of Terminology

While we will be concerned with the whole range of psychological terms for the springs of action, we can begin with issues surrounding the interpretation of *cetanā*, a term often translated as "intention." The history of translations of this term demonstrates the complexity of the issues before us in interpreting this moral theory. Reviewing this history also shows the entanglement of our interpretations of Buddhist ideas with Western philosophical assumptions, regardless of whether this entanglement is always made explicit. Our work thus requires some attention to Western theories of the will, intention, and motivation as they are embedded in their own intellectual histories, in order to clarify the distinctiveness of Buddhist psychological vocabulary and make space for distinctively Buddhist ideas to emerge.

Given her assertion that "Buddhism is so emphatically a philosophy, both in theory and practice, of the conscious will" and her considerable attention to the subject, it is fitting to begin with Caroline Rhys Davids's interpretation of Pāli *cetanā*.[28] In her early writings and translations, she interpreted *cetanā* in very cognitive terms and did not link it immediately to the workings of conation. Relying on its etymological links to the verbal roots of thinking and cognition (*ceteti*), she likens *cetanā* to "reasoning" or "deductive inference," translating it more generally, as "thinking" in her translation to the *Dhammasaṅgaṇī*, first published in 1900,[29] and she does not even mention the term in her short piece on Buddhist theories of will.[30] In her collaboration with Shwe Zan Aung on the *Abhidhammattha-saṅgaha* and at his prompting, she backtracks on this interpretation and instead finds *cetanā* to be better rendered "volition or conation."[31] She reverses course yet again in *The Birth of Indian Psychology* and regrets translating it as volition because it is "mainly cognitive."[32]

But most other scholars have translated *cetanā* as "volition."[33] This line of interpretation sees *cetanā* as the operation of the will, although some would distinguish between will and volition. In one of the more useful explorations of the term to date, W. S. Karunaratna describes *cetanā*'s range of meaning:

> The different aspects of meaning embodied in the term have been rendered variously as will, volition, intention, motivation, conation, drive, stimulus, disposition, determination, effort, choice, resolve, arrangement, organization, aspiration, purposive intellection, mental construction and formative tendency. In its more technical signification, however, *cetanā*, unless otherwise qualified, refers only to the self-centered, goal-directed and result-oriented volitional disposition which impels the worldly individual (*puthujjana*).[34]

---

28. Rhys Davids, *A Buddhist Manual of Psychological Ethics*, lxv.

29. Ibid., 8–9, n. 1.

30. Rhys Davids, "On the Will in Buddhism."

31. Aung and Rhys Davids, *Compendium of Philosophy*, 235–36.

32. Rhys Davids, *The Birth of Indian Psychology*, 276.

33. For example, Sadaw, "Some Points in Buddhist Doctrine"; Ñāṇamoli, *The Path of Purification*; Nārada and Bodhi, *A Comprehensive Manual of Abhidamma*; Pe Maung Tin, *The Expositor*; de La Vallée Poussin, *Abhidharmakośabhāṣyam*; Gethin, *The Buddhist Path to Awakening*; and Harvey, *An Introduction to Buddhist Ethics*.

34. Karunaratna, "*Cetanā*," 87.

He takes this term to refer to the volition or will that drives human action, though his essay demonstrates the many complexities of its technical definition.

A related line of interpretation construes *cetanā* as moral choice. Damien Keown likens *cetanā* to Aristotle's *prohairesis* in that it "stands at the crossroads of reason and emotion."[35] While for Keown no English word matches *cetanā* precisely, he describes it as a type of practical reasoning or a kind of deliberation and decision about ends. But he also suggests that *cetanā* contains some dispositional and affective aspects. In fashioning his comparison with Aristotle, Keown wants to see the mind divided into the classic tripartite division of cognitive, affective, and conative elements, where the conative function, *cetanā*, "is best pictured as the matrix in which the push and pull of the rational and emotional aspects of the psyche are funneled in the direction of moral choice."[36] For Keown, as for many other scholars, "ethics concerns choices" and "the distinctive function of *cetanā* is making choices."[37] Phra Payutto similarly says that *cetanā* "includes volition, will, choice and decision, or the energy which leads to action."[38] Michael Carrithers also depicts *cetanā* as "choice," as does Paul Fuller, who also adds "preference," and this interpretation has found its way to some of the more popular writing on Buddhist moral thinking.[39] In these modernist interpretations, choice, as a deliberative process of weighing options and choosing among them, is the distinctive feature of *cetanā*. For these interpreters, the Buddha's elevation of the individual's capacity for choice liberates the moral agent from a deterministic social and causal order and assigns human beings a substantial share of freedom and autonomy.

A similar line of inquiry on *cetanā* has been advanced by Richard Gombrich, though he prefers to translate *cetanā* as "intention." Gombrich

---

35. Keown, *The Nature of Buddhist Ethics*, 213.

36. Ibid., 216. In *Buddhism and Bioethics*, Keown appears to parse *cetanā* as "moral psychology," without specifying exactly what is meant by this beyond "the psychological factors which underlie moral choices." He goes on here to use the language of "moral will" (39).

37. Keown, *The Nature of Buddhist Ethics*, 54, 143. Note Dreyfus's criticism of Keown's claims ("Meditation as Ethical Activity," 8–9) and also that of Meyers, *Freedom and Self Control*, 169–74.

38. Payutto, *Good, Evil and Beyond*, 6.

39. Carrithers, *The Buddha*, 67–68; Fuller, *The Notion of Diṭṭhi in Theravāda Buddhism*, 150; Misra, *An End of Suffering*, 197–98.

has written extensively on intention and its significance in Buddhism. For him also, the Buddha's emphasis on *cetanā* makes space in Buddhist theories of karma for freedom of individual choice and self-determination: "since ethical value lies in intention, the individual is autonomous and the final authority is what we would call his conscience."[40] According to Gombrich, the Buddha's equating karma with intention revolutionalized moral thinking in his context because it interprets karma as an individual's mental decision making rather than as collective Brahmanical ritual activity. In particular, by liberating karma from a ritual framework and endowing it with a sense of free will,[41] the Buddha "turned the Brahmin ideology upside down and ethicized the universe." He argues that the Buddha's equating karma with intention was far and away one of his most significant teachings, since it introduced a radical notion of individual moral responsibility to ancient India, an idea that he says has rarely been accepted in human history.[42] Gombrich does not see how "one could exaggerate the importance of the Buddha's ethicisation of the world," which he regards "as a turning point in the history of civilization."[43]

In his work on Abhidharma, Herbert Guenther comes to these questions from a quite different direction and disputes the translation of *cetanā* as volition or choice. For him, the English word *volition* "designates merely the act of making a choice or decision, but it rarely suggests the determination to put one's decision or choice into effect." Emphasizing the active nature of the process of *cetanā*, he prefers something like "our idea of stimulus, motive, or drive."[44] *Cetanā* is not a process of making autonomous and deliberate choices, but rather is the psychological drive that projects and sustains human activity in the world. James McDermott also wants to include some aspect of motive or drive with his rendering of *cetanā* as "intentional impulse."[45]

---

40. Gombrich, *Theravāda Buddhism*, 68 and quoted verbatim in *What the Buddha Thought*, 13; see also *Precept and Practice*, 170; *How Buddhism Began*, 48–56. Keown also insists on the role of "personal conscience" in Buddhism (*The Nature of Buddhist Ethics*, 15).

41. Gombrich, *Precept and Practice*, 170.

42. Gombrich, *What the Buddha Thought*, 22.

43. Gombrich, *How Buddhism Began*, 51. Note, however, that Steven Collins has suggested that already in the Upaniṣads a shift toward a more ethical, rather than purely ritual, interpretation of action was underway (*Selfless Persons*, 82), and Nalini Devdas shows that the Upaniṣads had quite complex and sophisticated ideas about volition (*Cetanā and Dynamics of Volition in Theravāda Buddhism*, ch. 1).

44. Guenther, *Philosophy and Psychology in the Abhidharma*, 43–46.

45. McDermott, "Scripture as the Word of the Buddha," 27.

Very recently, Nalini Devdas has contributed substantially to our understanding of *cetanā*. Though she often translates *cetanā* as "purposive impulse," she resists a single translation, demonstrating its "protean" character and range of meaning in the Suttas and Abhidhamma. For her, the central question about *cetanā* is whether it is understood "primarily as a cognitive function of assessing possibilities and deciding on goals, or as a motivating function that initiates goal-oriented activity" or if it somehow functions both cognitively and conatively, how the texts describe this synthesis.[46] She shows that *cetanā* does not act as a sovereign will or decision-making process, but rather as a volitional process that intends, initiates, and directs action toward fulfilling a goal. It has both cognitive and conative functions, but it always operates with and through the myriad factors at work in dependent origination.

Of course, all of these English terms—*will, volition, intention, motive*—come to our aid with complex histories and genealogies of their own, and most scholars acknowledge that none of them matches the nuances of Pāli and Sanskrit *cetanā*. Although determining how best to understand *cetanā* and other terms essential to Buddhist conceptions of moral agency will unfold in the following chapters, a closer look at the English vocabulary will help us begin to refine our terminology. To translate the Pāli terms effectively requires us to clarify the genealogies and contemporary meanings of the English terms in question, to locate with some precision areas of both overlap and divergence.

A developed doctrine of the will (Latin, *voluntas*) first appeared in Western traditions in the work of St. Augustine. Although the Greeks had a number of different terms for certain aspects of conation—chiefly, *boulēsis*, a desire for an end judged to be good; *prohairesis*, a rational choice involving deliberation as to the best manner of achieving one's end; and various appetitive forces—they kept them conceptually distinct.[47] Augustine was the first to bring together diverse aspects of conation and describe them as a single faculty, reducible to neither cognition nor appetite. He does so in the context of theodicy and in an effort to absolve an omnipotent God from responsibility for the fallen human condition and for sin. Richard Sorabji shows that Augustine associates the will with the rational aspect

46. Devdas, *Cetanā and the Dynamics of Volition*, 369.

47. Dihle, *The Theory of Will in Classical Antiquity*; Kahn, "Discovering the Will." For an account of the freedom of the will in Augustine's *de libero arbitrio*, see Harrison, *Augustine's Way into the Will*.

of the soul, assigns it freedom and responsibility, connects it to the idea of willpower, finds it present in all action, and develops the notion of the perverted will. For Augustine, the will has many tasks. It

> performs some of the functions of paying attention. It unites perception with the perceptible, memory with internal vision, and intellect with objects taken from memory. It is responsible for imagination. Faith is also due to will. Belief depends on the assent of the will.[48]

Finally, as Aaron Stalnaker has argued, the will may be understood "as the sum or collection of a person's loves, which aim at delighting in some end or ends."[49] The clustering of these diverse functions and ideas under one faculty invented for it a robust role in morality, religion, and psychology unprecedented for any single term related to conation in previous philosophy. In Augustine's hands, the will acquired tremendous importance in the religious and moral life. As Albrecht Dihle puts it, for Augustine the "will became the point of reference in the doctrines of intellect and sensual life, freedom and determination, moral evaluation of purpose and action, and, above all, in that of fall and redemption."[50] The human will for Augustine was modeled on the divine will with its capacities for creative action and freedom of choice.[51] Augustine's intense interest in the will emerged from his own tormented self-examination and centered on the will's obedience and conformity to God's will. It is the errant human will that is responsible for evil, and so management of the will, aided by God's grace, became a central focus of much Christian moral thought.

It is on Augustine's scaffolding that medieval and early modern theories of the will were constructed. While retaining a strong conception of the human will modeled on the divine will, Thomas Aquinas departed from Augustine in returning to classical conceptions of the rule of the intellect over the appetites and, thus for him, over the will.[52] In this intellectualist position, the intellect commands the will; cases of moral error or sin are not the result of a wayward will but of a mistaken understanding

48. Sorabji, *Emotion and Peace of Mind*, 337.

49. Stalnaker, *Overcoming Our Evil*, 101–4.

50. Dihle, *The Theory of Will in Classical Antiquity*, 127.

51. Kahn, "Discovering the Will," 235, 259.

52. Fiering, *Moral Psychology at Seventeenth-Century Harvard*, 110–14.

of the good. Against this view, the voluntarist position, associated with Augustine and later Christian figures, argued that the intellectualists falter on the classic dilemma known as the Medean paradox: "I see and approve the better course; I follow the worse." This problem, although expressed here by Ovid, was also a central worry of both St. Paul and Augustine.[53] For the voluntarists, the dilemma seems to point to an unruly and intractable will that is not governed by the rational mind. For voluntarist Christian thinkers, the will is not closely connected with the intellect, and it can be mastered by the passions and appetites; sin is not a matter of rational error but of a perverse will.

The workings of the will and the passions went on to become central preoccupations for many Christian thinkers in the early modern period. Norman Fiering demonstrates that in Christian moral anthropology of the 17th and 18th centuries, there was a remarkable expansion in the exploration of the inner life; he describes a "renewed religious concern with the whole man, an immersion in the problems of the inner life, the realm of appetites, affections, passions, and inclinations, which the pagan moralists, by comparison, had only touched on."[54] In this context, the will becomes "almost synonymous with the inner essence of the whole man, the battleground of God and the devil," in which the "personal drama of salvation is enacted." Human salvation is seen as entirely dependent upon the quality of one's will, on the "fundamental disposition of his heart."[55] This "new moral science of the inward man," initiated by both Protestant and Catholic thinkers, led to further developments a century later in Christian morality and theology (most notably perhaps in Jonathan Edwards's treatment of the will) and, in a more secular or naturalistic direction, to the British moral sense theorists who began to develop a psychology of motivation untethered to the idea of the will.

Although the principal intellectualist and voluntarist debates about the will lost their vitality by the end of the seventeenth century, and the notion of the will itself became increasingly called into question in secular philosophy, certain legacies of these debates still influence modern thinking on intention, even in the study of Buddhist ethics. For example, the question

53. Ibid., 115. It is also one version of the classic problem of *akrasia*, referred to in modern philosophy as "weakness of the will."

54. Fiering, *Jonathan Edwards's Moral Thought and Its British Context*, 5.

55. Fiering, *Moral Psychology at Seventeenth-Century Harvard*, 117.

of whether *cetanā* is largely a matter of cognitive or rational decision making, or whether it is chiefly about emotion or impulse, may be a distant echo of the intellectualist-voluntarist dispute. But perhaps less obviously, this tradition of Christian thinking has bequeathed to us a certain set of presuppositions about the inner dimensions of moral knowledge that continue to inform modern treatments of Buddhist thought. Since the language of conscience has been invoked in reference to *cetanā*, it does not take us too far afield to examine it briefly here. Although the concept of a conscience as a special faculty (rather than simply a kind of moral knowledge) goes back to the 13th century,[56] early modern Protestant theologians elaborated an idea of, as Fiering puts it, a "determined construction of a sacrosanct personal inner space" that bears witness to and judges our actions.[57] While more recent conceptions of the conscience may have parted with their overtly Christian moorings, they nevertheless retain a sense of conscience as an inner guide to decision and action that is highly autonomous and individualized: each individual possesses within his or her own innermost resources a capacity for moral reflection and choice. In this conception, moral agency occurs as the individual consults his or her conscience and makes "free" choices accordingly. This is a very particular conception of human nature that has its own religious and intellectual history, and it may not have direct analogs outside the West; it is not, I argue, present in the Pāli sources.[58]

But to return to the will: Enlightenment scholars grew increasingly skeptical about the will as a separate faculty of human agency and about the tripartite division of faculties into the emotive, rational, and conative. John Locke dispensed with the notion of the will as a faculty as a "distinct being" or "distinct agent within us" and refashioned the will or volition merely as "a power to begin or forbear, continue or end several actions of our minds, and motions of our bodies."[59] Hobbes had already

---

56. The term *conscience* is a translation from Greek *syneidesis*, which describes a judgment of the mind concerning the moral value of a particular act.

57. Fiering, *Moral Psychology at Seventeenth-Century Harvard*, 55–56.

58. David McMahan offers an excellent analysis of the many different sides of the subjective turn in Western thought and its grafting onto Buddhist thought (*The Making of Buddhist Modernism*). The "inner light of the self" becomes the chief resource for morality not only via its Christian heritage but also through Romantic, rationalist, and psychological conceptions of the self developed in modernity (200).

59. Locke, *An Essay Concerning Human Understanding*, Bk II, ch. 21, 5–6.

reduced the will merely to "the last appetite in deliberating," an appetite or aversion leading to action, something in fact shared with the beasts.[60] Subsequent philosophy has more or less discarded a conception of the will, favoring a simpler idea of volition, defined as "an inner, mental event or act of consciousness which is the cause, accompaniment, or necessary condition for any outer action, that is, for any voluntary movement of the body."[61] While the will was reinvigorated in the hands of some—in its role as self-legislation in Kant's thought and in the robust senses granted to the will in the 19th century by both Schopenhauer and Nietzsche—in general it gave way to various systems of moral psychology that replaced a singular sense of the will with more diffuse sources of motivation. Throughout much of the 20th century, philosophical accounts of action tended to reduce volition or will to a matter of practical reasoning about beliefs and desires[62] or abandon it entirely in favor of other accounts of action.[63]

We have good reason to put some distance between Buddhist *cetanā* and the concept of the will as developed by Augustine and subsequent Christian thought. Augustine's clustering of so many psychological functions around the will and his investing it with so much religious and moral value bear little resemblance, as we will see, to *cetanā*; moreover, his vision of a unified self with separate competing faculties does not sit well in light of Buddhist theories of nonself. The pervasive division of cognitive, affective, and conative faculties, elemental to premodern Western moral philosophy, feels forced when read back into Buddhist thought. *Cetanā* is not a faculty or set of abilities that may be posited independently of any particular action, nor does it ever act as sovereign over or apart from the dynamic conditioned and conditioning factors that constitute human experience as described in dependent origination. *Cetanā* is not a site for battles of the will; nor is it the site for discussions of free agency. It is not appropriate to inquire into the weakness of *cetanā*, as one might in worrying about the moral problem of the weakness of the will (*akrasia*); nor would traditional Buddhist systems connect *cetanā* to the notion of willpower. All of these usages, so familiar to us in talking about the will, do not transfer in any clear way to Buddhist ideas of *cetanā*.

---

60. Hobbes, *Leviathan*, ch. 6, 45.

61. Kahn, "Discovering the Will," 235.

62. As, for example, Davidson, *Essays on Actions and Events*.

63. Ryle, *The Concept of Mind*.

It is also worth noting that the question of free will, for reasons that by now should be increasingly apparent, is not my main entry point into Buddhist theories of agency. Although how this philosophical problem as it might apply to Buddhist ethics has sometimes been taken up in modern scholarship,[64] it is not the chief way in which the Buddhist sources themselves examine questions about intention or, for that matter, human freedom. The preoccupation with the will's freedom is an artifact of particular Western philosophical reflexes initiated by Augustine.[65] It is not a question considered directly by the Buddhist texts: abstract formulations about human freedom are not attached to the term *cetanā*. Questions of freedom in Buddhism are best treated independently from the idea of the will or intention, and we do not want to tie questions of human freedom to this one term.[66] This is not to suggest that Buddhists were not concerned with the tension between the conditioned nature of human thought and action and the measure of freedom required for morally accountable action, and these worries are a key theme of this study. But these concerns are articulated in ways quite apart from the language of free will.

Thus, while it may be that the notion of the will (and its modern correlate, volition) is too heavily freighted with Western religious and philosophical assumptions to offer a useful entry into our interpretation of *cetanā*, we do have other options. Since Guenther identifies *cetanā* with the idea of motive or stimulus, it is important to clarify this vocabulary. *Motivation* as it is used in current philosophy is connected to needs, wants, and desires, whether this is articulated in a straightforward kind of psychological hedonism (all actions are motivated by a desire for pleasure and the absence of pain) or a more nuanced account of the varieties of drives, desires, and emotions that prompt action. The psychology of motivation refers, in a most general way, to all mental factors that stimulate and sustain behavior.

---

64. See, for example, Gómez, "Some Aspects of the Free-Will Question in the *Nikāyas*"; Wayman, "Discussion of Frederick Streng"; Harvey, "Freedom of the Will"; and Federman, "What Kind of Free Will Did the Buddha Teach?" Most successful in this approach is Karin Meyers's Chicago dissertation, *Freedom and Self-Control: Free Will in South Asian Buddhism.*

65. Kahn, "Discovering the Will," 251.

66. Sorabji argues that questions of freedom in Western thought, too, are best treated apart from the notion of the will (*Emotion and Peace of Mind*, 340); see also Murdoch, *The Sovereignty of Good.* Current work in neuroscience also complicates traditional notions of freedom of the will, particularly those studies that describe brain activity toward movement as occurring before such movement is registered in consciousness. See Pocket, Banks, and Gallagher (*Does Consciousness Cause Behavior?*) for a useful volume on neuroscience's advances in our understanding of agency and some of the implications of these findings.

Its modern history may be traced to the flourishing of the psychology of motivation in the 18th century, when various philosophers, in part reacting to Locke's empiricism and Hobbes's pessimism about human nature, developed complex accounts of the "springs of action."[67] Diverse senses, sentiments, and affections, advanced first by Shaftesbury and Hutcheson and later by Hume and Smith, described human beings as constitutively endowed with moral and benevolent feelings that prompt action, a move that made religious authority in morals unnecessary and reason's role largely supplementary. Their accounts of the moral sentiments are rich and complex, and while they do not directly map onto the language of *cetanā*, it may be fair to suggest that from a broader perspective of overall approach, the 18th-century moral sense theorists offer more direct analogs to certain Buddhist theories of motivation, emotion, and intention than many other Western systems.

Nevertheless, the term *motivation* would seem to be a good deal wider, strictly speaking, than is what is meant by *cetanā*. In the context of Buddhist moral and religious psychology, desire and feeling, though far from irrelevant to intention, are covered by quite different categories. A central question for this study will be how *cetanā* is related to the various feelings, desires, and promptings that are suggested by the English term *motivation*. There is considerable language in the Pāli sources for varieties of desire in reference to action and effort (*chanda*, the desire to do something; *adhimokkha*, resolve; *viriya*, *vāyāma*, effort). There are also factors of the mind that suggest motivational impulses or groundings of actions (*hetu* or *mūla*, the causes or roots, often very deeply planted, of action), as well as motivations concerning reward or punishment through karmic effects (*vipāka*, *phala*, result or fruit; *puñña*, merit). Feelings are described in many contexts and are in many instances the chief prompts of action and vital indicators of its moral value. And of course, there occur in diverse contexts in the Buddhist literatures many terms for disposition, character, and virtue, all of which may be seen to influence action. Although we will come to see the diverse ways all of these factors play into action, the term *motivation* will be used in this study primarily for

67. The term "springs of action," while perhaps most notably appearing in Jeremy Bentham's *A Table of the Springs of Action* (a fascinating taxonomy of the sources of motivated action), was frequently used in this period to describe the fonts of action. See McReynolds, *Four Early Works on Motivation*, xxxi. This volume makes available two of Hutcheson's works on motivation, Jeremy Bentham's *Table* and *An Enquiry into the Origin of the Human Appetites and Affections*, attributed to James Long.

the motivational roots (*hetu, mūla*), which prompt intentional action but should not be conflated with *cetanā*.

As already suggested, our closest match for *cetanā* may be the English word *intention*, though here, too, important divergences exist. *Cetanā*, like intention, is by definition connected to action.[68] This makes it narrower than desire or motivation, which can have many different types of content: one's motivation can be money or love, for example, whereas one's intention is always to perform some particular action. *Intention*'s history, in English, begins around the 14th century, when it conveyed "the action of intending or purposing; volition which one is minded to carry out; purpose" and, a century later, "the aim of an action."[69] Today, a useful working definition of *intention* and *intentionality* can be taken from Malle, Moses, and Baldwin: intentionality is "a quality of actions (those that are intentional or done on purpose), whereas intention is an agent's mental state that represents such actions."[70] We can modify this definition to fit *cetanā* more precisely to suggest that intention refers to the mental processes that *constitute* (rather than represent) purposeful action. *Cetanā*, as we will come to see, is creating and performing a purposeful and (usually) morally relevant action. Notice that it is the creating and doing of action; in the quotation with which we began defining action as intention, one does not occur without the other. In this it may bear some limited affinities with a recent construal of intention as "adopting a course of action."[71] But it does not refer merely to what are referred to as "future-directed intentions," or the *planning* aspects of action, as in Michael Bratman's theory of intention.[72] Buddhist texts have ways of talking about planning action, but they do not usually use *cetanā* to name that activity. Nor are there ready parallels in *cetanā* to the desire-belief model of intention that held sway in the latter half of the 20th century in Western philosophy until Bratman's work. And *intention* in the sense of wish or aim, or in the sense

---

68. Malle and Knobe, "The Distinction between Desire and Intention," 47.

69. Oxford English Dictionary.

70. Malle, Moses, and Baldwin, *Intentions and Intentionality*, 3. This book is a collection on recent interdisciplinary work that takes intention as an object of empirical research.

71. See Scheer, "The 'Mental State' Theory of Intentions," 123; also "Intentions, Motives, and Causation" and "The Origin of Intentions."

72. Bratman, *Intentions, Plans, and Practical Reason*. Bratman acknowledges the importance of present-directed intentions, but for him, "the future-directed case is central" (4).

of authorial intention or intended meaning, is covered by entirely different language in Pāli: *adhippāya*.

One advantage of the use of the term *intention* for *cetanā* is that it can suggest the phenomenological sense of intentionality, which concerns the property of a mental state that makes it *about* an object. If we develop the idea of this aboutness to consider the particular ways mental phenomena are related to and intertwined with their objects, there may be intriguing elements of this idea evident in *cetanā*. Martha Nussbaum is interested in the way intentional mental states are about their objects "not from a mechanical sort of directedness" but rather from one's "active ways of seeing and interpreting."[73] As we will see, *cetanā* often refers to the complex ways the mind actively interprets (and indeed constructs) its objects.

It is also worth noting at the outset that since *cetanā* is so closely tied up with karma, that is, morally relevant action, it is not easily separated from moral questions; this makes it difficult to treat it as a thing apart from ethics, as G. E. M. Anscombe and Donald Davidson do, for example, in their treatments of intention. Modern treatments of action investigate intention and action generically and then consider ethical action as a subset of action, if it is considered at all. The Pāli sources generally classify action, or karma, immediately into good, bad, and neutral action, as distinctions useful for thinking about how to live well and for thinking about the effects of action; to consider intention means that one is already immersed in questions of ethics or morality so conceived.[74] In addition, *cetanā* plays a very important role in Buddhist soteriological doctrines, an issue I will defer discussing to the next chapter.

Although it is not my aim to discern which, if any, Western system or thinker might best match Buddhist theories of moral agency, much less to engage systematically with modern theories, conceptual clarity has required reviewing, even if only briefly, the ways these terms have been understood in Western philosophy and psychology. All of these terms are part of historical traditions, and it would be surprising if they shared the

---

73. Nussbaum, *Upheavals of Thought*, 28. On the phenomenological view of intentionality in Brentano, Husserl, and Merleau-Ponty, see Glendinning, *In the Name of Phenomenology*.

74. The adjectives *moral* and *ethical* are used throughout the book in broad and general ways to get at the some of the ideas we will see introduced in the beginning of the next chapter concerning how to live well. These can then be juxtaposed against neutral values, on the one hand, and against soteriological values, on the other. But they do not indicate a single unified natural category that maps onto modern Western treatments of moral judgments as a single category. This will be discussed more thoroughly in chapter 1.

same meanings, given their particular genealogies and the vicissitudes of the diverse contexts in which they were attributed meaning. The best we might hope for is to achieve a language that is analogous enough to bring us close to the ideas in the Buddhist sources, while we stay on guard against assuming an overly uncritical equivalence. All of the English terms considered thus far may illuminate certain aspects of Buddhist moral psychology, even as they serve as points of departure for our evolving interpretations of it.

There is much at stake for ethical inquiry in these considerations about translation. Depending upon how scholars have translated the key word *cetanā*, they have also characterized Buddhist moral thinking more generally. For those who see in *cetanā* a sense of choice or rational deliberation, Buddhist ethics (still unfortunately treated in a holistic fashion by many scholars) is seen to be principally a matter of means-ends decision making. Those who see *cetanā* as a matter of conscience center Buddhist ethics more generally around a notion of an autonomous inner guide or set of moral convictions, often uncritically presuming a certain conception of moral agency that may be in evidence only in modern Western thought. A more fine-grained grasp of moral psychology as it is articulated in the various genres of Theravāda discourse will yield a more promising portrait of at least certain dimensions of this tradition of Buddhist thought.

Structure

As a term subject to technical definition and precision, *cetanā*, and related terms for conation, find their meaning and significance in diverse contexts and genres of Buddhist thought. Buddhaghosa describes the three branches of canonical texts—the Suttanta, the Vinaya, and the Abhidhamma—in a manner that can, in part, structure our own explorations of intention. He describes the Suttas—that is, the teachings of the Buddha in his many sermons—as teachings in the everyday or colloquial idiom that are straightforward and geared to people of various dispositions, inherent tendencies, and behaviors.[75] They are concerned with questions of meaning as it concerns self and other, with how the processes of mind and thought work, with how to abandon problematic states of mind and the defilements of

75. The following discussion is from a passage found in three places: Sv.i.17–22; As 19–24; Sp 17–23.

craving and ignorance, and with the refutation of wrong views. Where the Suttas are about colloquial meanings, the Abhidhamma, according to Buddhaghosa, is the teaching of the Buddha that analyzes things in their ultimate sense, and it is in this genre that we find the most technical meanings of the terms and ideas under consideration. The Abhidhamma, focused as it is on the "higher" wisdom of the Buddha's teaching, treats the ultimate factors of experience through analysis and defines the names of things and the physical forms of them. It is for those who see in the various factors of a person a robust sense of self and ownership, and who need to be disabused of this conception, since in the ultimate sense a human person is nothing more than "just a pile of factors" (*dhammapuñjamatto*).[76] The Vinaya or the monastic code is described as the Buddha's injunctions or commands about offenses and faults. Its strictures involve restraint on behavior, the higher morality of monastic practice, and the transgressions that imperil that practice. Concerned solely with monks and nuns who have taken the monastic vows, it instructs them about their faults and defilements in conduct.

Despite some overlap among genres, particularly in the commentaries, on these different emphases, we may look to these genres for quite distinctive treatments of intention. The Suttas and their commentaries provide us with several key passages on intention that form the core of our investigations in chapter 1, and we learn that *cetanā* is, in fact, a quite technical term even in the Suttanta. This chapter investigates some of the general ways in which the mind creates actions, referring not only to intentions but also to motivations, causes, and elements of disposition and temperament. Since moral considerations are almost always connected to discussions of *cetanā* in this literature, we also spend some time trying to understand what is meant by good (*kusala*) and bad (*akusala*) intentions, both in formal definitions of these terms and in actual actions. This chapter also locates *cetanā* in larger psychological frameworks in which intention is a chief component of the constructive activities (*saṅkhāra*) of the mind and considers the implications of this for Buddhist soteriology.

While there are similarities in content in the Sutta and Abhidhamma texts, there are differences in method. We turn in chapter 2 to the Abhidhamma texts and commentaries for our most technical and scholastic treatment of intention. In Abhidhamma, we find a catalog of mental factors that undergird moral agency; the commentaries on the canonical

76. As 21.

sources produce a complex moral phenomenology describing how moral and immoral actions occur. Our challenge in this chapter is to examine Abhidhamma styles of definition, including its prolific use of lists and metaphors, to interpret the processes of conation. Here we find *cetanā* not as an autonomous faculty of mind, but embedded in a matrix of processes, such as attention, feeling, and motivation, that condition and constitute action. The canonical Abhidhamma does not treat persons as such; rather, it treats the phenomena that comprise experience. It offers theories of action and mind that depict various mental factors working together through complex interrelations to produce actions. Intention is understood variously in this chapter: as the key constructive element in action, as a workmanlike mental activity that integrates and stimulates other processes of mind, and as one essential, if not sufficient, causal factor of moral action. This literature also provides a morally and soteriologically inflected psychology: factors of mind can be good, bad, or neutral according to a clear set of criteria.

Chapter 3 takes up the legalistic treatment of intention in the Vinaya and its commentaries. The *Atthasālinī* says that where the Abhidhamma teaches the discrete psychological factors (*dhammas*) that go into experience—perception, feeling, intention, and so on—in the Vinaya it is enough to talk more generally of "mind" or "thought" (*citta*) without feeling one has to parse the intricacies of the interior conditions that make up action.[77] Because much of this literature is concerned with infractions of the monastic code, the Vinaya treats intention largely from a legal standpoint. Often the intentional element in legal reasoning is an omission, or recklessness, or it is simply enough to say whether an act is done with knowledge or consent, and nothing more needs to be said about it as a psychological state. Since this material is highly attuned to the language of culpability and blame, and penalties are meted out according to intent, the Vinaya and its commentaries develop a highly nuanced set of presuppositions about the relation of actions to mental events. These presuppositions find expression in the interpretation of particular cases.

Other considerations occur in the Vinaya that are not as explicit as its concern with matters of culpability, but come to be readily apparent when we identify the texts' various techniques of self-formation. By its own account, the Vinaya governs acts of body and speech and does not regulate

77. As 68.

mental actions. At the same time, its rules and institutional norms create a certain type of sensibility and subjectivity in ways that the texts are sometimes quite explicit about, and thus, at least at the level of the ideal, the Vinaya creates or conditions a model type of moral agency. Thus in addition to attending to the way the Vinaya considers intention in matters of culpability, I also chart how the texts understood the ways that social, religious, and institutional processes shape intention.

Finally, in chapter 4, we turn to narratives. The narrative collections, of course, do not formally constitute a fourth *piṭaka*, but we do have some precedent with Buddhaghosa understanding them as a distinctive form of teaching, as I have already suggested. In particular, stories provide the very settings and histories that identify—and constitute—intention and action.

Many stories are interested in human intention and motivation—what makes people do what they do—but, like the Vinaya literature, they do not always use the language of *cetanā* to describe them and often speak more broadly of "mind." We turn in this chapter to the diverse ways that narratives treat the causes, reasons, and explanations for why people do what they do. What makes a good account of people's actions? The stories provide rich and varied possibilities for exploring how and why people ascribe intentions to others; bystander monks are almost always interested in figuring out why people do what they do, though they are often corrected in their interpretations by the omniscient Buddha, who knows all minds and can frame actions in a larger scope of time and personal narrative. Minds and intentions are *negotiated* in these stories by the characters' conversations. Intentions in this chapter are thus not so much a matter of private inner thoughts, but rather products of narrative and dialogue. I borrow from scholars in cognitive science, cultural psychology, and anthropology who see intention less as a psychological state of mind and more as an emergent social process, an irreducible unity of self in action with others, and a matter of negotiated social meaning.

Thus, while we begin our study with *cetanā* and other relevant factors of action, our interest in agency and intention extends substantially beyond exploring these terms and the system of moral phenomenology in which they operate, and it moves into the ways that social and discursive processes construct, mediate, and describe intentional action.

I

Constructing Experience

INTENTION IN THE SUTTAS

IN AN IMPORTANT teaching on the nature of karma, the Buddha encourages people to ask wise recluses and brahmans the following questions:

> What is good, what is bad? What is blameworthy, what is blameless? What should be practiced, what should not be practiced? What, when done, leads to my lasting harm and suffering, and what when done, leads to my lasting welfare and happiness?[1]

The sermon occurs, Buddhaghosa explains, when a young man is pondering the nature of rebirth, having been shocked to learn that his miserly father became a dog after his death, and that after his dog life, he will journey on to hell. The Buddha explains the workings of karma, how actions create the disposition and temperament that determine future births. Beings are, the Buddha explains, the "owners of their actions, the heirs of their actions; they originate from their actions, are bound to their actions, and have actions as their refuge."[2] Actions, in a fundamental way, create and condition and determine who and what beings are and are at the center, we might say, of their nature or identity. Because action makes us who we are and what we will experience, it is a matter of great urgency to ask wise people about what kinds of actions we should do. Buddhaghosa says that this is something one must inquire about because, "if one does not ask, one will not know what is to be done."[3]

---

1. This is the *sutta* on the Shorter Analysis of Action, M.iii.206. (This passage also occurs at D.iii.60 as advice about the kinds of questions a Cakkavatti king should ask and at D.iii.157 as describing the questions the Tathāgata asked in his previous lives, resulting in his eventually achieving the 32 marks of a great man.)

2. M.iii.203.

3. Ps.v.14.

Much of the Theravāda thought we will be concerned with can be located in this quest for happiness: how can I know what to do so that I can be happy and avoid sorrow? The search for knowledge about what is good and beneficial for human beings indicated here is not just a theoretical exercise, but is driven by pragmatic concerns, by people who want to discover and do what will lead to happiness instead of sorrow, what leads to good rebirths instead of hell. Buddhist reflection about what we would call morally relevant intention and action is located in this yearning to avoid the bad, the blameworthy, and the harmful and to practice the good and the blameless in order to find happiness. These concerns reflect some of the range of questions one might ask while engaged in what has been called in the Aristotelian tradition *ethics*—questions about how to live. It is in this spirit that the use of the adjectives *ethical* and *moral* throughout the book can be located; I do not use them to indicate a single unified category of morality that the book tries to unearth or glean from Buddhaghosa.[4]

Although this passage and others like it advise us to frequently turn to wise people with such questions, in another *sutta* we see a more empirical approach, suggesting that people can figure out for themselves what is good and which actions they should perform. We can come to know what is good for human beings through experiential study and observation, and this idea is perhaps nowhere more evident than in the well-known Kālāma Sutta, a favorite text of many modern interpreters (though Buddhaghosa appears to have been considerably less interested in it). This teaching captures the Buddha at perhaps his most empirical, where he invites this particular audience to come to know for themselves what is good and bad and to not rely on oral report, tradition, hearsay, scripture, logic, inference, reasoning, speculation, convention, or the authority of a teacher.[5]

---

4. As Charles Hallisey has argued, Theravādins often resisted a notion of offering generalizable criteria that would serve as a rationale for constructing a single category that would match anything like modern categories of "morality" (Hallisey, "Ethical Particularism in Theravāda Buddhism" and "A Reply to Kevin Schilbrack"). This is not philosophical laziness on their parts, but a distinctive choice in the direction of what Hallisey calls "ethical pluralism." It is also in keeping with what Walter Sinnott-Armstrong argues from the perspective of neuroethics, which is that morality is not a single unified category ("Keynote").

5. As important as it has been to modern interpreters, the Kālāma Sutta was not discussed much by Buddhaghosa and Dhammapāla, who do little but gloss its terms. I agree with those scholars who insist that the Kālāma Sutta must be taken in context as advice offered specifically to the Kālāmas, a well-educated but skeptical community of people who were not yet the Buddha's followers. To his own followers, the Buddha did not recommend a freewheeling empiricism of simply following one's own moral preferences (as this *sutta* has sometimes, anachronistically, been read).

A key part of what one will discover, the *sutta* suggests, when one attends empirically to one's action and its results is something about intention.

The Buddha offers, among other things, a number of assurances to the Kālāmas about the way that moral action leads to happiness, one of which brings up the equivalence of intention and action and suggests one important role it plays in how karma is interpreted. The Buddha sets up the assurance as a rhetorical question: "Suppose while acting, evil is done, but I did not intend (*cetemi*) evil for anyone. Since I did not do an evil action, how can sorrow touch me?"[6] This suggestion offers a sense of assurance or comfort: only what I *mean* to do is morally relevant and karmically fruitful. I may inadvertently bring about an evil effect while acting, but if I did not *intend* the evil, then a morally relevant action, that is, evil karma, did not take place, and I will not experience the sorrow that would otherwise follow it. This assurance responds to the anxieties one might have in a karmic reality in which one is acting all of the time and, all too often, doing actions that are morally problematic. What it appears to assert, on the face of it, is that the karmic laws of cause and effect are attuned to human intention. Moreover, the assertion is suggested in a larger teaching on discovering such things for oneself: one can observe that only what one intends is of moral consequence, leading to one's benefit or harm.

This is by no means obvious, for often it seems that bad consequences flow from even well-intended actions. The suggestion that karma is morally equivalent to intention may be regarded as positing something new or potentially controversial in its context. The idea that action is, at least for the sake of moral evaluation, solely a matter of mental processes (rather than the effects of action) is a bold one. The implications of this view are considerable for understanding the workings of karma and investigating how the tradition assigns moral culpability. Chiefly, though, they point us *inward* to discover just what those mental processes are that are deemed morally significant. It is through looking to the inner moral landscape of the mind that we can come to see how and why the Buddha thought that experience will demonstrate that it is what we intend to do that matters in creating our present and future condition.

We thus begin psychologically. The Buddha invites the Kālāmas to see what happens when they make their thoughts "free of enmity, ill will, corruptions, and pure," and thus he turns our gaze inward to discover how

---

6. A.i.192.

happiness and welfare follow from a purification of thought. But what is pure thought and intention? The Suttanta (and the Abhidhamma in an even more refined manner) provides a complex moral phenomenology to explore thoughts and intentions and how they are related to (what we would call) emotions, motivations, and dispositions. This phenomenology is part of a larger moral anthropology that investigates the moral capacities and limitations of human nature.

It is not an exaggeration to say that the amount of textual material in the Suttanta branch of the Pāli canon is huge—and doubly so when we consider the commentarial sources as well. Moreover, the interest this material displays in what might be very generally termed the "springs of action"—that is, the entire range of emotions, motivations, dispositions, and intentions that lead to action—is considerable. This chapter does not attempt to survey everything that relates to intention or motivation in this body of literature. Rather, I focus on several central passages about *cetanā*, investigate relevant ideas and terms raised in those passages, and then discuss other important usages of intention and how they can help us to understand moral thought in this branch of Pāli literature.

Cetanā

We begin with two important canonical passages that deal centrally with intention (*cetanā*) that can begin to guide us into how the Pāli tradition understood and used it. It is perhaps most appropriate to start by looking more closely at the well-known quotation from the *Aṅguttara* that opens this study where the Buddha links karma to *cetanā*. As we recall, the Buddha asserted that intention is karma and that, intending, one does karma with body, speech, and mind.[7] What exactly does this mean, and what is the context in which this assertion occurs?

According to this *sutta*, the Buddha taught this idea in a teaching described as a "penetrating method" (*nibbedhika-pariyāya*); the sutta is called "Penetrating Sutta." Buddhaghosa takes this to mean that this method causes penetration; it "pierces and penetrates" that which has not yet been

---

7. A.iii.415. *Cetanāhaṃ, bhikkhave, kammaṃ vadāmi. Cetayitvā kammaṃ karoti—kāyena vācāya manasā.* Karin Meyers quite rightly calls this line a "*mahāvākya*," a "sacred announcement" as it is used in modern scholarship on Buddhist ethics to encapsulate a modernist and Western preoccupation with reading karma in terms of inner freedom and moral responsibility, which she then criticizes (*Freedom and Self Control*, 138, 156–57).

pierced and penetrated.[8] It is a teaching expressed in analytical terms, puncturing through what had not yet been comprehended. And so we begin our study quite technically (rather than colloquially). The *sutta* defines and analyzes five topics in addition to action (karma): desire (*kāma*), feeling (*vedanā*), perception (*saññā*), the depravities (*āsavā*), and suffering (*dukkha*). These six topics are fundamental aspects of human experience, offering a somewhat expanded version of the five aggregates,[9] which itself is an analysis attempting to categorize all possible experience.

The text penetrates each of these phenomena by defining the phenomenon itself, its origin, its varieties, its fruit, its cessation, and the path to its cessation; this is a mode of analysis familiar to us from that of the Four Noble Truths. If we understand each of these as something that is present to us as a phenomenon and that can be analyzed according to its arising, its cessation, and the path to its cessation, we can see it in both temporal and soteriological lights. Karma and the other five phenomena are things that arise from certain conditions, bear fruit, and cease, a temporal sequence within a conditioned reality of other things that is crucial for interpreting what they are. Finally, the path to cessation for each of them is the Noble Eightfold Path, a soteriological trajectory that indicates that these experiences are undesirable and can be ended. This is not the only way these six things can be analyzed, and indeed the modes of analysis provided by lists are usually not intended to be comprehensive. But recognizing this mode of analysis goes some distance in helping us to understand each of these phenomena.

In addition, for each topic the text is concerned with the inner, subjective aspects of the phenomenon and says nothing about the external aspects of it; for example, in the case of desire, the *sutta* specifies that it is referring to desire as a person's passionate thoughts and not desire's objects or the ways it is expressed in the world.[10] The text is explicitly signaling that it is not offering an exhaustive definition of any of these items and instead is concerned solely with the interior or subjective aspects of each experience.

---

8. Mp.iii.406.

9. The six topics can be said to correspond to the five aggregates (*rūpa, vedanā, saññā, saṅkhāra*, and *viññāṇa*) that comprise human experience, with *kāma* corresponding to *rūpa, āsavā* and *karma* corresponding to *saṅkhāra*, and *dukkha to viññāṇa*. I am grateful to Steven Collins for pointing this out, as well as other key insights about this *sutta* in the following two paragraphs.

10. A.iii.411.

When he comes to karma, the Buddha first asks, "What should be said regarding karma?" And then he defines karma as *cetanā*: "I say that karma is *cetanā*" and that "intending, one does karma with body, speech, and mind." We can also translate this as "one does karma intentionally with body, speech, and mind," which offers a slightly different sense. Regardless, here we see the inward turn in defining the phenomenon according to the subjective dimension of physical, verbal, and mental actions. (Intention's relationship to mental action, which also is internal, requires further exploration.) The Buddha goes on to identify karma's "origin" as arising from sensory contact with the world and its "varieties" as the experiences that are had in hell, in animal lives, in ghost lives, in human lives, and in the divine realms. In this designation, the variety of action is something to be known or experienced (*vedanīya*) in these various locations in the rounds of rebirth. The *sutta* goes on to say that karma's "fruit" can occur either in the present, in the near future, or at some later time, its "cessation" as occurring at the ceasing of sensory contact, and the "path leading to its cessation" as the Noble Eightfold Path.

While what exactly the Buddha meant by *intention* here may be unknowable, Buddhaghosa offers a definition that suggests at least how he came to understand it: "here *cetanā* should be taken in the sense of arranging, in that it collects everything together."[11] He glosses the absolutive *intending* to mean that "an intention occurs at the doorway," which refers to a theory about action, discussed more thoroughly later, that involves *cetanā* occurring or located at a doorway or site of action according to whether the action is mental, verbal, or physical. But what does it mean that an intention "arranges" and "collects everything together"? Dhammapāla, author of the subcommentary, says that collecting everything together means *cetanā* holds together what is good or bad and that the "sense of arranging" means that its characteristic is arranging associated factors (*dhammas*).[12] These definitions are, of course, quite technical and even obscure at this point in our study and will require many pages in this and the following chapter to understand.

Another commentary on this passage, though brief, is worth mentioning here. In a section on a passage from his commentary on the Upāli Sutta in the *Majjhima* (a *sutta* later discussed briefly), Buddhaghosa quotes

11. Mp.iii.408.

12. Mp-ṭ.iii.139. Good (*kusala*) and bad (*akusala*) are discussed at length later, and *dhammas*, the momentary factors of experience, are treated in the next chapter.

this passage in the *Aṅguttara.* He brings this up in the context of a discussion on whether karma or intention is foremost. He says that some *suttas* say that karma is foremost (or the leading, prior part, *dhura*), and others say that *cetanā* is foremost. So what did the Buddha mean when he said that karma is *cetanā*? The answer, he says, is that *cetanā* is "the origin from which action springs" (*cetanāmūlakattā kammassa*), attempting to state more precisely their exact relationship.[13] The issue here, I think, is a subtle one, but it exposes a suppressed tension in these sources: is it mind that makes action (as the epigraph of this book suggests in identifying the mind as the forerunner of all things), or is it action that is prior and mind inherits its effects (as in the passage on humans as the "heirs of their actions" with which we opened this chapter)? Both are, of course, true when we consider an agent across time, but here, and I think most often, Buddhaghosa comes down on the side of intention being the root of action, suggesting its priority (priority in terms of importance, not temporal relation, since they occur simultaneously). But this tension should be noted when in evidence, and there will be certain moments in which actions are evaluated independently and prior to the intentions that constitute them.

The second passage we will consider here, the Intention Sutta in the *Aṅguttara,*[14] offers a more extensive treatment of *cetanā.* In a general way, this *sutta,* too, is concerned with the arising and ceasing of action and the subjective dimensions of it. It asserts that pleasure and pain arise subjectively as they are conditioned by intention in all three types of actions: physical, verbal, and mental. They cease at the cessation of ignorance. The *sutta* is also interested in how one's own and others' intentions create one's experience of pleasure and pain, recognizing that one's experiences are often conditioned by others' intentional actions. Finally, it says that these processes may be either deliberate (*sampajāno*) or not and yet still have the same effects in producing pleasure or pain.

We will parse each of these claims in turn, but first it is important to discuss the distinction invoked in both *suttas* between physical, verbal, and

13. Ps.iii.54.

14. Subsequent passages are quoted from this *sutta,* the *Sañcetaniyavaggo* (A.ii.158–60; the commentary is Mp.iii.143–48 and Mp-ṭ.ii.345). This *sutta* does not describe a context of the circumstances of its teaching, and the commentators do not provide one. Compare this passage to S.ii.34–40 and Spk.ii.56–58, where a similar passage occurs in the context of explaining dependent origination, and to M.iii.209, where the aim is to show how pleasure and pain arise. *Sañcetanā* and *cetanā* are used synonymously.

mental action, as it is pervasive in the tradition's thinking about action. The threefold division of action appears to have been part of the intellectual landscape of the Buddha's day, though the precise workings and moral weight put on each of the types were often points of contention, at least as matters are represented in the Buddhist texts. The Buddhist texts regard themselves as distinctive among their rival teachers, especially Jains, in emphasizing mental action as the most important of these, though all three are morally significant in the sense of being karmically fruitful.[15]

According to the account of action sketched in the Pāli sources, one has an intention that manifests itself at one of three doorways—body, speech, or mind—resulting in three types of action. Buddhaghosa took this quite literally to mean that intention is occurring in movements of the body in the case of bodily actions and in the movements of the jaw for verbal actions, while mental actions occur invisibly in the mind.[16] Sometimes he offers the example of giving a gift. A mental action of giving involves thinking of or planning an actual gift and recipient entirely in one's mind, a verbal action is when one orders someone else to give on one's behalf, and a bodily action is giving the gift oneself. Each of these is considered an action with an intention that occurs at the doorway of its respective location.[17] Buddhaghosa attempts to define how this works quite technically, specifying that *cetanā* is the accumulating of what should be collected together at the three doorways of action.[18] The meaning of this sentence is not fully explained here, but we will come

---

15. The Upāli Sutta describes a discussion between a Jain ascetic and the Buddha about evil action, where the Buddha argues that mental action is more morally significant (in the sense of leading to present and future effects) than verbal or bodily actions, whereas the Jain emphasizes bodily actions (M.i.372–78). See Devdas for a careful comparative treatment with Jains on issues of intentional agency (2008, ch. 2). Another *sutta* in the *Majjhima* describes Buddha arguing with a teacher who has misrepresented the Buddha's view to the effect that only mental actions are real. In this *sutta*, the Buddha reaffirms the significance for one's experience of all three types of actions and their future consequences (M.iii.207–15).

16. Ps.iii.104.

17. As 77–81 provides extensive examples like this; it says, too, that in the case of mental actions, "one would later do the actual verbal or bodily deed" so that it is not just a thought (77). This passage also makes a distinction between Vinaya and Abhidhamma exposition, suggesting that Abhidhamma takes mental actions more seriously than Vinaya does; the latter, as legal discourse, is concerned solely with verbal and bodily actions.

18. Mp.iii.145. "Accumulating" is a specialized sense of *āyūhana*, connected with the processes of "making a heap, making a pile" (*rāsiṃ karoti piṇḍaṃ karoti*) elsewhere (Mp.ii.191) and discussed by Bodhi, *The Connected Discourses of the Buddha*, 342, n. 2; Cone, *A Dictionary of Pāli*, 323; and Devdas, *Cetanā and the Dynamics of Volition*, 345–49. As we will see, accumulating indicates a key function of *cetanā* of gathering together other mental factors in initiating action; this has karmic implications because it is the gathering together of conditioned

to see that *cetanā* is the gathering together and animating of other mental factors in the construction of experience through action.

It is important to note that a mental action (*manokamma*) is not identical to *cetanā*; rather, one has *cetanās* for each of the three actions. Certain types of purely mental activity are considered mental actions and have karmic results even if there is no bodily or verbal behavior involved. In particular, there are six types of mental actions: covetousness, malice, wrong view, the absence of covetousness (such as one might experience in planning a gift), the absence of malice, and right view. This can be confusing because these mental actions, though considered complete actions, can also (though they need not) have motivational force leading to bodily or verbal actions in addition to the mental activity. But they are not to be conflated with *cetanās,* which are the central component of all three types of action.[19]

This location of intention in body, speech, and mind closes the gap between action and intention. Intention does not come first and then culminate in action; intention cannot fail to issue in action.[20] If intention is an essential element of action, I cannot say things like this: I intended to get to class on time but then stopped and chatted with a friend and so failed to do so. Intention and action are joined at the hip, as it were, making philosophical discussion around intention very different than the treatment of it in certain modern Western philosophical treatments, where, following Bratman, for example, we can speak of future-directed intentions as the planning part of an action but not the actualization of it.[21] Here, *cetanā* is part of every karmic action and does not occur independently of action; action, however, will have other components as well.

experience that keeps us in the round of rebirth. Devdas suggests that in addition to its specialized meaning of accumulating, *āyūhana*'s sense of striving or exertion should be preserved in translating it. However, in this passage (*idāni tīsupi dvāresu āyūhanacetanā samodhānetabbā*), the idea is that *cetanā* is accumulating and gathering together other mental processes to galvanize action at the three doorways. This is further discussed later.

19. As 87–90. Devdas is helpful on this, and she shows how the Theravādins' view was regarded as controversial among other Buddhist schools (*Cetanā and the Dynamics of Volition*, 371, 387–96).

20. Note that his close link between intention and action at this level of theory will be in tension with how intention is treated practically in the Vinaya sources.

21. Bratman, 1987. Since the Buddhist conception identifies action with intention, a whole host of philosophical problems that would only occur if the two were deemed separate, such as *akrasia*, do not come up.

The Intention Sutta goes on to emphasize that there are feelings "subjectively" or "inwardly" (*ajjhattam*) experienced in these three types of action: "there arises subjective pleasure or pain" caused by each of these three kinds of intentions. Intentions produce effects experienced as feelings, and the nature of the intention determines whether one feels pleasure or pain. The idea that intentional actions produce felt experience (a basic "hedonic tone," pleasurable, painful or neutral) and that those feelings are to be noted by those who seek a guide for their actions is echoed elsewhere. The feelings accompanying an intentional action are crucial in this moral psychology: in performing an action, if one feels pain, one can know directly and empirically that the action leads to bad results. For example, according to a similar passage in the *Majjhima*, one who kills living beings feels a kind of pain that is in keeping with the violence of the act and its results for the agent facing future karmic repercussions.[22]

Moreover, the Intention Sutta asserts, these intentions are ultimately conditioned by ignorance. In this section, interestingly, the term *saṅkhāra* ("mental constructions") and a verbal form of it, *abhisaṅkharoti*, are used interchangeably with *cetanā*, pointing to an equivalence or overlap that will occupy us at some length later.[23] For now, it is enough to note that the language of *saṅkhāra* and the references to *cetanā* being bound up with felt experience and ignorance signal *cetanā's* role in two essential doctrines—the five aggregates and dependent origination.

The *sutta* then goes on to make a further set of distinctions about *cetanā*. Intentions may occur either on one's own or another person's initiative: "either one intends one's own bodily intention and subjective pleasure or pain arises from that condition, or others intend a bodily intention

22. M.iii.209–10. This text says that feelings associated with actions can be pleasurable, painful, or neither. The subjective nature of our experiencing the fruits of karmic action was an issue contested by other Buddhists; the Theravādins insist that karmic fruit is subjective; that is, it is how we experience our actions and what they lead to. For more on this as it was debated in the *Kathāvatthu*, see McDermott, "The *Kathāvatthu* Kamma Debates," 426.

23. In addition, once the language of *saṅkhāra* is introduced, Buddhaghosa and Dhammapāla tally up the numbers of different kinds of mental, verbal, or bodily *saṅkhāras* or *sañcetanās* according to whether they are good or bad, whether they are located in the realm of sense desire or the realms of form and formlessness (the latter only in the case of certain mental intentions), and whether they are "prompted" (*sasaṅkhārika*). We consider these distinctions further in the Abhidhamma chapter, but a helpful manual to them can be found in the *Abhidhammasaṅgaha* (see Nārada and Bodhi, *A Comprehensive Manual of Abhidhamma*, 32–40). On the 20 bodily, 20 verbal, and 29 mental volitions, see Bodhi, *The Discourse on Right View*, 65.

and subjective pleasure or pain arises from that condition." This is surprising: how can someone else's intention shape my action and experience of it? While the *sutta* itself does not elaborate, Buddhaghosa explains that people can do things by "being aroused and commanded by others."[24] Moreover, the *sutta* goes on to say that other people's intentions can determine our rebirth.[25] How can this be so? Buddhaghosa describes how deities in one of the lower heavens become envious of one another; unless one is protected from such envy, it spreads to both sides.[26] When this happens, both deities fall from that heavenly state. He goes on to suggest that this phenomenon is even more serious among humans who "fall due to their own intentions and others' intentions," because their anger can lead to actual violence. This suggests that our intentions are shaped by others' intentions in a direct way. Although not elaborated with as much precision and detail as we might wish, this recognition of intersubjectivity, occurring either in one acting at the prompting or command of others or in the way the text sees one's own fate as bound up with the intentions of others, may be striking to readers accustomed to seeing intention as a principal site for autonomy and self-determination.

The *sutta* draws a further distinction about intentions: they may be either deliberate or not. What does this mean? Buddhaghosa says that acting deliberately means that one knows that what is good is good and that what is bad is bad, and what the effects or fruits are of one's actions.[27] He illustrates this with the example of young children who, copying their parents, worship shrines and the Saṅgha, make offerings, and so on, without really knowing that what they are doing is good. And animals, too, seem to listen to Dhamma talks and worship shrines and the Saṅgha without really knowing what they are up to. Conversely, children can do mischief without knowing that what they are doing is bad. Such behavior, while not deliberate or done knowingly (*jānanta*), is still intended, and its effects are

24. Spk.ii.57 explains that when acting on one's own initiative, one acts with an unprompted mind (*asaṅkhārikacitta*), and when acting by another's initiative, one acts with a prompted mind (*sasaṅkhārikacitta*). Bhikkhu Bodhi suggests that this passage may be the basis for the Abhidhamma distinction between *sasaṅkhārikacitta* and *asaṅkhārikacitta*, which we will take up in the following chapter (Bodhi, *The Connected Discourses of the Buddha*, 749).

25. There are four ways of attaining birth as a living being: through one's own intention, through another's intention, through both, and through neither (A.ii.159; cf. D.iii.232).

26. Mp.iii.147.

27. Ibid. Again, the terms here for good and bad are *kusala* and *akusala*, to be discussed later.

experienced. Dhammapāla's subcommentary on this passage emphasizes that *knowing* here refers to whether one is aware of the karmic fruits of action. Children act from a readiness (*kammañña*) to imitate their parents without knowing that their actions have future consequences.[28]

It is worth pausing briefly to notice the presence of deities, children, and animals in these interpretations. We discover the nature of ordinary mature human intentions by considering these cases. When even deities in their heavenly conditions act out of envy and anger, we learn something about human intersubjectivity, since humans are even more prone to such failings engendered by contact with others in our fraught and messy social world. Children do not have full mature moral agency, and we can see in their behavior intentions that lack deliberation and knowledge.[29] This tells us that intention does not have to entail deliberation and that moral agency varies in the course of human development. (We might be aware that many empirical investigations of mind and agency in our own time also focus heavily on children.) And the doings of animals, a rich object of moral reflection in the Pāli literature, also help us discern what is uniquely human in our experience while we see that we share much with them, even in their limited moral capacities.[30]

From these two *suttas* and their commentaries, which together give the most extensive discussion of *cetanā* in the Suttanta, we learn several things about intention. First, we see that *cetanā* tends to be discussed in rather technical treatments of psychological factors of experience. *Cetanā* is a mental activity of collecting and arranging mental experiences in the performance of bodily, verbal, or mental action. *Cetanās* are accompanied by subjective feelings of pleasure or pain for their agent and may occur

---

28. Mp-ṭ 2.345.

29. Mil 310–12 discusses the moral and religious capacities of animals and young children. Both can practice well, even though they have no comprehension (*abhisamaya*) of the Dhamma. The minds of children under seven are weak, powerless, limited, small, little, trifling, ignorant, and without clarity, and they cannot grasp the profundity of *nibbāna*. At the same time, children do not have passion, hatred, delusion, conceit, wrong view, discontent, or thoughts concerning sensual pleasure. Indeed, it is for these very reasons that the child is unable to discern what is good or bad or to comprehend the Dhamma; that is, lacking passion and hatred, for example, they do not have enough in their experience to discern what is good (*kusala*) or bad (*akusala*). The *Milindapañho* also says, in the context of a discussion about whether Vessantara's children were old enough to consent to his giving them away, that until age seven, children are not old enough to properly to give their consent (Mil 275).

30. See Jaini, "Indian Perspectives on the Spirituality of Animals," 252–66, on the moral capacities of animals in Indian literatures.

at either the agent's own or by another's initiative. Finally, intentional actions occur with or without deliberation; one can perform an intended act without knowing its moral significance.

Constructing Experience

It is highly significant that the Intention Sutta uses the term *saṅkhāra* synonymously with *cetanā*. This usage gives us the opportunity to further investigate this important term, which is one of the most challenging in Buddhist thought, and to work out its exact relationship to the processes of intention. It should be mentioned at the outset that while on certain occasions *cetanā* and *saṅkhāra* are used synonymously or interchangeably (as here),[31] they do not always overlap entirely, and the two terms should be held conceptually distinct even as we become aware of where they intersect.

Here is not the place to review exhaustively the entire range of *saṅkhāra*'s meaning, but we may outline the main contexts in which it is used.[32] If we look chiefly at its etymology, *saṅkhāra* is derived from the prefix *saṃ* and the verb *karoti*, which means "to put together, construct, and compound other things, *and* the things that are put together, constructed, and compounded."[33] The *Samyutta* says that *saṅkhāras* "construct the conditioned," where "the conditioned" refers to the five aggregates, or the

---

31. De Silva suggests that they are often synonymous (*An Introduction to Buddhist Psychology*, 20). Karunaratna says they are "equivalent" and that "the fourth aggregate *saṅkhāra* is directly and unambiguously defined in terms of *cetanā*" ("*Cetanā*," 87). Bhikkhu Bodhi suggests that *saṅkhāra*, when understood as an aggregate, is treated as an "umbrella category" where *cetanā* is "mentioned only as the most important factor in this aggregate, not its exclusive constituent" (Bodhi, *The Connected Discourses of the Buddha*, 1065). This is affirmed in the commentary on the Abhidhamma text the *Vibhaṅga*, which says that "*cetanā* is the principal *saṅkhāra*" because "of its well-known sense of accumulation" (VibhA 20). S.iii.60 defines *saṅkhāra* in terms of the six types of *cetanā*: *cetanās* regarding forms, sounds, odors, tastes, tactile objects, and phenomena (*dhamma*). A.ii.232 describes a person intending (*abhisaṅkharoti*) a bodily, verbal, or mental *saṅkhāra*; later, the *sutta* mentions this process in terms of *cetanā* and its commentary glosses *kāyasaṅkhara* as *kāyadvaracetanā*, an intention that occurs at the doorway of the body (Mp.iii.312). Beginning with Vibh 170, the *Vibhaṅga* repeatedly identifies *saṅkhāra* with both *cetanā* and what is intended (*yā cetanā sañcetanā sañcetayitattaṃ ayaṃ vuccati saṅkhāro*).

32. For more exhaustive treatments of *saṅkhāra*, see Jayatillake, "Some Problems of Translation and Interpretation," 208–24; Boisvert, *The Five Aggregates*; Payutto, *Buddhadhamma*; Bodhi, *The Connected Discourses of the Buddha*, 44–47; and Devdas, *Cetanā and the Dynamics of Volition*.

33. Bodhi, *The Connected Discourses*, 45.

compounded things that make up human existence.[34] *Saṅkhāras* are also said to be the intentions (*cetanā*) connected to each of the five senses and the factors of mind; *saṅkhāras* put together the sensory data and factors of thought, and refer to the things so constructed.[35] A. B. Keith suggests that *saṅkhāra* "denotes the making ready or complete something for an end" and also "the result of the activity when achieved."[36] It is purposive activity aimed at an object or end that it constructs, as well as those constructed objects. Nalini Devdas shows how *saṅkhāra* can refer both to conditioned responses and habits and to the dynamic capacities for creative and goal-oriented action.[37]

Drawing on these basic senses, scholars have used various terms to translate it: *formations, volitional formations, determinations, compounded things*, and *constructions*. Phra Payutto is perhaps the most concrete in his treatment of *saṅkhārā*. They are the "mental formations, predispositions or volitional activities" that are the

> psychological compositions, or the various qualities that embellish the mind making it good, bad, or neutral, and they have intention (*cetanā*) as their guide. Put very simply some of these good and bad thoughts are as follows: confidence (*saddhā*), mindfulness (*sati*), moral shame (*hiri*), moral fear (*ottappa*), loving-kindness (*mettā*), compassion (*karuṇā*), joy (*muditā*), equanimity (*upekkhā*), wisdom (*paññā*), delusion (*moha*), ill-will (*dosa*), greed (*lobha*), conceit (*māna*), perspective (*diṭṭhi*), envy (*issā*), and avarice (*macchariya*), for example.[38]

The term captures at once the psychological forces and activity of the mind as it makes sense of and acts in the world, as well as the existing dispositions, habits, memory traces, and patterns that predispose us to construe the world in the way that we do. In a general way, it has the sense of both occurrences and dispositions.[39]

---

34. S.iii.87.

35. S.iii.60. The next chapter on the Abhidhamma lists the 52 factors of mind (*dhammas*) that the *saṅkhāras* put together and that are then also called *saṅkhāras*. They include dispositions, emotions, habits of thought, and, of course, *cetanā* itself.

36. Keith, *Buddhist Philosophy in India and Ceylon*, 50.

37. Devdas, *Cetanā and the Dynamics of Volition*, 121–28.

38. Payutto, *Buddhadhamma*, 54.

39. De Silva, "Theoretical Perspectives on Emotions in Early Buddhism," 110.

While I translated it as "intention" where it is used synonymously with *cetanā*, I prefer to translate *saṅkhāra* in its general sense as "construction," which points to the feature of the mind that creates our experience through putting together and compounding other things. *Construction* also conveys in one word both *saṅkhāra*'s active and passive senses—that which constructs and that which is constructed. Like karma, *saṅkhāras* are both tendencies inherited from the past and the activity of creating new experiences. In this, both karma and *saṅkhāra* imply both *patiency* (our experience is acted upon and shaped by past constructions) and *agency* (our minds construct experience), and different contexts bring either of these senses to the fore.[40] Through both of these rubrics, the category of *saṅkhāra* allows us to see a person as a temporal process. The mind is a changing dynamic of shifting factors, not a static enduring collection of states. Change is a matter of previous conditions constructing present experience, which in turn is an active process of creating the future.

In perhaps its most prominent role, *saṅkhāra* is one of the five aggregates, that is, the main collections of events and factors that make up a person, which we further discuss later. In this context, Buddhaghosa takes *saṅkhāra* primarily in its active sense as collecting and constructing what is compounded. He defines its characteristic as "constructing," its function as "accumulating," its manifestation as "work," and its proximate cause as the other aggregates. He also says that *saṅkhāras* are good, bad, and indeterminate.[41] We see now quite clearly *saṅkhāras*' links to the idea of *cetanā*, in particular in how the first commentary we considered defines *cetanā* as that which "collects everything together."[42] Buddhaghosa makes this explicit when he says that *saṅkhāras* are manifested as *cetanā*, and these same processes—accumulating, working, and so on—are common to both.[43] Elsewhere, he glosses bodily *saṅkhāra* as an "accumulation of *cetanā* at the doorway of the body" and says that the verbal form *abhisaṅkharoti* is

---

40. Sometimes the texts talk about "old karma" and "new karma." Old karma is what is generated by karma, and new karma is what one does now (S.ii.65, iv.132, for example). Other passages assert that one is the heir of one's past actions and encourage a subjectivity of seeing oneself as the result of previous actions (M.iii.202, 206; A.iii.72).

41. Vism 462. Here I follow the *Mahāṭīkā*, which glosses *vipphāra* as *vyāpāra*, "work" (Vism-mhṭ 484).

42. Mp.iii.408.

43. Vism 528; Vism-mhṭ 571.

working, making a heap, accumulating.[44] The *Milindapañho* suggests that *cetanā* is distinguished by "*abhisaṅkharaṇa*," which may be best understood in this context as "making a preparation," since the text offers a simile of an intention being like a man preparing poison by taking and mixing other stuff, and drinking it himself or making others drink it. This action would lead to bad future results because what has been concocted or accumulated is harmful.[45] *Cetanā* and *saṅkhāra* are the active processes of the mind that accumulate experience and thereby construct reality.

Saṅkhāras are placed at the heart of Buddhist teachings about the person and the nature of human experience in *saṃsāra*. Since, according to Buddhist thought, all experiences except *nibbāna* are constructed and compounded, *saṅkhāra* in its widest sense has very broad scope indeed. As Bodhi puts it, "this notion of *saṅkhāra* serves as the cornerstone of a philosophical vision which sees the entire universe as constituted of conditioned phenomena."[46] Passages that assert the impermanence of, and the suffering entailed by, all conditioned things use this term.[47] *Saṅkhāra* in this broad sense leads us directly to the soteriological project of the Buddhist path, which is to gain insight into the nature of our suffering and to find release from it. That which is conditioned, constructed, and impermanent ultimately entails loss and frustration; the religious path seeks what is not conditioned and thus leads to the final cessation of sorrow.

There are two main doctrinal contexts in which *saṅkhāra* functions that situate it in the context of the soteriological teachings of the tradition: as a link in the chain of dependent origination and as one of the five aggregates. In the context of dependent origination, *saṅkhāra* is the second link in the 12 links that determine our existence in *saṃsāra*.[48] Produced

---

44. Mp.ii.191: *Kāyasaṅkhāranti kāyadvāre cetanārāsim. Abhisaṅkharotīti āyūhati rāsiṃ karoti piṇḍaṃ karoti*. In the context of rebirth, these processes of "making a heap" and accumulating are considered a specialized sense of *āyūhana*, which also means "doing work" (*vyāpāra*) according to the *Mahāṭīkā* (Vism-mhṭ 571; on *āyūhana* see Bodhi, *Connected Discourses*, 342, n. 2; Cone, *A Dictionary of Pāli*, 323). Mp.iii.312 says that *abhisaṅkharoti* means to accumulate (*āyūhati*) and combine (*sampiṇḍeti*). See also note 18 here.

45. Mil 61.

46. Bodhi, *Connected Discourses*, 46.

47. *Sabbe saṅkhārā aniccā* (S.i.200; D.ii.157).

48. The 12 links are, of course, ignorance (*avijjā*), *saṅkhāra*, consciousness (*viññāṇa*), mind-and-form (*nāmarūpa*), the six sense bases (*saḷāyatanā*), sensory contact (*phassa*), feeling (*vedanā*), craving (*taṇhā*), clinging (*upādāna*), becoming (*bhava*), birth (*jāti*), and decay and death (*jarāmaraṇa*) (S.ii.1–11).

by ignorance, *saṅkhāras* in turn generate consciousness. Ignorance drives the process of putting together the factors of experience that allow us to be aware or conscious of the world and to react to it.

It is significant that consciousness is not prior here to either ignorance or the intentional momentum of constructing experience, but is, in fact, generated by them. In an explication of dependent origination, the *Saṃyutta* elaborates on *saṅkhāra*'s role in generating conscious experience explicitly through the language of *cetanā* and adds to it the notion of biases or latent tendencies (*anusaya*). It says that "intending (*ceteti*), planning (*pakkappeti*), and having biases (*anuseti*)" establish consciousness. The mental activities of intending and planning, which are the very constructing and fashioning of the objects of conscious experience, as well as the underlying proclivities or obsessions that underlie or accompany such intentions, establish conscious experience.[49] This suggests that this prior putting together of the world makes consciousness possible and gives it its object.

But *saṅkhāra* is conditioned not only by ignorance; like all the links of the chain of dependent origination, *saṅkhāra* is conditioned by and conditions all of the other links and is embedded in a complex and mutually conditioned system. *Saṅkhāra* is the work of our minds, which take our sensory data and thoughts, motivations, feelings, and other psychic phenomena and put them together to create our conscious experience, through the radically causal processes of dependent origination. It is a process impelled by ignorance and confusion and is a fundamental operation of the mind that traps us in *saṃsāra*. Bhikkhu Bodhi explains:

> As the second factor in the formula of dependent origination, *saṅkhāras* are the kammically active volitions responsible, in conjunction with ignorance and craving, for generating rebirth and sustaining the forward movement of *saṃsāra* from one life to the next. *Saṅkhāra* is synonymous with *kamma*, to which it is etymologically related, both being derived from *karoti*.[50]

The restless, active nature of *saṅkhāra/cetanā* to collect sensory and psychic data and thoughts to construct our experience is the very karma that

49. S.ii.65; Spk.ii.70–71.

50. Bodhi, *Connected Discourses*, 45.

propels *saṃsāra*. In this regard, passages that see *cetanā* as a kind of food (*āhāra*) get at this sense of how our intentions nourish and fuel our existence, trapping us in a conditioned and compounded reality.[51] The path to *nibbāṇa* involves ceasing craving for this food. Another passage sees intention (*cetanā*) and aspiration (*patthanā*) as keeping humans established in the realm of rebirth.[52]

In this sense, *saṅkhāra/cetanā/kamma* are highly problematic from a soteriological standpoint. Because of this, the cessation of *saṅkhāra* and the cessation of karma are identified with achieving the Noble Eightfold Path that brings our turmoil in *saṃsāra* to an end.[53] When we stop our intentional activity, we cease constructing and grasping our conditioned and thus impermanent fabrications, and suffering ceases.[54] An awakened person (*arhat*) no longer generates or is subject to *cetanā* or karma in this sense.

As we have seen, the other main doctrinal context in which *saṅkhāra* plays a starring role is as one of the five aggregates (*khandhas*) that make up a person. Briefly, a person is comprised of nothing more or less than five constantly changing and conditioned collections: body, feeling, perception, *saṅkhāra*, and consciousness. *Saṅkhāras'* role as an aggregate consists of all intentional activity pertaining to the six senses.[55] This doctrine of the five aggregates is another way of describing the nonself teaching; it dismantles any notion of a permanent self by defining a person as nothing more than these complex bundles of constantly changing and conditioned phenomena. There is no self beyond these five processes; no person or self stands apart from the five aggregates and directs the show,

51. There are said to be four "nutriments" or "foods" (*āhāra*): food for the body, contact with the world, mental intention (*manosañcetanā*), and consciousness. Themselves arising from craving, they nourish and sustain our experience (M.i.47; S.ii.11–12; S.ii.98–100; D.iii.228). Buddhaghosa says that these foods are the special conditions for the continuity of existence; just as material food is the fundamental condition for sustaining the body, intention is the special condition that sustains consciousness (Ps.i.209); see also Bodhi, *The Discourse on Right View*, 41–45, for a translation of this passage of commentary.

52. There is an extended metaphor being worked out here: karma is the "field," consciousness is the "seed," and craving is the "moisture" that together make us exist in *saṃsāra*. For beings hindered by ignorance and yoked to craving, intention and aspiration (that is, our ceaseless grasping and goal-oriented constructing of the objects of experience) keep us in the lower realms of *saṃsāra* (A.i.224).

53. S.iii.60; A.iii.415.

54. S.ii.65; S.ii.81–83.

55. S.iii.60.

as it were. Nor should one identify with any of the five; none of them constitutes some sort of essential nature of a person.[56]

For these reasons, *saṅkhāra* is not seen as a site for a sovereign or autonomous agency; one *sutta* recounts how when one identifies with *saṅkhāras* (or any of the other aggregates), one has no power over them so that one could say, "Let my constructions be thus, let them not be thus."[57] Even when we identify with our intentional processes, we have little control over them. They are not what they are just for the willing of them, just as our bodies and feelings and other compounded experiences are the results of previous conditions, even as they are dynamic shapers of our present and future experiences. Though *saṅkhāras* are the constructive and agentive capacities of our minds, their creative work is conditioned (though not exhaustively determined) by the other causal factors in dependent origination.

These considerations locate *saṅkhāra/cetanā* as a psychological process that occurs quite a few steps before choice and decision making. Rather than imagining the mind as possessing a faculty or capacity that stands apart from various options, deliberating, weighing, and choosing among them, these texts see moral agency as occurring at a deeper and more elemental level of constructing experience in a radically conditioned way. Experience is constructed and shaped through the processes of dependent origination. Additionally, as we saw in the Intention Sutta, it occurs even without our explicit deliberation or knowledge, and it can occur as the result not only of one's own initiative but also at the promptings of others. The Buddha's equivalence of karma with *cetanā* identifies this collecting and managing sensory and psychic experience with action, and it is these processes that determine, as karma does, our present and future experience.

"Good" Intentions

The foregoing discussion has alerted us to the idea that intentional processes are, from a *soteriological* point of view, at the heart of our condition of suffering in *saṃsāra*. They are, as indeed karma is, the problem that

56. S.iii.2–5 describes how the ordinary person falsely and obsessively identifies with each of the five aggregates as oneself.

57. M.i.233.

the Buddhist path addresses: how to cease our endless construction and manufacturing of experience that only compounds ultimately ephemeral things, producing yet further constructions that are themselves impermanent and subject to decay and discontent. The solution is the Noble Eightfold Path of retraining our orientation to the world (right view and thought), transforming our actions (right speech, action, and livelihood), and developing effort, mindfulness, and concentration.

Yet, from an ethical point of view—which is our central interest—*cetanā*, *saṅkhāra*, and karma can all be said to be good, bad, or neutral, and many passages are preoccupied with describing intentional action in such terms. The distinction between the ethical and the soteriological is a complex one. We do not want to always hold them apart, and certainly sometimes they are seen as part of the same continuum. Yet the tradition does make a distinction between mundane (*lokiya*) and supramundane (*lokuttara*) thought and action, and thoughts and actions can be ethically good at the mundane level, in that they conduce to a life well lived, without necessarily embodying advanced levels of meditative and spiritual wisdom or achievement.[58] The Eightfold Path is religious or supramundane action;[59] as one passage puts it (which we consider later at some length), this path is karma that is neither bright nor dark and thus leads to the destruction of karma.[60]

One place in which the distinction between ethical and spiritual accomplishment is particularly sharp is in the Brahmajāla Sutta, where "ordinary people"[61] are said to praise the Buddha for "small and mundane" matters concerning moral precepts (*sīla*), but wise people will recognize

58. For example, Vism 13 says that virtue (*sīla*) subject to the depravities (*āsavas*) is mundane; virtue free of *āsavas* is supramundane.

59. Sometimes a distinction is made between the mundane (*lokiya*) and supramundane (*lokuttara*) levels of the Path factors (M.iii.72–78); the mundane are affected by the taints (*āsavas*), considerations of merit, and how they ripen into rebirth, while the supramundane are noble, without taints and free of considerations of rebirth and merit.

60.A.ii.234.

61. Often the term "ordinary people" (*puthujjana*) is used derogatorily because as regular folks (not on the Buddhist path), they are still mired in the depravities, wrong views, and so on, but in fact there are different types of them. For example, some are "blind," while others are "virtuous" (*kalyāṇa*); of the virtuous, there are two kinds: those virtuous due to their actions and those virtuous due to inner reasoning. Still, even these good folks practice a low *dhamma* that contravenes the Ariyan *dhamma*, and they keep with common or vulgar custom (Sv.i.59).

and praise him for his spiritual insight into deep and subtle matters.[62] The "small and mundane" matters of morality are then said to include following the 10 precepts and ideals of monastic decorum and livelihood, points of practice that are by no means treated as minor in other contexts, but here pale in importance on a scale of value that considers the Buddha's religious achievements. We are thus alerted to shifting scales of value; sometimes from a soteriological perspective—when the texts are interested in the pursuit of *nibbāna* or trying to communicate the Buddha's level of insight—workaday ethical concerns of good (*kusala*) and bad (*akusala*) action get minimized. In other contexts, however, as the passages with which we began this chapter show, it is fitting and appropriate to ask how to be good, to be concerned with moral precepts, and to learn how to eschew actions harmful to one's worldly happiness.

But what then is meant by good in these texts? What are good intentions? The term *kusala*, translated here as "good," and its opposite, *akusala*, "bad," are of paramount importance both in the sources themselves and for our understanding of how intention is interpreted. *Kusala* and *akusala* are usually used to describe *cetanā*, karma, conduct (*ācāra*), and more generally the *dhammas*, or factors of experience (which we discuss at much greater length in the next chapter).[63] One can also ask in a general way, as does the *Dīgha* passage with which we began this chapter: "what is the good (*kusala*), what is the bad (*akusala*)?" This is a question that the omniscient Tathāgata can answer, but so can the wise "wheel-turning emperor," a repository of knowledge on primarily temporal affairs.[64]

In an extended discussion of the term in his commentary on the *Dīgha Nikāya*, Buddhaghosa says that *kusala* should be understood as fivefold: the state of health, the state of blamelessness, the state of arising from proficiency (or skillfulness), freedom from distress, and bringing about pleasant results.[65] Good thoughts and actions are faultless, salutary, skillful, and free of trouble, and they produce felicitous results. In contrast, *akusala* thoughts

62. D.i.3–13.

63. It is surely significant that the *Dhammasaṅgaṇī*, which describes all the factors of experience, frames its entire discussion in terms of asking which factors are good, bad, and neutral (Dhs I).

64. D.iii.157, iii.62.

65. Sv.iii.883–84. The terms in question here are: *ārogya* (health), *anavajja* (blamelessness), *kosallasambhūta* (produced by proficiency or skill), *niddaratha* (freedom from distress), and *sukhavipāka* (pleasant results). (Compare to As 38 and Paṭis-a i.205, which drop *niddaratha*).

and actions are quite the opposite—unskillful, blameworthy, and leading to bad and insalubrious results, misfortune, and disease. Notice that these distinctions do not map in any clear way onto modern Western distinctions between moral and immoral. I agree with Walter Sinnott-Armstrong that it is not useful to see morality as a "unified natural category" and that Buddhist thought, like current work in neuroethics, does not support significant universal generalizations about the category of morality as such.[66] Here we see a broader category of *kusala*, where nonmoral values—health and freedom from distress—are included that do not offer any obvious rationale for being considered as comprising a single category of morality. *Good* and *bad* work in a more general way to get at the range of possibilities suggested by *kusala* and *akusala*, some of which are not, strictly speaking, moral. Abandoning a quest for morality as a unified category will help us avoid many tangles in trying to shoehorn Buddhaghosa into categories that developed in the modern West.

In the *Atthasālinī*—here we glance ahead to an Abhidhamma commentary—he defines *kusala* with its standard fourfold hermeneutical device of stating *kusala*'s characteristic, function, manifestation, and immediate cause,[67] and he adds as well a quality of purification and the attribute of being caused by careful attention:

> [*Kusala*'s] characteristic is its blameless and happy result, its function is the shattering of what is bad (*akusala*), its manifestation is purification, and its immediate cause is careful attention (*yoniso manasikāra*). Alternatively, *kusala* has blamelessness as its characteristic because of its being opposed to blame, its function is the arising of purification, its manifestation is a pleasing result, and its immediate cause is as was already mentioned [ie. careful attention].[68]

---

66. Walter Sinnott-Armstrong, "Keynote." He argues that Buddhists' failure to make a distinction between moral and nonmoral as natural categories (in the ways that are often taken for granted in the modern Western tradition following from Kant) "is not a bug, but a feature." We return to this point in the discussion of the 10 good and bad deeds.

67. This standard device employed by the commentaries and derived from the *Nettippakaraṇa* defines a word by explaining its characteristic (*lakkhana*), function (*rasa*), manifestation (*paccupaṭṭhāna*), and immediate cause (*padaṭṭhāna*); these terms are defined at As 63. Note that *rasa*, a term with a wide semantic range in Indic systems, has a technical meaning in Pāli commentary: Buddhaghosa defines it as "duty" or "function" (*kicca*) or "attainment" (*sampatti*).

68. As 62–63: *ārogya* (health), *anavajja* (blamelessness), and *kosallasambhūta* (produced by proficiency). A second definition gives *ārogya*, *anavajja*, *cheka* (skillfulness), and *sukhavipāka* (pleasant results) (As 38).

This definition adds elements of careful mental cultivation to the term—learning to attend to the world properly[69] and a purifying or cleansing of bad experiences and mental dispositions.

Keeping in mind that there are usages of *kusala* that are nonmoral, as when it refers to skillful artists,[70] and usages that are soteriological, as when referring to the factors of enlightenment (*bodhipakkhiyadhamma*), collectively these definitions of *kusala* constitute a large part of what we could call ethically good in Buddhist thinking. When *kusala/akusala* modify karma, intention, and conduct, they are reflecting ethical concerns of how one should act and think in mundane life. Moreover, *kusala* is something discerning people can come to know directly because actions that are *kusala* or *akusala* have results or fruits. Certain passages in the canonical sources assert that *kusala* is something ordinary people can know about their actions. As we have seen, in several passages, including the Kālāma Sutta, the Buddha suggests that people can know for themselves whether actions are *kusala* or *akusala*, blameless or not, and whether their effects are pleasing or not.[71]

An important instance of the Buddha teaching that people can figure out the differences between good and bad actions occurs in a conversation he has with his son, Rāhula.[72] This passage suggests that reflection is a way to discern good and bad actions. The Buddha begins by asking Rāhula: what is the purpose of a mirror? Rāhula answers that reflection is the purpose of a mirror. The Buddha then says that actions of body, speech, and mind should be done with reflection. One should reflect on whether the action will lead to affliction for self or others and on whether it is *kusala* or *akusala* due to leading to happy or painful results. One should reflect about these things before, during, and following the action. As in English, the Pāli term for reflection (*paccavekkhana*) can mean the reflection of a mirror and reflection in the sense of considering and reviewing, but there

---

69. *Yoniso manasikāra*, careful attention, is attention that involves right means and the right path and sees the impermanent in the impermanent (Ps.i.64). See also Bhikkhu Ñānamoli's n. 19 in his translation of the *Khuddakapāṭha*, 260, where he emphasizes that *yoniso* means "from the womb" or from its origin or cause, and thus *yoniso manasikāra* means attention to conditions and to the conditionality of existence. We will discuss attention more thoroughly in the next chapter.

70. The *Atthasālinī* suggests that *kusala* in the sense of health can refer to physical health, and professional singers and dancers can be said to be *kusala* in the sense of skillful (As 38).

71. A.iii.65; A.ii.190.

72. M.i.416–20.

is also a sense here in which the two senses come together: actions shine back their effects in a visible way. Buddhaghosa says that one uses a mirror for looking at a blemish on the face.[73] Similarly, the faults in actions will shine back at us.

Lance Cousins has argued that in the earliest layer of the canonical tradition, *kusala* referred to the skillfulness of meditation practices, which connects it to wisdom and the soteriological path, and that the moral sense of *kusala* came later. But he does acknowledge that even in the canonical Suttanta there are "a considerable number" of contexts in which *kusala* is associated with karma, good conduct (*sucarita*), and *sīla*, and in "the great majority of cases" when other terms are associated with it, the term immediately next to *kusala* is *blameless*, an apparently ethical concern.[74] That *kusala* should sometimes be restricted to meaning skillful in a contemplative sense, as when it is referring to factors (*dhammas*) that conduce to awakening (*bodhipakkhiya*), is a point well taken. But given the numerous instances in the *canonical sources* in which *kusala* is referring to conduct, intention, and karma in what is clearly a sense of blamelessness and good results, I am not persuaded that the sense of good, blameless, and salutary was only a later development occurring at the Abhidhamma or commentarial stages.[75] Nor should we always hold skillfulness and ethics apart conceptually; there are ways that moral sensitivity and awareness can be conceived of as skillful, and ethically good action as well crafted.[76] Again,

---

73. Ps.iii.128.

74. Cousins, "Good or Skillful? *Kusala* in Canon and Commentary," 147–48; on Cousins's genealogy, see Harvey, *An Introduction to Buddhist Ethics*, 42–43; Clayton, *Moral Theory in Śāntideva's Śikṣāsamuccaya*, 67–72. All are, of course, correct to reject Keown's linking of the idea of skillfulness to utilitarian approaches to ethics and his subsequent position that therefore *kusala* cannot mean "skillful" in most ethical contexts (Keown, *The Nature of Buddhist Ethics*, 118–20).

75. Examples of *kusala/akusala* modifying karma, conduct (*ācāra*), or *sīla* with this clear ethical sense can be found in descriptions of the 10 good and bad courses of action (M.i.415f.; M.i.489f.; M.i.46), the good conduct rulers are interested in (M.ii.114f; D.iii.157), bodily, mental, and verbal karma (A.i.104; A.i.292; M.i.402), and other examples of good and bad deeds or habits (M.ii.104; D.i.115; and M.ii.26, all modifying *sīla*).

76. For example, in Robert Desjarlais's ethnographic work among Buddhists in Nepal, morality and skillfulness are closely linked: "virtuousness and virtuosity go hand in hand" (*Sensory Biographies*, 262). While wanting to see skillful as morally valuable, Gombrich takes a different tack: skillful is the primary sense of *kusala* "because good moral choice is an intelligent and informed choice" (*What the Buddha Thought*, 15). In this view, skillful means something like informed and reasonable moral decision making, which is taking it in a different direction than Cousins's treatment of it as a contemplative skill and Desjarlais's seeing it as an aesthetic aptitude.

using the terms *ethical* and *moral* in a more provisional sense of being associated with living life well keeps us from having to impose artificial boundaries around terms like *kusala*, and we can attend more sharply to the tradition's own distinctions.

For example, despite the *Atthasālinī*'s passage about attention and purification, there are places in which its sense of skillfulness (and its connections to wisdom) appears to fall by the wayside. There emerged the curious fact that one can have *kusala* intentions that are without knowledge (or undeliberate), as we saw in the Intention Sutta commentary, for example. In addition, and as Cousins also points out, while skillfulness's connection to knowledge and wisdom is prevalent throughout the sources, the Pāli Abhidhamma does allow for *kusala* consciousness that is without knowledge.[77] The *Atthasālinī* recognizes that this may be a problem: how can what is disassociated from knowledge be called *kusala* (since knowledge seems to be implicit in the idea of skillful)? Buddhaghosa offers two answers to this. The first is that one can take *kusala* in a figurative or popular sense. Just as people call even fans not made of palmyra leaves "palmyra fans," so, too, *kusala* can apply even when knowledge is absent. The second, nonfigurative answer is that *kusala* is used in this case only in the senses of blameless and healthy, not skillful.[78]

Buddhaghosa thought that some senses of a term are appropriate in some contexts but not others and that context will determine which sense is appropriate. His exegetical choices favor relevance, whereby he likes to put in front of him all the different meanings a term can have and then decide which is relevant, on the basis of context, in a particular instance. He lists the full range of possibilities for the meaning of a given term, but then his sensitivity to context will guide him to argue which meanings are appropriate in each case. We can say that he favors a contextual approach to deciding the meaning of terms rather than a historical chronological approach of the sort that Cousins sketches out. Buddhaghosa also uses general guidelines for which sort of contexts or even genres of knowledge favor which meanings. For example, he argues that the different kinds of instruction in the different genres favor one or the other of the senses of *kusala*—the sense of healthy prevails in Jātaka instruction, the sense of blamelessness in the Suttanta, and the senses of skillful, free of distress,

77. Dhs 147; Cousins, "Good or Skillful?" 142.

78. As 63.

and producing pleasant results prevail in the Abhidhamma.[79] Note that this characterization of the diverse meanings of the term does not map easily onto Cousins's chronology of the development of *kusala*. Moreover, it emphasizes the quality of blamelessness (rather than skillfulness) for its meaning in the Suttas.

Good Intentions and the Path to Nibbāna

If the idea of good and bad intentions developed into an interest in primarily ethical matters rather than soteriological concerns, what then is the relationship between *kusala* intentions and actions to the Noble Path and *nibbāna*? Do morally good intentions and actions lead to arhatship? And how do we understand the activity of arhats (awakened people)? Are they performing intentional actions when they do good things in the world? Can they be said to be doing good actions, or are they somehow beyond such dualistic considerations? The tradition's treatment of these questions is more highly textured than is usually allowed in modern scholarship on them, and, in fact, the canonical sources seem to suggest conflicting views on how to characterize the intentional actions of arhats and those on the Noble Path. One important passage says yes, good action (*kusalakamma*) leads to the cessation of karma and does not lead to the arising of further karma,[80] which indicates that *kusala* action can lead to *nibbāna* (though it does not describe an arhat's actions in the language of *kusala*). But other passages suggest that the Noble Path is about ceasing even *kusala* thoughts and habits.[81] If, as we have seen, *kusala* is defined in part as productive or generative of pleasant results (*sukhavipāka*), then how can it properly define an arhat's activity that does not generate, nor is generated by, karmic results? An important passage, which we will discuss at length later, describes a kind of karma that is beyond the usual distinctions of morality, and the commentators tended to favor and develop this line of interpretation.

---

79. Sv.iii.883. This is not, however, a hard-and-fast determination of meaning, and As 62–63 sees it differently; Cousins has commented on this passage (Cousins, "Good or Skillful?" 140).

80. A.i.263. Unfortunately, Buddhaghosa does not discuss this passage with any detail.

81. M.ii.26–27; Ps.iii.268–70. "Thoughts" are *saṅkappo*, and "habits" are *sīla*.

There is also the deeper issue of whether it is appropriate to describe the activity of arhats in terms of the language of *cetanā* and *karma* at all. It would seem that the direct connections of *cetanā* and karma with *saṅkhāra*, the constructing activities that are constitutive of life in *saṃsāra*, would preclude an arhat's involvement in them. Intentions are that very purposive constructing of experience that keeps us in *saṃsāra*, and arhats are surely free of them. And since *cetanā* is principally defined as "accumulating" experience, how can it be an agency that leads to freedom from karma? But in fact, there are certain moves that the texts make to allow for distinctive types of karma and *cetanā* that are conducive to and constitutive of *nibbāna*.

The key canonical treatment of this issue is a distinction made about four different types of karma that occurs in two places in the Suttas.[82] Action can be dark (*kaṇha*), bright (*sukka*), both dark and bright, and neither dark nor bright. Dark actions lead to dark or afflictive results in future lives, and bright actions lead to bright or nonafflictive results; the *Aṅguttara* says that violating the five precepts are dark actions, and refraining from violating them are bright actions, while the *Majjhima* commentary says they are the 10 good (*kusala*) and bad (*akusala*) deeds respectively.[83] Actions that are both dark and bright lead to mixed rebirths. These first three kinds of actions are firmly located in a strict karmic logic of like-begets-like: one will be reborn according to one's actions. And the Buddha repeats several times, "Beings are the heirs of their actions."[84] Moreover, both *suttas* use the language of *saṅkhāra* in these processes, which by now should be expected: action is the constructing of intentions.[85]

The fourth kind of karma is action that is neither dark nor bright; as such, it does not lead to either dark or bright fruits, and both *suttas* say that this kind of karma leads to the destruction of karma. The *Aṅguttara* goes on to say that the karma that leads to the destruction of karma is

---

82. The passage in the *Aṅguttara* concerns a close treatment of karma (A.ii.230–36); the passage in the *Majjhima* occurs in a debate with a non-Buddhist ascetic about karma and its fruits (M.i.389–91).

83. We will discuss the 10 *kusala* and the 10 *akusala* deeds below.

84. M.i.390–93.

85. For example, in the case of committing a bodily action, the text equates karma with *saṅkhāra*, saying "one constructs a bodily intention" (*kāyasaṅkhāram abhisaṅkharoti*). And likewise for constructing verbal and mental *saṅkhāras*, all of which then can be seen as dark or bright or neither (A.ii.232–33; M.i.390–91).

following the Noble Eightfold Path. Both *suttas* say that this kind of karma is the "intention for abandoning"[86] dark and bright and mixed actions with their dark and bright and mixed results. The *Majjhima* commentary says that action that is neither dark nor bright is action that has as its intention (*cetanā*) the four paths leading to the destruction of karma. (The "four paths" refers to the soteriological goals culminating in arhatship: stream-entry, once-return, nonreturn, and arhatship). What both the *suttas* and this commentary indicate is that there is a type of intentional action that involves abandoning morally good and bad intentions, actions, and their fruits. And this action is conducive to the highest religious path and goal, which entails the destruction of karma. This move was necessary in part due to the inherent logic in *saṅkhāra/cetanā/karma* that defines them as "accumulating";[87] ordinary karma is the relentless accumulation of experience in *saṃsāra*, and so some other kind of agency of a very different order must occur to break this logic of grasping and constructing further experience.[88]

If we take this seriously, we have to conclude that approaching the highest soteriological goal involves intentional action that is not, strictly speaking, evaluated as morally good or bad (at least in terms of the distinctions between dark and bright in the canonical passage or *kusala* and *akusala* for Buddhaghosa).[89] The path to *nibbāna* is *not* paved with good intentions.

86. *Tassa pahānāya yā cetanā* (this is also stated at Ps.iii.105).

87. In addition to the passages we have already seen that use the language of accumulating (*āyūhana*), A.v.292, for example, says that intentional actions performed and accumulated cannot be wiped out without experiencing their results. Also Ps.i.211 states that because *cetanā* involves accumulation of good and bad actions, it nourishes our condition in *saṃsāra* (this is the commentary on the Sutta on Right View, in its discussion of *cetanā* as a food).

88. In another place in which this issue comes up, Buddhaghosa says that all courses of action, good and bad, are the Noble Truth of suffering, and their roots are the Noble Truth of the arising of suffering. And, he says, the Noble Truth of the cessation of suffering is the nonarising of both good and bad courses of action (Ps.i.205). We will discuss in the next section what is meant by the good and bad courses of action (*kusalākusalakammapathā*).

89. Another place that the idea that the Noble Path and arhatship do not entail *kusala* actions is in the commentary on the Intention Sutta that we have already considered (A.ii.156–57; Mp.iii.147). The *sutta* says that for arhats there is no body, voice, speech, mind, field, object, occasion, or reason whereby the subjective pleasure or pain associated with karma could arise. "Field," Buddhaghosa elaborates, refers to *kusala* and *akusala* actions that give rise to fruits; thus arhats are not operating in the field of good and bad actions and are not engaged in "productive action" (*karaṇakamma*). Buddhaghosa is strikingly at odds on this point with modern interpreters like Keown, Velez de Cea, and Adam who want to see *kusala* karma as "nirvāṇic." In his treatment of the *sutta* on bright and dark actions, Adam says that the fourth category of neither bright nor dark actions are *kusala* actions, which is simply not a

The idea of an "intention for abandoning" refers to an intention that has as its purpose or object the abandoning or destruction of karma (which is equivalent to arhatship). Buddhaghosa speaks of "desire-realm *cetanās*" and "Path *cetanās*" to distinguish them, and desire-realm *cetanās* can characterize one's experience in some of the meditation stages, but they will not be present in achieving the Noble Path.[90] He says that Path intentions are neither dark nor bright and that they are different from even the "whitest" mental factors (*dhamma*). "Path *cetanā*" is a specialized sense of *cetanā* that is not the same as the *cetanā* identified with the constructing activities (*saṅkhāra*) that keep us in *saṃsāra*, nor is it the *cetanā* that the Buddha was referring to when he identified karma with it. It should be kept conceptually apart from *kusala* and *akusala* distinctions about action.[91]

None of this should be taken to suggest that the Noble Path does not involve other morally relevant factors of mind (*kusaladhammas*) or skillful meditation states; rather, it does not entail *kusalakamma* or *kusalacetanā*.[92] In the context of factors of mind, Buddhaghosa distinguishes between two meanings in *kusala*: one that leads to the round of rebirths, the other referring to the 37 factors (*dhamma*) of enlightenment that lead to the destruction of rebirth.[93] Nor can it be said that an arhat behaves in a manner that cannot be described, in some important sense, as moral; in fact, arhats and the Buddha are said to be virtuous (*sīla*).[94] My suggestion is much

tenable notion for Buddhaghosa, as I argue throughout this section (Adam, "Groundwork for a Metaphysic of Buddhist Morals"; Velez de Cea, "The Criteria of Goodness"). Keown ignores this *sutta* and argues that "all kammic actions stand in a relationship to the *summum bonum* and the moral status of this relationship is defined by the terms *kusala* and *akusala*" (Keown, *Nature of Buddhist Ethics*, 127).

90. Ps.iii.105. All four *jhānas* abandon *akusala* intentions, but it's only in the second *jhāna* that the cessation of *kusala* intentions occurs (see also M.ii.28–29 for more about how the second *jhāna* involves the cessation of *kusala* intentions, and Ps.iii.54 for more about the distinction between Path intentions and meditation intentions).

91. See also Karunaratna, "*Cetanā*," 94.

92. For example, M.ii.116 states that the Tathāgata has abandoned all *akusaladhammas* and possesses all *kusaladhammas*.

93. Sv.iii.848. This passage is a commentary on the Cakkavatti Sutta, where Buddhaghosa is commenting on the general question "What is the good?" As Premasiri argues about this passage, the sense of *kusala* that is conducive to the round of rebirths invokes the term *puñña*, meritorious action (Premasiri, "Interpretation of Two Principal Ethical Terms in Early Buddhism," 72–73). Buddhaghosa also says that for *kusala* in this sense there is the seeing of results, emphasizing two matters that I have stressed here: *kusala* actions have *visible* results that shine back their effects, and rebirth *kusala* is all about results, which cannot characterize the Noble Path or arhatship.

94. D.i.174. Since *sīla* is the absence of any wrongdoing, this is to be expected.

narrower: some of the canonical texts and certainly Buddhaghosa resisted the language of *kusala* to describe *intentions* and *actions* in characterizing the activity of the supramundane Path and arhatship. Instead, when describing the intentions and activity of a highly advanced practitioner, they devised a particular kind of Path karma and *cetanā* that does not have all of the constructive and constructed associations that these terms' usual linkages to *saṅkhāra* bear. Moreover, this kind of action involves *abandoning* the habits and constructions of accumulating and gathering experience. I suggest later additional ways in which the Noble Eightfold Path is articulated in terms of abandoning, desisting, and leaving off.

There is more to say about Path karma and intention as it developed in the hands of the Abhidhammikas and the commentators. The commentary on the *Majjhima* passage does some important work with these ideas in pointing to a doctrine that was developed in the Abhidhamma. This doctrine asserts that some kinds of factors of mind, called *kiriya*, are fruitless; that is, they are neither the fruits of action nor do they lead to further fruits.[95] At the very start of the commentarial passage on the fourfold division of bright and dark actions with which we began this discussion, Buddhaghosa asks, "Why did the Buddha undertake this teaching?" He answers that the Buddha taught it so that *kiriya* will become clear, and he says that this teaching is arrived at through the notion of a certain type of karma called *kiriya*.[96] Moreover, knowing this teaching is suitable for those who take refuge, those who ordain, and those who have attained arhatship. Although Buddhaghosa does not define *kiriya* here, his immediate move to connect these four types of karma with the idea of *kiriya* and his insistence on its relevance for all types of practitioners suggest that for him this theory of fruitless intention was important and its meaning was well-known enough to require no explanation.

Kiriya factors of mind, we learn from the canonical Abhidhamma and the commentaries, are neither the result of karma nor productive of it. As Lance Cousins puts it, the term "designates a type of mentality which does not take part in the kammic process."[97] Path intentions and karma are thus

95. I follow Gethin in not translating it in order to signal that it is a highly technical term (Wijeratne and Gethin, *Summary of the Topics*, xx). Translated, it can mean acting, doing, or merely acting, and, as we will see, is getting at action that is not karmically produced or productive.

96. Ps.iii.102. See also Spk.ii.57, where he says that the action of arhats is neither good nor bad, but is *kiriya* because it is fruitless.

97. Cousins, "The *Paṭṭhāna* and the Development of the Theravādin Abhidhamma," 26–27. For more on *kiriya*, see Wijeratne and Gethin, *Summary of the Topics*, xx, and also throughout

one kind of *kiriya* karma. *Kiriya* is further clarified in a list of four types of intention that differs (but in certain overlapping ways) from the four dark and bright karmas we have just seen. The four types of intention are good (*kusala*), bad (*akusala*), resultant (*vipāka*), and *kiriya*. The distinction is also mentioned in the *aṭṭhakathā* on a different *sutta*,[98] where it appears in the context of the Buddha arguing against various non-Buddhist teachers who argue either that pain and suffering are entirely predetermined by previous karma, that they are the result of divine power, or that they are purely random events. Here Buddhaghosa brings up this fourfold distinction about the four kinds of intention. He argues that the Buddha rejected the first position, that of determinism, because it only accepts the notion of *cetanā* as a result and denies the view that *cetanā* can also be productive, that is, good or bad, and it denies the possibility that karma can be neither produced nor productive of results, that is, *kiriya*. Part of this distinction may be understood in terms of my language of *patiency* and *agency*: some *cetanās* are best understood as agentive in that they are productive of good and bad experience, and others are patient in that they are the fruits or results of previous actions (which is what determinists hold about all intentions). Yet others, namely, *kiriyā cetanā*, are neither: they are neither the result of previous karmic causality nor productive of it. *Kiriya* actions are mere actions or pure activity without all of the purposive constructions we bring to our usual karmic action.

This idea was developed because Buddhist thinkers grew increasingly curious about how to characterize properly the action of arhats. Surely arhats have some sort of intentional agency and are seen to do good actions. But by definition, they must also be entirely free of the karmic process constitutive of *saṃsāra*. Dhammapāla states and resolves the issue succinctly:

> When an arhat worships shrines, preaches the Dhamma, or attends to a meditation subject, why is there no bodily karma for him? Because there is no condition of being resultant. For karma done

their translations of the *Abhidhammatthasaṅgaha* and its commentary; see also Karunaratne, "*Cetanā*," 94; and Carter, "Beyond 'Beyond Good and Evil,'" 50–51. In the Abhidhamma, which I treat in the next chapter, *kiriyā dhammā* are morally indeterminate (*avyākatā*) (Dhs 566, 568). The fourfold distinction is mentioned at Dhs 993, where *kiriya* factors are neither *kusala, akusala,* nor the fruits of karma (Cf. Vibh 106, 182).

98. A.i.173; Mp.ii.274.

by an arhat is not *kusala*, nor *akusala*, nor resultant, but is merely *kiriya*.[99]

Arhats are engaged in intentional actions that are neither the results of previous karma nor generative of further karma. But the category also provides a name for actions by nonawakened people that are morally neutral, and it is somewhat surprising that more is not made over this use of the term, given how much activity this category would presumably cover. Surely we do actions all the time that are not morally charged, such as when I walk into the kitchen for a glass of water. In fact, probably much of our ordinary action and behavior of getting through the day falls into this class of action.

Ten Good and Ten Bad Deeds

We can leave Path and *kiriya* intentions and actions here and return to the ethical plane of distinctions of *kusala* and *akusala* actions. One place that the texts try to sort out the role of intention and other mental factors in action in a much more concrete fashion than we have seen so far is in their treatment of what are called the "courses of action" (*kammapathā*). There are said to be 10 bad courses of action and 10 good courses of action, and each list classifies these deeds according to whether they occur through body, speech, or mind. The 10 bad courses of action are, first, three bodily actions: taking life, taking what is not given, sexual misconduct; then four verbal actions: lying, malicious speech, harsh speech, and frivolous speech; and finally three mental actions: covetousness, ill will, and false views. The good courses of actions are the opposites of these, generally stated negatively as refraining from the 10 bad courses of action.[100] These are considered complete courses of action because they are carried out

---

99. Mp-ṭ.ii.346 on the Intention Sutta, A.ii.156, Mp.iii.135.

100. There are several places where the 10 good and/or the 10 bad courses of action are listed and discussed: D.iii.74, 269, 292; M.i.46–47, 286–87; M.iii.46–53, 209–10; S.ii.166–68; S.iv.321–22, 343–44, 350–51; A.v.292–94, 258, 264–68; As 95–104; and Vin.v.138. The 10 good deeds are sometimes called the "*dāsa sīla*." The Sādhu Chapter in the *Aṅguttara* is given over the 10 good and bad deeds (A.v.273–303), where the bad deeds are referred to as *asādhu*, not in keeping with the Ariyan Dhamma, bad, disadvantageous, non-Dhammic, connected to the taints, blameworthy, mortifying, tending toward accumulation, yielding suffering, and having suffering as their fruit; and the good deeds are the opposite of these. It describes the results in this and the afterlife for these deeds and their importance for men and women.

fully, and the criteria for establishing the completeness of each of these actions are discussed case by case, as we will see.

The courses of action and the discussions around them suggest that one thread of Theravāda moral thinking is concerned with an action-based ethics, rather than an ethics solely based on intention or character. There are some actions, 10 in fact, that are just bad to do, and the wrongness of them in some sense lies in the action primarily rather than in some vice in the agent. To be sure, we will see that since action (by definition) always has internal components that shape what it is, action, in theory at least, can never be interpreted entirely apart from the inner experience of the agent who performs it (and the analysis of these courses of action will bear this out). For his part, Buddhaghosa tries in a consistent fashion to interpret action in terms of its internal dimensions. Despite this, there is a small but steady suggestion in some of the discussions that follow of a moral order in which some actions are simply bad in ways that can be talked about independently of agents' particular inner experience while performing them. Such considerations might well be in tension with the more psychologically oriented approach to action dominant in the sources, but they evince a kind of moral naturalism also prevalent in Buddhist thought, where the world is just structured in such a way that bad things will follow from bad actions. These tensions help us to see the internally diverse threads apparent even in Buddhaghosa's own systematic thought.

The 20 actions are listed in various contexts. They are sometimes listed in teachings to householders as actions that are either in keeping or not with the Dhamma. In the Sāleyyaka Sutta, for example, when teaching householders how one's conduct may lead to fruits in the next life, the Buddha describes the courses of action.[101] The 10 bad courses of action lead to bad future destinations in hell or lower realms of life, and the good ones lead to fortunate human births or lives in the heavens. The Sutta on Right View describes the 20 actions in the context of Venerable Sāriputta teaching about right view.[102] Other *suttas* describe actions that are to be practiced and those that should not, on the basis of how these actions cause good or bad factors to arise, and they chart how killing and thieving, for example, bring nothing but further bad experiences.[103] These actions are evaluated on the basis of their results.

101. M.i.286–89.

102. M.i.46–47.

103. M.iii.47–53, for example.

A particularly fascinating context in which the 10 good deeds occur is the Cakkavatti Sīhanāda Sutta, which describes the catastrophic destruction of the human moral order in the future when all religious and moral knowledge will be destroyed, human life spans will be reduced to a 10-year period, and nearly all people will have killed one another off in a great cosmic cataclysm of violence. Only a small remnant of people will remain who are able to hide away from the violence and then emerge to rediscover and reestablish a moral order that will make it possible for them to survive. They figure out, for themselves on the basis of what has occurred, that killing, the first of the 10 bad deeds, is bad as it has nearly destroyed them. By refraining from killing, their life spans increase, and they gradually expand their body of moral knowledge to include refraining from taking what is not given, sexual misconduct, and the other bad courses of action.[104] This context suggests that these good actions can come to be known through experience about what humans need to do to survive and flourish. Knowledge of them is not dependent on scripture, but is something that humans, even those in the most adverse circumstances possible, can come to know empirically. Moreover, these actions are not the result of any apparent prior goodness on the part of those who commit them: they just happen to commit actions that lead to beneficial results.

We can look more closely at these good and bad deeds to see what they are more specifically and how they are defined in relation to intention. Since the bad actions are usually described first, and the good actions are then simply their opposites, we may begin with the bad actions. What are the bad actions? And what does it mean to abstain from them?

The 10 bad deeds are described by a *Majjhima* passage with some detail beginning with murder.[105] One who kills living beings is "murderous, bloody-handed, bent on killing and striking, without pity for living beings." One who takes what is not given is a thief who seizes the wealth and property of others. One (a male agent is assumed) who engages in sexual misconduct has sex with women who are "protected" by their parents, brother, sister, or relatives; have a husband; are protected by law; or are engaged to be married.

As for the four bad verbal deeds, speaking lies is interpreted primarily as bearing false witness, either in court or in an important meeting,

---

104. D.iii.74.

105. M.iii.47–50; cf. A.v.264–65.

"in full awareness one tells a lie for one's own ends, or another's, or for some small gain."[106] Malicious speech is a matter of repeating things one has heard in order to divide people and to create discord. Harsh speech is "uttering words which are sharp, hard, harsh, painful and offensive to others, bordering on anger, and not conducive to concentration." And frivolous speech is gossip: "speaking at the wrong time, speaking untruths, speaking what is not helpful, speaking against the Dhamma or the Vinaya, and saying worthless things."

Bad mental deeds are three: covetousness is the desire for someone else's property; malice is not merely disliking someone, but wishing for their destruction; and wrong view involves championing doctrines that deny the value of giving and sacrifice, the workings of karma and rebirth, that parents are important, and that good recluses and Brahmans are present in the world. These are amplifications of the three toxic roots or motivations (*mūla, hetu*) at the heart of our suffering in *saṃsāra*: greed, hatred, and delusion. They involve more fully developing into thoughts these basic motivations.

A much more extensive treatment of the 10 bad deeds is given in a section of commentary that was used in a number of places, including in the Abhidhamma commentary.[107] This commentarial passage gets into some technicalities concerning the factors that contribute to the culpability of each of these actions.[108] Taking life, for example, "is the intention to kill (*vadhakacetanā*) applied at either the doorways of body or speech, for one who is aware that life is present in a living being, and who generates an attack which cuts off the faculty of life." It says that there are five constituent parts of it: life, awareness that life is present, the thought to kill, the attack, and death of the victim:

---

106. For more on lying, see Derrett ("*Musāvāda-virati* and 'Privileged Lies' "), particularly his argument that Buddhism does not allow for a category of lies he calls "privileged lies," lies that are excusable and commonly overlooked.

107. Sv.iii.1048–50 (on D.iii.269); Ps.i.196–206 (on M.i.47–50); Spk.ii.143–51 (on S.ii.166–68); As 97–104; Paṭis-a.i.219–25. Bhikkhu Bodhi has a very helpful translation of both the *sutta* and *aṭṭhakathā* of the Sammādiṭṭhi Sutta, which includes this commentarial passage (*The Discourse on Right View*).

108. This and the following passages from the commentaries are all taken from Ps.i.196–203, but this passage is more or less identical with the commentarial citations in n. 107. Harvey discusses some of these factors, as well as factors present in other texts (e.g., *Milindapañho* and the *Vinaya*) that were used to assess culpability ("Criteria for Judging the Unwholesomeness of Actions," 143–44, and *An Introduction to Buddhist Ethics*, 46–49). Vibh-a 382–83 offers a precise ranking of creatures according to size and virtue.

> Moreover, the fault can be greater or lesser depending upon the size or status of the victim.
>
> In the case of inferior life, such as among animals, etc. who lack virtues (*guṇa*), the fault is small, but in the case of large bodies, the fault is great. Why? Because of the greatness of the effort (*payoga*), or because of the greatness of the object (*vatthu*) when the effort is the same. In the case of humans who possess virtues, the fault is small when the virtues are small, and great when the virtues are great. When the virtues of the body are equal, it should be understood that the fault is small for those whose attacks on the defilements (*kilesa*) are weak and great for those who are stronger.

These considerations indicate that intention should not be confused with the idea of moral responsibility. All of these deeds depend on intention being present and evident in clear terms, but intention is not the only morally relevant factor in the morality of action. Fault can be greater or lesser depending on the nature of the victim and other criteria. The language of "effort" is interesting; presumably, it takes greater effort to strike down an elephant than an ant, or a more virtuous person than a less virtuous one, and attributions of fault take this into consideration. Effort refers to the means of the action and is said in the case of killing to be sixfold: effort can occur through one's own hand, by giving an order, by weapons that are thrown, by weapons that are held, by the arts [of battle], and by magical power.

Theft and sexual misconduct are treated in similarly technical terms that indicate interest in not only intention and awareness of what one is doing but also the nature and status of the object or victim of the deed and the effort in performing it. We might look at sexual misconduct more closely for its assumptions about gender, in particular the text's ready assumption of a male subject and the meticulous classification and objectification of women. Sexual misconduct is "the intention of transgressing ground where one should not go, occurring at the doorway of the body." And there is just one type of effort: "with one's own hand." There, "ground where one should not go" refers to 20 types of women: married women (of which there are 10: a wife bought for money, a wife married according to her will, a wife living in wealth, a wife who possesses [just] her clothes, a water pot wife, a wife relieved of carrying water vessels, a slave wife, a servant wife, a wife captured as booty, and a temporary wife),[109] those protected by others (mother, father, both parents, brother, sister, relatives, or her clan), a woman protected by the Dhamma (that is, her monastic companions), a woman who is engaged, or one promised to a man and whose engagement is enforced by law. This fastidiousness presumably leaves some women out with whom sexual relations are not considered misconduct, such as widows. "But," the text goes on to say, "the misconduct is a small fault in regard to forbidden ground that is lacking in qualities such as morality, and a great fault in regard to those endowed with qualities such as morality." The culpability of sexual misconduct for men depends, to a substantial degree, on how the woman's virtue is judged.[110] In addition, the care with which the object of the sexual transgression is scrutinized *deflects* attention from the perpetrator of it, which promotes, at least in this instance, an action-based or results-based ethical logic rather than an agent-based one.

We need not go through the close parsing of all four varieties of bad speech acts, except to note generally that these four actions demonstrate a close ear for what speech can do and the variety and nuances of its damaging effects and also to note several intriguing comments about them. "Malicious speech" is a very particular kind of speech that is said to "empty someone else's or one's own heartfelt love for another." One says it deliberately to cause a breach in relationships. It can occur because one wishes to endear or ingratiate oneself to someone by tearing someone else apart. Buddhaghosa uses his exposition of "frivolous speech" to mention not only silly gossip but also telling meaningless stories such as the *Mahābhārata* and the *Rāmāyana*. He adds as well that the full course of action is not

109. Dhammapāla helps explain some of these distinctions (*Ṭīkā* 1.301), as does Collins, "Remarks on the Third Precept." The classification occurs also in the Vinaya (Vin.iii.139; Sp.iii.554–55). Several of these marriages regard the social and economic status or advancement of the woman, such as the wife living in wealth, the wife possessed of clothes, and the wife relieved of carrying water vessels. The temporary wife is a prostitute (Collins, 265). The water pot wife is a woman who has been married according to a ceremony of touching water (Bodhi, *Discourse on Right View*, 29).

110. Curiously, as Collins ("Remarks on the Third Precept") has shown, while all 10 women and all 10 kinds of wives are "forbidden zones," for men who violate the precept in having sex with them, the first eight women protected by their families do not violate the precepts in having sex with men (only the last two, those engaged, violate the precept). Collins suggests that the reason that having sex with women who are engaged is wrong is because it is a transgression not against her but against the husband or prospective husband who "owns" her sexuality. By this logic as well, prostitutes do not violate the precept.

complete if such talk is rejected by the listeners: only when people accept and believe frivolous or meaningless talk is there the full deed.

"Harsh speech" is worth lingering over, because Buddhaghosa treats it with an intriguing story. The story offers up a small detail that shifts analysis of action back to the agent and intention, but also shows something about Buddhaghosa's own voice. Harsh speech is described as "bodily or verbal effort to stab a soft spot in another," and the text says, "A story will make this clear." He goes on to describe a young disobedient boy, who against his mother's instructions runs off into the forest. Fed up with him and not able to catch him, she shouts after him, "May a fierce buffalo chase you!"—an apparent example of harsh speech. And in fact, a buffalo does appear and chases him. But the boy makes a vow of truth, saying, "Let not what my mother said with her mouth come to pass, but what she thought with her mind." The buffalo stops in its tracks, and the boy is safe. Buddhaghosa says this:

> Thus even though there was a stabbing of a soft spot in effort, there was no harsh speech because of its being suppressed by the mind. For parents sometimes say to children, "may thieves cut you to bits," but in fact they do not want so much as a lotus petal to fall on them. And teachers and preceptors sometimes say to their students, "what can be done with these shameless, fearless [students]! Throw them out!" but they do want them to attain knowledge of the scripture.[111]

The passage indicates that here, regardless of the apparent action, the actual thought underlying it is the essential criterion of the moral quality and results of the action. The anecdote illustrates an awareness that people say things they do not mean and that we can expect them to be divided in this way.

The voice of the commentator is equally interesting. Buddhaghosa notices an everyday sort of situation between a mother and her son, knows that mothers do not want any harm to come to their children, and knows that sons know that, too. She says something, she's fed up, but at the very bottom of it is something else altogether (the truth act shows what is really real). Parents may say harsh things, but we know, of course, that they do

111. As 100.

not want so much as a lotus petal to fall on their babies. We should also note Buddhaghosa's fascination here with the "innermost interiority" or psychological reality of ordinary human experience, reflecting in his own distinctive way the usual Buddhist refusal to stop with a description of mere action and his insistence on attending to the way that moral experience is actually being constructed underneath action.

The three mental actions are covetousness, ill will, and false views (we have already met with mental actions in an earlier section when we distinguished them from *cetanā*). Buddhaghosa echoes the *Majjhima* passage in asserting that these are not just equivalent to the three motivational roots—greed, hatred, and delusion—that lie at the heart of so much of what we do. Rather, they are fully worked-out mental actions, motivations realized or activated in the mind: not merely desiring someone's property but having the thought, "would that it be mine"; not merely harboring anger or hatred toward another but having the thought "this one should be destroyed"; and not merely being mistaken but advancing the view "there is nothing given," which denies the value of giving, causality, and action.

Buddhaghosa concludes his treatment of the 10 bad actions with an additional parsing of five aspects: each can be understood as factors, groups, objects, feelings, and roots.[112] These dimensions of action get at many of the (sometimes competing) criteria by which it may be evaluated. As factors (*dhamma*), the first seven are *cetanās*, actual intentions, and the last three, the mental actions of covetousness, malice, and wrong view, are *cetasikas*. We may defer discussion of the significance of this point to the next chapter since the issues in this designation are quite technical and Abhidhammic. As groups, the first seven and false views are considered as belonging only to the group "courses of action"; covetousness and malice are considered both courses of action and roots (i.e., greed and hatred). *Object* (*ārammaṇa*) refers here to the object of the action since all action has an object, whether (in the most reductive sense) that object is a capacity (*saṅkhāra*) or (in a more customary sense) a being or person affected by the action. Taking life, for example, has as its object the faculty of life (that is, a *saṅkhāra*), which is the chief property of the victim that is aimed at; harsh speech has as its object the person or being affected.[113]

---

112. The *Khuddakapāṭha* and its commentary are also interested in these five factors and several others besides in assessing the culpability of actions, in this case the 10 training precepts (see Ñāṇamoli's translation in *The Minor Readings*, 17–36).

113. See Ñāṇamoli, *The Minor Readings*, 29, n. 16, on "objects."

The designation of feelings (*vedanā*) attached to these deeds is important for the larger point in the texts that feelings are a useful agent-based guide to action. There are three feelings—pleasure, pain, and neutral feeling—that attend actions. Taking life, for example, can have only pain associated with it. Even if kings may laugh when a thief is caught and they command that he be killed, Buddhaghosa asserts, "The intention in the decision is associated only with pain for them." Actions can have mixed feelings, such as in stealing one may first be excited and pleased at taking the property of another, but then pain follows as one considers with fear the fruits, outcomes, and consequences of the deed. There may even be a neutral feeling of indifference at the moment of committing the theft. Lying can also be mixed in this way, but harsh speech will be only painful. Covetousness involves pleasure toward the idea of the object desired but indifference or neutrality toward the person who owns it, and so, too, with false views. Malice is only painful.

Frivolous talk can be complicated: when telling the Hindu epics (a paradigmatic example of frivolous talk), one is initially excited and pleased when people shout "well done" and toss their garments. But then after the bard's fee has been paid and someone comes along and asks that the story be repeated, one thinks, "Should I tell a random and disconnected story or not?" and then at the time of telling the story for one so distressed, there is a feeling of pain.

The idea that feelings invariably accompany action in these specified ways points to a moral anthropology in which humans are connected emotionally to their actions in certain identifiable and necessary ways through feeling. This dimension emphasizes once again the subjective nature of the experience of karma and its fruits. We act and experience the results of our action subjectively in terms of pleasure or pain.

Finally, each of the 10 bad deeds is motivated by one or more of the three roots: greed, hatred, and delusion.[114] These vary according to the action and circumstances. For example, lying can be a matter of either greed and delusion or hatred and delusion, depending on the nature of the lie. It is difficult to overstate the importance of the motivational roots as the basis of actions, and a brief word on the motivational system operative here is in order (it will be covered more extensively in the next chapter). Other passages emphasize that these three toxic roots are the cause of the 10 bad deeds and lie at the bottom of all our wrongdoing. They are the seeds that

114. See also A.v.261, which also states that the 10 bad deeds are due to greed, hatred, and delusion.

bring forth fruits,[115] and like actions, can be classified as good or bad.[116] Roots are causes, and Buddhaghosa brings out much of the considerable arsenal of terms for causality to describe the way they cause karma and thus rebirth: greed, hatred, and delusion are roots (*mūla*), causes (*hetu*), sources (*nidāna*), origins (*samudaya*), and reasons (*kāraṇa*) for continuing in the cycle of rebirth.[117]

But what about the 10 good deeds? Buddhaghosa's treatment of these is considerably shorter than his discussion of the bad deeds, for reasons that are instructive on numerous levels.[118] Chiefly, they are described as merely "abstaining" (*virati*) from the 10 bad deeds that have already been described. But he goes on to describe the varieties of abstaining. There are three types of abstaining: abstinence despite opportunity, abstinence one acquires from resolution, and abstinence of giving up.

The first is abstaining when an opportunity for transgression occurs by people who have not taken any formal moral precepts and who just think "to do such a wicked thing is unsuitable for me," when they consider their birth, age, learning, and so on. Buddhaghosa gives a story to illustrate this kind of resistance to temptation. When his mother became ill and close to death, Layman Cakkana of Lanka was instructed by the physician and his brother to fetch hare's meat for her, and so he went to the fields to catch a hare. As he snared one, Cakkana first thought, "I will make medicine for my mother," but then he reconsidered, "It is not right that I deprive another of life for the sake of my mother's life." And so he freed the hare and urged him to join the other hares in the forest enjoying grass and water. When he returned empty-handed, his brother scolded him, but Cakkana went to his mother and took a vow of truth to the effect that he had never, since he was born, knowingly deprived a creature of life. And his mother recovered on the spot. (We may note in passing the fortuitous recourse to vows of truth, evident also in the harsh speech story, that saves the situation and keeps people from what might otherwise be unhappy consequences of their decisions.)

The second kind of abstinence is when one has made a resolution, such as the precepts. What appears to be important here is that a person

115. A.v.261–62.

116. D.iii.214; A.i.201.

117. Mp.ii.209.

118. Ps.i.203–6.

makes a formal precept in a face-to-face ritual with a senior monk that keeps him from acting on his impulses; this is an intention that is a kind of promise. Buddhaghosa describes a certain layman living on Mount Uttaravaḍḍhamāna who took the five precepts with the elder Piṅgalabuddharakkhita and went out to plow his fields. Searching for a lost ox, he was menaced by a snake. His first thought was to cut off the snake's head, but he then recalled, "Since I have taken the precepts in the presence of a respected teacher, it is not right for me to break them," and so he preferred to give up his life rather than strike the snake. Of course, the snake conveniently obliges the moral of the tale, releasing him and slithering away.

Finally, the "abstinence of giving up" should be understood as the abstaining of someone following the Noble Path. For them, the thought "I will kill a creature" does not even arise. Thus the highest kind of abstinence is not resisting temptation or following precepts, but being so advanced that the thought to commit a bad action never even enters one's head. This idea is in keeping with the earlier discussion of dark and bright deeds; as action that is neither dark nor bright, following the Noble Path does not involve the construction of either *kusala* or *akusala* intentions, but rather the abandoning or absence of them. This kind of abstinence, unlike the first two varieties, has no thought or restraint associated with it. Cakkana's refraining from killing the hare comes from an act of self-awareness that to do a wicked act is "unsuitable for me." In the second example, the elder invokes a precept and his fidelity to it. This third "good deed," however, is quite different: it involves no awareness of even the possibility of committing a wrong act. It is a pure absence of intention and action altogether.

As with the 10 bad deeds, the 10 good deeds can be classified by five aspects—as factors, groups, objects, feelings, and roots—and these are classified much the same way as the bad deeds. But feelings will be a matter of either pleasure or indifference since "there is no feeling of pain in following the good." And the relevant motivational roots of moral actions are the opposites of the bad roots: nongreed, nonhatred, and nondelusion.

Although the 10 good deeds are given relatively abbreviated treatment here, the brevity should not divert us from the significance of what is being said. Chiefly, it is important to note that these full courses of action are all abstentions, that is, *nonactions*. Buddhaghosa describes them entirely in the negative, what one could do or think but does not do or think. They are not given positive description here or, for the most part, elsewhere in the canonical texts.

An exception to this choice to define the good deeds as simply refraining from the bad ones is the passage from the *Majjhima* with which we began our discussion of the 10 good and bad deeds.[119] It defines the 10 good deeds largely negatively, describing in detail, for example, a person refraining from all of the bad things involved in taking life or in harsh speech, but also adding a few more positive descriptions as well: one "lives with rod and weapon set aside, conscientious and kind, compassionate toward all living beings," and not speaking harshly, one "utters such words as are pleasing to the ear, affectionate, heartfelt, polite, beloved and delightful to many." Here we have a sense that these acts are not just refraining from the bad deeds, but involve specific actions that display the opposite values. Other texts discuss what is possible when one has abstained from the three mental bad deeds; for example, when one is free of them one experiences lovingkindness and the other *brahmāvihāras*, expanding in all directions.[120]

Whether these positive descriptions are always implied in the abstentions as given in the commentary or elsewhere where the 10 good deeds are described is hard to say—certainly the texts do not say so. They are content to describe a large part of moral action as abstaining from breaking precepts[121] and from committing the 10 bad deeds. This indicates that much of morality lies in refraining from bad actions, and where morality lies, so, too, the flourishing of human life, at least as much as may be possible in the *saṃsāric* existence of good and bad experience. As the people in the Cakkavatti Sutta learn through hard experience as they piece together their world after its near-total destruction, it is by *refraining* from evil actions, from killing, stealing, lying, and the rest, that the moral order is restored.

The Presence of Absences

As we have begun to see, a curious feature of moral thought and action, particularly in a system that emphasizes so strongly an ethic of intention, is that many of these Buddhist descriptions of moral experience involve

119. M.iii.47–49; cf. A.v.266–89.

120. S.iv.322.

121. Pj I. 24–37 describes the five precepts as abstentions (*veramaṇi*), for example, and offers a long discussion of what it means to "undertake" an abstention and what the "object" of an abstention could be said to be. It also mentions the *Vibhaṅga*'s treatment of undertaking abstentions, which we consider in the next chapter (Vibh 285).

abstaining, refraining, abandoning, and relinquishing immoral thought and action. *Sīla*, or the five precepts, is largely defined as *not* violating certain actions,[122] and the 10 morally good deeds are *not* performing the immoral actions and thoughts listed in the 10 immoral deeds. At the psychological level, much moral (and, of course, meditation) work is a matter of clearing away and abandoning problematic states of mind. The texts are interested in what is possible morally and psychologically when certain things are absent or refrained from, and substantial energy and effort are trained on generating absences and desisting from certain behaviors. For example, the "right effort" factor of the Eightfold Path is described in part as "generating zeal for nonarisings"—a phrase well worth mulling over—which entails resolving and exerting the mind to not permit bad mental factors to emerge.[123]

In fact, all of the Noble Path's eight factors—right view, thought, speech, action, livelihood, effort, mindfulness, and concentration—are distinguished by their *abandoning* and *abstaining* from ordinary perspectives and actions. We have noted that Path *cetanā* are "intentions for abandoning." For example, right thought (*sammāsaṅkappa*) means three thoughts: renunciation, nonmalice, and noncruelty, which means *stopping* our usual thoughts of desire, malice, and cruelty.[124] Right speech, action, and livelihood, the three factors that are normally taken "to pertain to ethics or morality (*sīla*)," as Payutto puts it, were seen as, principally, abstentions (*virati*).[125] Right action (*sammākammanta*) means abstaining from killing, taking what is not given, and sexual misconduct; it is a kind of

---

122. Vism 10 says that, among other distinctions, *sīla* is of two kinds: (actual) practice (*cāritta*), which refers to what one should do, and avoiding, not doing, what is prohibited, a distinction that would seem to give *sīla* both positive and negative senses. But even this positive definition of *sīla* of practicing good conduct is then defined as following the precepts, which involves *refraining* from wrong actions. Buddhaghosa defines *sīla* as a matter of (1) intentions (of one who abstains from killing, etc.), as (2) the three mental factors of noncovetousness, nonmalice, and right view (which involves *rejecting* wrong view), as (3) restraint, and as (4) nontransgression, which are again all defined as what one does not do or think or feel (Vism 6–7). He says, too, that the function of *sīla* is its work (*kicca*) of *stopping* misconduct, and its achievement (*sampatti*) is blamelessness one enjoys when one accomplishes this (Vism 8).

123. M.iii.252.

124. *Sammāsaṅkappa* is sometimes translated as "right intention," which is in some sense appropriate, but as we can see, it is conceptually very different from *cetanā*, and I have preferred to keep the two ideas distinct by translating it as "right thought."

125. Payutto, *Buddhadhamma*, 239. The *Abhidhammasaṅgaha*, for example, classifies these three as abstinences; see Nārada and Bodhi, *A Comprehensive Manual*, 79, 88–89.

action (*kamma*) that is really a matter of ceasing from other actions. The Noble Path as a matter of abandoning (*pahāna*), leaving off (*ārati*), abstention (*virati*), refraining (*paṭivirati*), and abstaining (*veramaṇī*)—these terms for abandoning and ridding oneself of problematic thoughts, intentions, and activity are characteristically pervasive in the textual treatments of the Noble Path.[126] And Buddhaghosa gets even more elaborate in glossing the myriad ways one can pull back and desist: leaving off means keeping back, abstaining is without taking pleasure, abstinence is not taking pleasure having turned away, and refraining is crushing and destroying hostile action.[127]

Noting that descriptions of the Path as pulling back and desisting pervade the texts need not lead us to characterize the soteriological path or goal as essentially pessimistic, passive, or quiescent.[128] Nor does pulling back and desisting exhaust the experience of advanced practitioners and arhats; rather, it may be that abandoning problematic thought and action makes space for good states to arise and permeate their experience. But the importance of restraint, abstinence, and the configuring of good actions as the sheer *absence* of bad action should be recognized.

While I cannot treat or even fully outline here the philosophical and interpretative challenges of what I will call the "presence of an absence" (and it will appear in various forms in subsequent chapters), we can begin to see some of the questions it raises by a close look at a curious *sutta* in the *Aṅguttara* called the No Need for an Intention Sutta.[129] The *sutta* describes how, in the presence of one thing (which is, in fact, itself often an absence), there is no need for an intention (*cetanā*) for the arising of something else. For example, the *sutta* begins with the Buddha instructing that when one possesses virtue (*sīla*, the *nonviolation* of the five precepts), there is no need for the intention "may non-remorse arise for me," because in someone who is virtuous, nonremorse will naturally (*dhammatā*) arise. And for one who has nonremorse, there is no need for the intention "may joy arise for me," because it will naturally happen that those who have nonremorse experience joy. Joy then leads to delight, delight to calm, calm to happiness, happiness to *samādhi*, *samādhi* to seeing the way things

126. As, for example, in M.iii.72–78.

127. Ps.iv.133.

128. See Phra Payutto's critique of such misinterpretations (*Buddhadhamma*, 234–35).

129. *Cetanākaraṇīyasutta*, A.v.2.

truly are, then to disenchantment, to dispassion, to release, and finally to *nibbāna*. This formula gives the entire soteriological path in a nutshell, as it were, and it begins with *sīla*, the *not* doing of five bad things.

Now, while it may make for a smoother English translation to say something like "freedom from remorse occurs for those who practice *sīla*," I have deliberately kept the translation as literal as possible here to show how these absences are things that arise: nonremorse arises for people not violating the precepts. Nonremorse is an absence of remorse that arises—is present, as it were—coming about as the result of certain processes (specifically, not committing immoral acts), and in turn making possible other things (joyful experiences). I believe that the language of absences is not just a quirk of the Pāli, but rather an important feature of this moral psychology that identifies experiences of absence as the conditions for other experiences that cannot otherwise occur. Pāli is fully equipped with a rich vocabulary for positive states and factors of mind that could easily be deployed to offer positive content, and yet in so many places in the texts the language of absence is preferred. I believe then that we should take seriously the idea that nonremorse is an experience.

In addition to introducing the idea that absences are importantly present in some way (an idea by no means restricted to this one example but pervades the moral psychology of much of this literature), this particular *sutta* also, and quite pointedly, indicates that these processes occur "without the need for an intention," as Buddhaghosa puts it.[130] This suggests that much occurs morally and soteriologically (in meditation perhaps in particular) when intentional processes are laid aside. Nalini Devdas has also noticed this "remarkable" passage and the way it sets aside the purposive impulse of *cetanā* in favor of a natural development based on dependent origination; the withdrawal of *cetanā* allows "the mind's development (*bhavanā*) to proceed according to its own inner impulse."[131]

As far as I know, the experience of absences has not been much explored in Buddhist ethics, at least as a philosophical problem of learning how to take the presence of absences and abstinences seriously or even learning how to talk about them in adequate philosophical language.[132]

130. Mp.v.2.

131. Devdas, *Cetanā and the Dynamics of Volition*, 219–21.

132. But note Collett Cox's "Attainment through Abandonment," which offers a careful study on how the Sarvāstivādin Abhidhamma tradition interpreted the abandonment of the defilements and fluxes as part of the path structure of practice.

We need to know more about the various types of absences, the ways of making them possible (through restraint, abandoning, nonarising, etc.), and how they may be identified, or not, with positive states or factors of mind and action. But most pertinent from the standpoint of this project, where intention is said to figure so centrally in morality, is to come to see the places and processes in which morally significant activity and experience occur *outside* of intention.

Conclusions

The Suttanta treatment of *cetanā* has introduced some important theories about intention and action, which are subtle, technical, and complex and worth briefly recapping here. *Cetanā* is usually linked to *saṅkhāra*, our constructive activity in the world through which our minds generate our experience. As such, *cetanā* works with and arranges our psychological factors, motivations, and feelings to create all of our experience in *saṃsāra*. This can be a process that occurs without deliberation, and it can occur as the result of the influence others have on us. The texts see these processes as good (*kusala*), bad (*akusala*), or neutral (*abyākata*), and they explore our karmic activity both abstractly and concretely in these terms.

Since action is what it is constructed to be, we now have a clearer account of what the Kālāma passage with which we began was getting at. It asserts, we will recall, that if one does not intend evil when acting, then one is free of the sorrow that may attend evil effects of one's activity. Since, in theory, there is no gap between intention and action, between *cetanā* and karma, then, to state the obvious, the experience one constructs in intended action is in fact what one experiences. Because there is no gap between intention and action, there can be no misfiring of intentions so that what we intend results in a quite different action or result. We are the makers of our experience, and karma, *cetanā*, and *saṅkhāra* name that very process of world making. Moreover, these processes in a fundamental way are tied into good and bad (*kusala* or *akusala*) experience. They describe what is important to us in leading our lives: will our actions create healthy, skillful, blameless, distress-free, and pleasing experiences, or not?

At the same time, probably because of karma's connections to the operations of *saṅkhāra*—which are intrinsically *saṃsāric* activities—both canon and commentary made moves to define a very distinctive type of *cetanā* and karma that does not participate in these constructive processes but instead entails abandoning them (*maggacetanā* as one type of *kiriyacetanā*). This is the intentional action of the Noble Path and arhatship. This way we can still say that arhats act with intended action—they have agency in this sense—without seeing them as tied up in the constructed and constructive activity of *saṅkhāra*.

Early on in the project, we dispensed with the notion of free will as an analytical category useful for framing these Buddhist sources; as we have seen, attributing freedom abstractly to *cetanā* or, indeed, to any of the other intentional or motivational processes described so far does not come naturally to these sources. I argue instead that the language of *agency* and *patiency* can help us discern the dual nature of karma and *cetanā*, which are at once agentive and passive. The enormous emphasis on intended action as generating our present and future experience captures their agentive aspect. Even so, as the Buddha repeatedly says, we are the heirs of our karma, and our intentions are constructed by our own past psychological proclivities and conditioned by all of the factors of dependent origination. This language of agency and patiency can allow us to focus closely on those places in which agency is possible, even while we are aware of the constraints and conditions on the way it is realized.

Patiency, or our sense of being acted on and constrained by karmic conditions (whether of our own making or otherwise), is featured prominently in descriptions of a person in the doctrines of dependent origination and the five aggregates. To know these doctrines is to grasp fully our human condition of suffering—the true horror of *saṃsāra* is just that very fact of being conditioned and thus subject to constant loss. One purpose of these doctrines is to show how we are conditioned and lack any permanent dimension of self. As both doctrines describe persons as dynamic processes and constantly changing events (rather than more substantial entities), they emphasize our human experience as constructed and conditioned. *Cetanā*, *saṅkhāra*, and karma are conditioned events that we do not stand apart from and direct, even while they are also essential instruments of our creative activity in making the present and the future. Mind may make experience, but it is conditioned by previous karma.

But in related doctrines, such as the soteriological project of the Noble Path, we discern a sense of agency, in fact, a quite strong one. It is here that even as conditioned beings, we can effect a new trajectory for ourselves. But curiously, that agency is often found in pulling back and desisting from our ordinary thought and action. The term *saṅkappa* (often translated as "intention" or "thought") is one example where we see a robust sense of agentive possibility. Right *saṅkappa* refers to thoughts of renunciation or that lack malice and cruelty. These thoughts have conditions, most prominently right view as well as the other factors of the Path, but they also demonstrate that our thinking can pull back from sensuality, hatred, and violence. Similarly, the other factors of the Path all entail strong agency, whether in changing or stopping one's views, actions, or thoughts. Right effort (*sammāvāyama*), for example, refers to a host of terms connected to resolve (*chanda*), energy (*viriya*), power (*bala*), exertions (*padhāna*), and other forces that help one guide the mind to relinquish bad mental factors and cultivate good ones. Not only the Noble Path but also the other path factors[133] cultivated in meditation display an enormous optimism in the human capacity to move toward the experience of complete freedom once we learn to relinquish our ordinary constructions of experience.

133. I refer here to the 37 factors of awakening, which include the Eightfold Path, discussed most exhaustively in Gethin, *The Buddhist Path to Awakening.*

2

The Work of Intention

MENTAL LIFE IN THE ABHIDHAMMA

WE OFTEN EXPERIENCE a strong sense of agency: we make decisions and choices and do so with a least some measure of freedom. But when we look more closely at what lies behind the choices we make, we see a more complicated state of affairs: I may be free to choose what I will, but what makes me will what I will? When we consider the *causes* lying behind our choices (rather than the *reasons* we offer for them), we get a more complicated picture psychologically, one that points us inward to feelings, motivations, and dispositions that in subtle but pervasive ways undergird our agency.

We have already learned that the Theravāda sources see moral agency lying not so much at the moment of choice or decision but at the moment when our minds put together and arrange our mental factors to experience the world in the particular and distinctive ways that we do. It is this process that defines intentional action. Strikingly, neither the Buddha nor his commentators describe this process of constructive world making as a matter of rational deliberation; rather, it lies prior to rational processes as a fundamental mechanism of the mind that creates our conscious awareness.

We turn in this chapter to a deeper and more systematic analysis of the precise mental factors operative in this moral phenomenology to see how *cetanā* works. What are the feelings and motivations that intention arranges and animates as we construct our experience and act in the world? What role does deliberative thinking play in intentional action? The Abhidhamma probes these questions through a remarkably precise and exacting psychology. It offers a model of mind that treats the factors of mental experience and the intricacies of their interactions with a level of detail that is distinctive in the history of human thought.

The Abhidhamma

The mental and material constituents of experience that the Abhidhamma charts are called *dhammas*, translated here as "factors." Of course, there are many different meanings of the word *dhamma*, and Buddhaghosa lists several: scripture, root cause (*hetu*), virtue (*guṇa*), and something that lacks an essence or life. He says that it is this last sense of a phenomenon lacking essence or life that is used in the Abhidhamma.[1]

I suggest that *factor* begins to get at this phenomenon because it does not, at least to my ear, seem to bear the same substantive or static sense conveyed by the term *state*, which is often used to translate it. The Abhidhamma texts claim that all experience is composed of these irreducible factors that are conditioned by and that condition other factors. Though they are not reducible to other factors, they are also not sealed off or self-contained units; as Nyanaponika puts it, they are "open" to the past and the future, and their functions, direction of movement, intensities, and karmic qualities are "variable in accordance with the relational system" to which they belong.[2]

In the Pāli Abhidhamma, there are 82 *dhammas* that comprise all our experience: 28 are material (*rūpa*), 52 are mental (*cetasika*), 1 is conscious awareness or mind (*citta*), and 1 is unconditioned and enduring (*nibbāna*). All of them, except *nibbāna* (which exists outside space and time), are momentary events rather than things or states. These events are known through analyzing conceptual experience to its most irreducible parts through meditative techniques and in grouping and classifying them in various ways. As Bhikkhu Bodhi puts it, when meditative techniques are applied:

> the familiar world of everyday perception dissolves into a dynamic stream of impersonal phenomena, flashes of actuality arising and perishing with incredible rapidity. It is the thing-events discerned in the stream of immediate experience, the constitutive mental and physical phenomena, that are called *dhammas*, and it is with their characteristics, modes of occurrence, classifications, and relationships that the Abhidhamma is primarily concerned.[3]

---

1. As 38.

2. Nyanaponika, *Abhidhamma Studies*, 40–41.

3. Bhikkhu Bodhi in Nyanaponika, *Abhidhamma Studies*, xvii. On *dhamma* theory, see also Karunadasa, *The Dhamma Theory*; Gethin, "He Who Sees Dhamma Sees Dhammas" and "On the Nature of Dhammas"; and Ronkin, *Early Buddhist Metaphysics*.

The first two books of the Abhidhamma, the *Dhammasaṅgaṇī* and the *Vibhaṅga*, are largely devoted to enumerating the various factors of mind that contribute to good, bad, and neutral thought and action. In these texts, together with their commentaries, our questions concerning the nature of the springs of action—what intentions are and what goes into forming them—are treated more systematically and, according to Buddhaghosa, more deeply than any other branch of the Pāli literature. They offer a moral psychology that addresses in a very central way some of our most nuanced questions about intentions.

The range of questions the Abhidhamma asks and the possibilities and limitations of its capacities to answer them are closely tied up with its methods and styles of analysis. The relationship between the Sutta *piṭaka* and the Abhidhamma *piṭaka* is rather subtle and, in certain ways, overlapping. The two genres are distinguished not so much for their content, but for their method, although there is slippage on both sides of any clear distinction of method since the Suttas often form matrices and treat phenomena quite abstractly, and the Abhidhamma and certainly its commentaries often treat persons more conventionally than its own disclaimers suggest.[4] Nevertheless, the canonical Abhidhamma does have a distinctive method that involves forming lists and groupings of the factors of experience in prolific and often repetitive fashion. The *Dhammasaṅgaṇī* and the *Vibhaṅga* are primarily lists of items in different arrangements and taxonomies. These lists present the ever-changing dynamic factors that constitute both the material and psychological experience of human beings.

Buddhaghosa sees the canonical Abhidhamma as a body of work that "exceeds and is distinguished from the Dhamma" ("Dhamma" here means the teaching of the Buddha, and he takes the prefix *abhi* to add the sense of "exceed"). Here he does some careful footwork. The Abhidhamma exceeds the Dhamma in that it offers fuller classifications of things than are often provided by the Suttanta.[5] It is an expansion of it principally through a method of classification. At the same time, he insists that Abhidhamma is the word of the Buddha: even if some of its texts were expounded centuries after the Buddha's lifetime, the Buddha forecasted that they would emerge, and he knew what their contents would be, so

4. There is, in addition, very frequent overlap in both canonical and especially commentarial passages between all three *piṭakas*.

5. As 2–3.

in this sense they are his words.[6] Moreover, the *Dhammasaṅgaṇī*, according to Buddhaghosa, contains sections that classify, summarize, or provide commentaries (*aṭṭhakathā*) on the three *piṭakas*, and he classifies the Abhidhamma as a kind of exposition (*veyyākaraṇa*).[7] That Buddhaghosa considers these elaborations of summary and commentary that constitute the canonical Abhidhamma texts to be part of the Buddha's words suggests that the lines between canon and commentary were less sharply drawn than modern scholars often treat them.[8] Buddhaghosa also says that though the *Dhammasaṅgaṇī* and the other Abhidhamma texts are finite in how long it takes to recite them, they are, in fact, "endless and immeasurable when expanded."[9]

Buddhaghosa returns many times to this idea of the endlessness of the Dhamma and the Buddha's words. He says that to picture the depth of the Abhidhamma method, one should consider the oceans. As vast and seemingly endless is the sea for one out in a lonely boat drifting on it, one knows that it is still bordered by land below and on all sides. But the limits of the Abhidhamma (particularly the method of the *Paṭṭhāna*) cannot be known. This is a cause of endless joy and happiness for those who fathom it.[10] (Intriguingly, those who can plumb its depths are not terrified by its endlessness, but enraptured by it.) Buddhaghosa also says that the Dhamma, in the sense of "the teaching as thought out in the mind," is endless and immeasurable. He plays also with ideas of its temporal boundedness and infinitude. Even though the Abhidhamma was taught straight through without stopping in three months' time, which must have

6. As 3–6. Here the worry concerns the status of the *Kathāvatthu*, which is said to be authored by the Elder Tissa, Moggalī's son, 218 years after the Buddha's *parinibbāna*, and is not accepted by the other schools. The idea that the Buddha, upon his awakening, knew the entire set of the Abhidhamma books and their "endless methods of exposition" occurs also in the *Jātakanidāna* (see Jayawickrama, *The Story of Gotama Buddha*, 104). On the matter of *buddhavacana*, Buddha's word and authority, and on the particular case of the *Kathāvatthu*, see McDermott, "Scripture as the Word of the Buddha," 26–31.

7. As 26.

8. The *aṭṭhakathā* section at end of the *Dhammasaṅgaṇī* is also called the *atthuddhāra*, synopsis of the meaning. The *Niddesa* is another text that though treated as canonical in the Suttanta, is really a commentary, and the *Suttavibhaṅga* is a "canonical commentary" on the Pāṭimokkha. The processes of canon formation and how these commentaries got into the canon is still not fully understood, but see Collins, "On the Very Idea of the Pali Canon."

9. As 7.

10. As 10–12.

seemed like a single moment, the Dhamma that was taught is endless and immeasurable.[11]

The infinitude of the teachings suggests the idea of the "surplus of meaning," mentioned earlier. The canonical texts are infinitely expandable, even as they report the Buddha's words. The Buddha's words are expansive by their very nature: they do not end, and the canonical texts are never fully closed. Commentaries, classifications, and summaries are very natural expansions of meaning embedded in the root texts. For us, knowing that the ideas are inherently expansive and open is crucial for how we learn to read these texts; it is particularly helpful for how we come to think about lists, as well as the expansive possibilities for human experience that the lists describe. This is an anthropology that resists closure in depicting human nature and moral possibility.

The Abhidhamma is engaged simultaneously in open-ended possibility and reductive analysis. The Abhidhamma's work with the Dhamma takes us deeply into ultimate matters (*paramattha*) and into the irreducible factors of our experience that cannot be analyzed further, even while the relations between them can extend and vary almost infinitely. Buddhaghosa says that the Abhidhamma is taught expressly for those who falsely hold onto a sense of self in what is really just a collection of changing factors; it is a distinctive training in wisdom[12] or, we might say, a kind of therapy for those confused about what really exists. It dismantles a static and enduring sense of selfhood in favor of a dynamic system of constantly changing and interrelated events. With the Abhidhamma then, in particular, we learn how to think about a complex sense of agency without any notion of ultimate selfhood. This complex agency is explored through lists and classifications of mental factors.

Abhidhamma's analysis of a person involves breaking down conscious awareness (*citta*) and material phenomena; we will be concerned primarily with *citta*. *Cittas* are discrete momentary units of conscious awareness—we can call them "thoughts"—that, when analyzed at the closest level possible, are seen to be made up of any number of the 52 mental factors (*cetasikas*).[13] This knowledge is not easy to come by. For one thing, the duration of a *citta*

---

11. As 15.

12. As 21.

13. *Citta* is also a *cetasika* that characterizes itself (all *cittas* are consciously aware), which is in keeping with the idea that all *dhammas* are characterized by themselves. *Citta* can also be translated as "mind" (it is a synonym of *manas* according to the *Atthasālinī*, As. 123). Mind should never be thought of as an enduring or static thing, however. Instead, it consists of a series of distinct moments of consciousness.

(and the other *dhammas*, for that matter) is incredibly minute, traditionally described as a billionth part of the duration of a flash of lightning.[14] As evanescent as these thought events are, they are comprised of many factors in complex relationships with one another. Although our ordinary experience of our mental processes involves a continuous stream of awarenesses, the Abhidhamma breaks down the series into discrete and irreducible parts, even while it acknowledges that these parts always show up in groups with other parts. The Buddha's analysis of mental processes into discrete components, a direct knowledge he attained on the night of his awakening, was said to be an even more difficult project than a person at sea scooping up a handful of water and determining which drops in it came from which rivers.[15] Thus, the *Dhammasaṅgaṇī*'s analytical method to discern, list, and classify these fleeting mental phenomena is quite removed in this sense from our ordinary conceptions of experience. That said, this is a type of moral phenomenology in the sense that it names phenomena available, at least in theory, in direct experience: it is based on the Buddha's first-person account of direct experience, and this account is, according to the tradition, available directly through meditation practice.

Scholars are still learning how to appreciate the Buddhist affinity for lists exemplified so assiduously in the Abhidhamma, and the apparent endlessness of its classifications has not always evoked "endless joy and happiness" in modern Western scholars. Erich Frauwallner found the Pāli Abhidhamma "monotonously mechanical," "tedious," "overrun" with formalism, "pedantic," and in many places silting up into a degenerate and "rampant scholasticism."[16] Rupert Gethin offers a much more careful and sympathetic treatment of the Abhidhamma use of lists. He shows how summary lists allow the Dhamma to be expressed both in brief and extensively, how they ingeniously articulate the structure of the Dhamma, and how they stimulate further exposition. Lists give license for improvisation and creative work: the term for list, *mātikā*, also means "mother," and in this sense, a list is "pregnant with the Dhamma and able to generate it in

---

14. Nyanaponika, *Abhidhamma Studies*, 100. Note, though, that the *dhamma nibbāna* is not characterized in terms of duration.

15. As 142; Mil 87.

16. Frauwallner, *Studies in Abhidhamma Literature*, 57, 79, 89, 45. But see Collins's criticism of Frauwallner's treatment of the Pāli Abhidhamma ("Remarks on the *Visuddhimagga*," 6, n. 22).

all its fullness."[17] In this view, the Abhidhamma propensity for extensive elaboration of lists and new arrangements of concepts is not a superficial or senseless rehashing of the material, but an exercise in fashioning new ways to interpret the relationality of existence.

Gethin also suggests that the Abhidhamma method must be understood in the context of meditation and mindfulness exercises. Other scholars as well have pointed to the inherent dynamic and living quality of the Abhidhamma and the way its dynamic interpretative impact can be fully appreciated only in the context of meditation and introspection.[18] Gethin advises that the Abhidhamma's method is, in the end, practical. Its analysis or breaking up of wholes into parts undermines our constant and fruitless tendency to grasp and fix the world of experience. The restless reexamination of these arrangements through proliferating lists is itself a method for destabilizing our yearning for a fixed and stable sense of the world.

> Of course, the danger is that when, in our attempts to undo our reifying of the world, we break it up into parts, we might then take the parts as real and begin to reify the world again, if in a different way.... It seems to me that the early Abhidhamma authors sought to avoid precisely this same danger through the elaboration of the various *mātikās*. Try to *grasp* the world of the *Dhammasaṅgaṇī*, or the *Paṭṭhāna*, and it runs through one's fingers. In short, the indefinite expansions based on the *mātikās* continually remind those using them that it is of the nature of things that no single way of breaking up and analyzing the world can ever be final.[19]

This is moral phenomenology of a unique sort. As much as it advances a model of mind—and we do come to know what the elemental components of mental life are and how they interact to produce action—its very method destabilizes an overly fixed or final version of it.

Buddhaghosa explains that as useful as it is from the standpoint of ultimate reality, the Abhidhamma method is simply not helpful when

17. Gethin, "The *Mātikās*," 161. Gethin is here referring to a later commentator, Kassapa, who says that lists (*mātikas*) are like mothers "because of begetting, looking after and bringing up without end or limit."

18. Nyanaponika, *Abhidhamma Studies*, for example.

19. Gethin, "The *Mātikās*," 165.

considering conventional behavior, such as that described in the Vinaya or in instruction on lay ethics and moral responsibility. In such contexts, it is best to speak of minds or thoughts in a more conventional sense, and we will see more conventional or everyday accounts of mind in the next two chapters.[20] Conventional use of language does some things that ultimate language cannot; the two kinds of teachings have different purposes and impacts on their audiences.[21] Ultimate teachings refer to analysis that is reductive and deeper in the sense that it pushes on things until they are dissolved into the smallest parts possible. Abhidhamma is useful for a generic analysis of human nature and experience (referred to as *nippariyāya* knowledge) but not for understanding the thick contextual and particular circumstances in which people live their lives (*pariyāya* knowledge).[22] As both Charles Hallisey and Y. Karunadasa have argued, the Theravādins do not see ultimate (*paramattha*) teachings as truer than conventional (*sammuti*) teachings.[23] They have different purposes but are equally truthful ways of describing the world, and the Theravāda sources do not place them in a hierarchy.

While the canonical Abhidhamma offers generic accounts of human experience, at the commentarial level, Buddhaghosa deals with lists by contextualizing them, elaborating on them, and explaining them, and thus he develops the material in a more conventional or everyday direction. He expands points by offering metaphors and similes of mental processes to

20. As 68–69.

21. See Hallisey, "In Defense of Rather Fragile and Local Achievement," 130–33, in response to Paul Griffiths's view that Abhidhamma, as a type of "denaturalized discourse," is an ideal type of philosophical discourse ("Denaturalizing Discourse," 69). For Griffiths, denaturalized discourse is an intellectual practice that renders its asserted truths "in a decontextualized, abstract, fleshless discourse, a discourse that pretends to stand nowhere solid, to be located nowhere specific, and to have its utterance by any thinking subject as an accidental property rather than an essential one" (58). It is normative and universalizable in its claims, austere in its ontology, and "aimed primarily at making available to its users what really exists, a function that, from the viewpoint of a user of such discourse, cannot be performed by ordinary, nondenaturalized discourse." Hallisey argues that Buddhaghosa and the later Theravāda thinker Gurulugomi did not see Abhidhamma as a superior type of philosophical discourse and were well aware of its limitations, particularly in the kind of impact it has on people. Moreover, while there are some elements of Griffiths's description that might be usefully applied to the canonical Abhidhamma method, Buddhaghosa is at pains to provide a context for when and why it was spoken, and it is very important to him that it be understood as the Buddha's words taught in a specific time and place; for him, not denaturalized or decontextualized (As 27–35).

22. Hallisey, "In Defense of Rather Fragile and Local Achievement," 131–32.

23. Ibid.; Karunadasa, *The Dhamma Theory*, 35–40.

help us understand how mental factors work. And he sometimes introduces stories that allow us to see how this moral psychology operates in the actions of flesh-and-blood agents in particular contexts. In general, at the commentarial level there are not the sharp distinctions between genres that Buddhaghosa is at pains to assert for the canonical texts (and, in fact, many of the same passages are used in both Sutta and Abhidhamma commentaries).

Moral Phenomenology

A central concern of the *Dhammasaṅgaṇī* is to determine the precise factors (*dhammas*) that go into moments of conscious awareness or thoughts (*citta*). These moments of conscious experience are known subjectively and through introspection. The account of this phenomenology is inflected by moral concerns as it classifies thoughts from the outset as good (*kusala*), bad (*akusala*), and neutral (*abyākata*). The opening line of the text's first chapter asks this question: "Which factors are good?" It goes on to claim that when a good thought arises in the sensory realm and is directed to an object (either an object of the senses or another mental object), and when it is accompanied by joy and associated with knowledge, 56 mental factors (*cetasikas*) may occur.[24] Morally good consciousness can also be accompanied by disinterest rather than joy, and dissociated from knowledge, and the *Dhammasaṅgaṇī* provides lists of these variants. Thought, or conscious awareness, should be understood as a momentary event that contains, at the very least, rudimentary perceptual and cognitive processes; it can also contain varieties of affect and quite refined moral sentiments. Since all consciousness is directed to an object, it is *intentional* in the modern technical sense of being *about* something.

Just as the *Dhammasaṅgaṇī* lists the factors that go into a morally good thought, it also lists the factors that go into bad and neutral thoughts. An immoral or bad (*akusala)* thought is not *kusala* and thus is unskillful, blameworthy, and leading to bad and insalubrious results, misfortune, and

24. The 56 *cetasikas* in this kind of moral consciousness are drawn from the 52 *cetasikas*, with some of them repeated. The text also states that this moral consciousness occurs in the "realm of sense desire." The realm of sense desire is that reality experienced by ordinary people who have no advanced spiritual insight. Highly advanced humans and deities have experiences in the other two realms: the realm of form and the realm of formlessness. While these distinctions among possible realities are very important, my concern in this book is with ordinary human experience, and thus, the higher realms will fall, for the most part, outside our purview.

distress. It fortifies mental defilements and impurities. Neutral (*abyākata*) thoughts are neither moral nor immoral, either because they are ordinary experiences of everyday consciousness not productive of karma, such as sense experiences toward that to which one is indifferent, or because they are the experiences of arhats, awakened ones, whose actions are not characterized in terms of *kusala* and *akusala*, as we saw in the last chapter.

Table 2.1 shows the *Dhammasaṅgaṇī*'s lists of the 56 moral mental factors, the 32 immoral factors, and the 10 neutral factors that can go into the first variety of the three types of thoughts. These thoughts will comprise combinations of such mental factors.

A few general remarks about the items on these lists are necessary, since most of them can be seen to contribute, in one way or another, to moral agency, before we go on to examine more closely those that are particularly relevant for conation.[25] The first five in all three lists are traditionally taken to be rudimentary perceptual and prerational functions present in every conscious moment: the barest impacts of sensory contact, sense impression or feeling, perceptual awareness (which also comprises an element of judgment), intention (*cetanā*), and conscious awareness itself. Nyanaponika suggests that these five omnipresent factors form the most primitive functions of conscious awareness, perhaps even shared with the higher animals.[26] For our particular interest in *cetanā*, this is interesting and seems to depart from many of the expectations we might have about intentions, and we will explore the commentary's exegesis on it at some length. But at this juncture, we note only that some element of intention is, necessarily, a part of every conscious moment and that it exists prior to the processes of cognition (initial and sustained thinking).

The next five items on the lists of both good and bad factors are "factors of absorption" that intensify and differentiate awareness in ways that are cognitive (initial and sustained thinking), affective (joy, that is, both

25. Nyanaponika, *Abhidhamma Studies*, chs. 3–4, discusses the good factors in more breadth than possible here.

26. Ibid., 55–57. This list of five was later expanded to seven in the Pāli tradition. Both the *Milindapañha* and the *Abhidhammatthasaṅgaha* list seven universal factors present in every consciousness: contact, feeling, perception, intention, oneness of mind, the faculty of vitality, and attention (Mil. 56; Bodhi and Nārada, *A Comprehensive Manual of Abhidhamma*, 78). Vasubandhu names 10 mental factors in every thought: feeling, intention, perception, the desire for action (*chanda*), contact, discernment (*prajñā*), remembering (*smṛti*), attention (*manaskāra*), resolve (*adhimukti*), and concentration (*samādhi*, glossed as oneness of mind with the object) (de La Vallée Poussin, *Abhidharmakośabhāṣyam*, vol. 1, 189–90).

Table 2.1 Good, Bad, and Neutral Mental Factors in the First Types of Good, Bad, and Neutral Thoughts[1]

Good Mental Factors	Bad Mental Factors	Neutral Mental Factors
Contact (*phassa*)	Contact (*phassa*)	Contact (*phassa*)
Feeling (*vedanā*)	Feeling (*vedanā*)	Feeling (*vedanā*)
Perception (*saññā*)	Perception (*saññā*)	Perception (*saññā*)
Intention (*cetanā*)	Intention (*cetanā*)	Intention (*cetanā*)
Conscious awareness (*citta*)	Conscious awareness (*citta*)	Conscious awareness (*citta*)
—	—	—
Initial Thinking (*vitakka*)	Initial Thinking (*vitakka*)	
Sustained Thinking (*vicāra*)	Sustained Thinking (*vicāra*)	
Joy (*pīti*)	Joy (*pīti*)	Equanimity (*upekkhā*)
Pleasure (*sukha*)	Pleasure (*sukha*)	
Oneness of mind (*cittassekaggatā*)	Oneness of mind (*cittassekaggatā*)	Oneness of mind (*cittassekaggatā*)
—	—	—
Faculty of faith (*saddhindriya*)		
Faculty of energy (*vīriyindriya*)	Faculty of energy (*vīriyindriya*)	
Faculty of mindfulness (*satindriya*)		
Faculty of concentration (*samādhindriya*)	Faculty of concentration (*samādhindriya*)	
Faculty of wisdom (*paññindriya*)		
Mental faculty (*manindriya*)	Mental faculty (*manindriya*)	Mental faculty (*manindriya*)
Faculty of happiness (*somanassindriya*)	Faculty of happiness (*somanassindriya*)	Faculty of equanimity (*upekkhindriya*)
Faculty of vitality (*jīvitindriya*)	Faculty of vitality (*jīvitindriya*)	Faculty of vitality (*jīvitindriya*)
—	—	—
Right view (*sammādiṭṭhi*)	Wrong view (*micchādiṭṭhi*)	
Right thought (*sammāsaṅkappa*)	Wrong thought (*micchāsaṅkappa*)	
Right effort (*sammāvāyāma*)	Wrong effort (*micchāvāyama*)	

continued

Good Mental Factors	Bad Mental Factors	Neutral Mental Factors
Right mindfulness (*sammāsati*)		
Right concentration (*sammāsamādhi*)	Wrong concentration (*micchāsamādhi*)	
——	——	——
Power of faith (*saddhābāla*)		
Power of energy (*vīriyabāla*)	Power of energy (*vīriyabāla*)	
Power of mindfulness (*satibāla*)		
Power of concentration (*samādhibāla*)	Power of concentration (*samādhibāla*)	
Power of wisdom (*paññābāla*)		
Power of shame (*hiribāla*)	Power of shamelessness (*ahiribāla*)	
Power of apprehension (*ottappabāla*)	Power of fearlessness (*anottappabāla*)	
——	——	——
Non-greed (*alobha*)	Greed (*lobha*)	
Non-hatred (*adosa*)		
Non-delusion (*amoha*)	Delusion (*moha*)	
Non-covetousness (*anabhijjhā*)	Covetousness (*abhijjhā*)	
Non-malice (*abyāpāda*)		
Right view (*sammādiṭṭhi*)	Wrong view (*micchādiṭṭhi*)	
——	——	——
Shame (*hiri*)	Shamelessness (*ahirika*)	
Apprehension (*ottappa*)	Fearlessness (*anottappa*)	
——	——	——
Tranquility of body (*kāyapassadhi*)		
Tranquility of mind (*cittapassadhi*)		
Lightness of body (*kāyalahutā*)		
Lightness of mind (*cittalahutā*)		
Softness of body (*kāyamudutā*)		
Softness of mind (*cittamudutā*)		
Workableness of body (*kāyakammaññatā*)		
Workableness of mind (*cittakammaññatā*)		

Good Mental Factors	Bad Mental Factors	Neutral Mental Factors
Proficiency of body (*kāyapāguññatā*)		
Proficiency of mind (*cittapāguññatā*)		
Uprightness of body (*kāyujukatā*)		
Uprightness of mind (*cittujukatā*)		
Mindfulness (*sati*)		
Meta-attention (*sampajañña*)		
Calmness (*samatha*)	Calmness (*samatha*)	
Insight (*vipassanā*)		
Exertion (*paggāha*)	Exertion (*paggāha*)	
Balance (*avikkhepa*)	Balance (*avikkhepa*)	
"and other factors":	*"and other factors":*	*"and other factors":*
Attention (*manasikāra*)	Attention (*manasikāra*)	Attention (*manasikāra*)
Initiative (*chanda*)	Initiative (*chanda*)	
Resolve (*adhimokkha*)	Resolve (*adhimokkha*)	Resolve (*adhimokkha*)
Impartiality (*tatramajjhattatā*)		
Compassion (*karuṇā*)		
Sympathetic joy (*muditā*)		
Abstention from bodily misconduct (*kāyaduccaritavirati*)		
Abstention from verbal misconduct (*vacīduccaritavirati*)		
Abstention from wrong livelihood (*micchājīvavirati*)		
	Conceit (*māna*)	
	Envy (*issā*)	
	Avarice (*macchariya*)	
	Rigidity (*thīna*)	
	Sluggishness (*middha*)	
	Agitation (*uddhacca*)	
	Remorse (*kukkucca*)	

1 Dhs 1; 75; 87; these are the potential contents of only the first types of thoughts (*citta*) in each category. Buddhaghosa adds additional factors to these canonical lists as "other factors" in As 131, 250, and 264. See also Nyanaponika, *Abhidhamma Studies*, 31–35.

rapture and interest, and pleasure, that is, a pleasant feeling as opposed to a painful one), and focusing (oneness of mind with the object).[27] These items can be either good or bad, depending on which other factors are present in the awareness. Similarly, other functions are shared by both lists: certain varieties of energy (and effort and exertion) and concentration (and balance), stated in different ways, are part of both good and bad consciousness. These good and bad thoughts alike require a certain energy toward their object, as well as a certain focus on or conscientiousness toward it. These factors are not good or bad in and of themselves; their moral valence is variable or open and determined by other factors that occur in a given thought.

The affective resonances in good and bad thoughts are especially interesting: both can be joyful and pleasurable, but only bad thoughts can be distressing and painful. We might expect some morally good thoughts to be painful, as when one does something that is disagreeable but morally right, such as diving into a cesspit to save the life of a child who has fallen in or lying to save a person's life. But in this psychology, *kusala* thoughts—skillful, felicitous, salutary—are simply never painful or distressing, though they can be neutral. (They are felt as neutral when they are experienced through equanimity and disinterest or are the thoughts of spiritually advanced adepts.) We might also note that the Abhidhamma generally does not set up its reflection about morality in terms of conflicts or dilemmas, such as when one is confronted with a dilemma between two morally problematic options—lying or allowing someone to be killed—neither of which is appealing. This may make it easier to see that moral thoughts and actions are not presented here as particularly fraught with the conflict, ambiguity, and pain that such dilemmas often engender. We will encounter a different moral psychology when considering the Vinaya and narrative texts that do consider moral dilemmas and the pain sometimes accompanying them.

The remaining items on the list of moral factors are parts of groups of morally and soteriologically valuable mental activities or states familiar from other contexts, such as the mental elements of the Eightfold Path, certain faculties (three of which, faith, mindfulness, and wisdom, are particularly conducive to changes in character and conduct), and the seven powers (which overlap with the first five faculties and add the important capacities of shame and apprehension). Although faculties exert a certain controlling influence over other mental factors, powers provide an additional firmness or steadfastness of the disposition.[28] Some factors are

27. Nyanaponika, *Abhidhamma Studies*, 53–55.

28. Gethin, *The Buddhist Path to Awakening*, ch. 4, provides a helpful discussion of the faculties and powers.

listed twice, treated here under their different aspects as powers and faculties, as, for example, mindfulness and concentration.

The several instances of repetition of items on the list may seem unsatisfactory, given the precision with which the topic is approached: why should concentration, for example, occur four times, as a faculty, a power, a Path factor, and separately? Buddhaghosa takes up this problem and argues that by repeating items in their membership in different groupings, attention is drawn to their functions and aspects in those groupings; just as a king hires an artisan who may be able to offer several kinds of crafts and belong to several different guilds, so the same factor can perform different functions according to its membership in groups. Since classification is a key instrument of the development of meaning, seeing which groups each item belongs to suggests important variations in its qualities and intensities.[29]

Shame and apprehension are two important powers and moral sentiments with particular value for conation. Shame (*hiri*) is a complex feeling of embarrassment and mortification in the face of one's wrongdoing, and apprehension (*ottappa*) is a fear or horror of one's own potential for evil and attracting the blame of others. These are features of our mental lives that, when cultivated, make us shrink from wickedness. They are called the "guardians of the world" because they protect the world from our potentially harmful incursions upon it.[30] While shame may have a rather negative ring in modern ears, evoking either a corrosive assault on the self, a primitive disgust at human vulnerability and animality, or a destructive internalization of rigid social norms, in this system it is considered a morally valuable sense of bashfulness and self-awareness of one's capacity for wrongdoing. (Some uses of the English word *shame* hint at some positive moral value in it, as when we disapprove of those who are shameless.) As I have argued elsewhere, *hiri* is regarded as a sensitivity to how one is perceived by others that generates a morally praiseworthy self scrutiny and regard.[31] *Ottappa*, or apprehension, is a sensitivity to blame and censure from others and fear of the consequences of evil action. Their opposites,

29. As 135–36. Nyanaponika offers a very helpful and sympathetic amplification on Buddhaghosa's treatment of factors according to function or application or degree of intensity among these factors (*Abhidhamma Studies*, 37–42, 88–92). Again, Nyanaponika's point that these factors are "open" means that they are really "potentialities" whose quality and intensity will be determined by the other factors by which they are relationally constituted (90).

30. Vism 465.

31. Heim, "Shame and Apprehension," 237–60.

shamelessness and fearlessness, are present in all bad thoughts and allow our wicked propensities to wreak harm on the world unchecked.

The motivational roots (*mūla* or *hetu*) are of particular importance to conation, as we have seen in chapter 1. Among the morally good factors, three motivational roots are listed—nongreed, nonhatred, nondelusion—together with their intensified states, noncovetousness, nonmalice, and right view. We should also notice that motivations comprise both affective conditions (nongreed and nonhatred, for example) and cognitive clarity (nondelusion and right view). In this psychology, the condition of possessing clarity and truth has motivational force. The importance of these factors of mind is hard to overstate. The first three are, according to Nyanaponika, "the main criteria by which a state of consciousness is determined to be wholesome," that is, *kusala*.[32] The latter three are considered to be "intensified states"[33] of the first three and are also the three good mental actions on our list of 10 *kusala* deeds. Except for right view, all are described in the negative; that is, they are the opposites of the bad roots (greed, delusion, malice) or the abstentions from the bad mental actions (covetousness, malice, and wrong view). Their statement in the negative is significant; chiefly, they are the absence of or abstinence from the bad motivations and bad mental actions. While Phra Payutto argues that stating virtues in the negative with the use of the "*a*" prefix covers more ground than a positive term would ("it carries both a negative meaning and encompasses all opposites"),[34] neither the Abhidhammikas nor Buddhaghosa typically elaborate on them in a positive direction. The texts themselves treat these "nonaffirming negations" as irreducible factors that need not imply positive content.

The bad motivations listed are greed, delusion, covetousness, and wrong view, opposites of the good motivations. Notably absent in the table are the motivational roots hatred and malice; this is because this particular listing is for bad thoughts that occur accompanied by joy (*somanassa*). Hatred and malice are such unpleasant experiences that they never occur in such a moment. The *Dhammasaṅgaṇī* gives another list of bad factors that occur in the presence of distress (*domanassa*): many of the same items are listed but instead of elements of joy, pleasure, happiness, greed, and covetousness, we find suffering, distress, and the motivational roots hatred and malice.[35] Thus a bad thought can either be joyful, such as when one is

32. Nyanaponika, *Abhidhamma Studies*, 69.

33. Jaini, "The Sautrāntika Theory of *Bīja*," 221.

34. Payutto, *Buddhadhamma*, 235.

35. Dhs 83.

greedy and lustful, or it is distressing, as when it is comprised of hatred or malice. In contrast, good thoughts are, as we have seen, always joyful or disinterested: ordinary good thoughts are joyful, but as they become more rarefied and attain to other realms achieved through meditation, they transcend joy, and the experience is characterized instead by equanimity.

The list of good factors includes six pairs of qualities that can describe both body and mind, for a total of 12 qualities that always arise together: tranquility (being quiet and composed), lightness (agility and buoyancy), softness (being pliable, resilient, and adaptable), workableness (the right balance of softness and firmness "which makes the gold—that is, the mind—workable"), fitness (health and competence), and uprightness (sincerity and straightforwardness).[36] These dispositions are not treated with much detail, but they suggest attributes that dispose one to moral action through mental and physical composure, malleability, health, readiness, and rectitude. Following them, we have several potentialities: mindfulness, mental clarity, and insight, which refer to distinctive aptitudes in the development of mental culture. Last, calmness, exertion, and balance (present in both good and bad thoughts) are synonyms or amplifications of some of the earlier items and provide the steadiness, energy, and concentration required for moral agency.[37]

In the last line of each passage listing the factors, the *Dhammasaṅgaṇī* allows that other factors not listed may contribute to each type of consciousness, making room for "whatever other factors" may also arise in mutual dependence with the others.[38] This asserts that these lists are not meant to be exhaustive; they do not complete the process of elaboration or classification, and, I would suggest, we cannot understand the nature of Abhidhamma lists if we think that the lists, or the moral phenomenology they depict, are always meant to be complete. Gethin is correct to describe a good thought as having "at least" 56 factors: his inclusion of "at least" shows the resistance to closure built into the structure here. He suggests

36. See Nyanaponika, *Abhidhamma Studies*, 71–81; As 150–151.

37. Nyanaponika, *Abhidhamma Studies*, 82–83.

38. Dhs 8, 75, 87.

39. Gethin, "The *Mātikās*," 165. Izmirlieva (*All the Names of the Lord*, 2008) offers a careful and thoughtful treatment of lists of the names of God in early Christian contexts; some of her insights about lists may be helpful here. She argues that a list is a "symbolic imposition of a particular vision upon reality" (7), and when a list is open-ended, it makes possible a view of the world that "is open to a 'yonder,' to the possibility of becoming something that it is not." Its order is temporary, and it "means living not with definitive answers but with provisional assumptions" (153). To experience the canonical Abhidhamma lists as open is to destabilize and make provisional even what the Buddha taught about mental experience.

that the lists are given as invitations to others to discover through meditation what else might be there in their experience.[39]

The door is thus left open for expanding the list, and Buddhaghosa is quick to step in and add additional factors. He suggests an additional factor of attention (*manasikāra*) is also present in all three types of consciousness.[40] Attention "makes the mind differently than it was before," and it leads the mind to its object.[41] Like a coachman, it drives other mental factors to an object, whether the object is a sense object, a cognitive process, or an impulse to act. We should not underestimate the importance of attention in consciousness, a point increasingly recognized by the tradition.[42] And we may recall the mention of "careful attention" in the *Atthasālinī*'s definition of *kusala* discussed in the previous chapter, which also indicates its importance specifically to moral agency.

Besides attention, Buddhaghosa includes eight additional good factors: initiative, resolve, impartiality, compassion, sympathetic joy, and three abstentions, that is, abstaining from physical and verbal misconduct and wrong livelihood.[43] Certain of these are particularly pertinent to our interest in conation and merit further definition. Initiative (*chanda*) is a desire for an object of an action, likened to the mind stretching out its hand toward that desired object.[44] Resolve (*adhimokkha*) is something like a firm decision, the "making up of the mind" in conviction and determination. The *Sammohavinodanī* defines *resolve* thus: "the mind is resolved in regard to the object by means of it and arrives at a conviction through the absence of doubt."[45] Impartiality balances the factors of energy and concentration and adds an important element of equanimity where necessary in moral action: it

40. As 131–33, 250, 262.

41. As 133. Attention has for its characteristic remembering, its function is joining associated factors to their object, its manifestation is its nature of turning toward an object, and it is included in the *saṅkhāra* aggregate.

42. Ānanda's *Abhidhammasaṅgaha* treats attention (*manasikāra*), oneness of mind, and vitality as universals, and unlike the *Dhammasaṅgaṇī*'s list, it omits *citta*, for a total of seven universals (Nārada and Bodhi, *A Comprehensive Manual of Abhidhamma*, 79–81).

43. As 131.

44. The *Sammohavinodanī* offers an intriguing detail about *chanda* (Vibh-a 461). It says that the people of Uttarakuru have entered into a place without *chanda*, this desire to act. Uttarakura is, in traditional Buddhist cosmology, the land to the north where people live fantastically long, beautiful, and pain-free lives; however, they are incapable of attaining awakening and seem to have limited moral agency. This may be due, as suggested here, to their lack of *chanda*, initiative.

45. Vibh-a 210.

46. As 133.

"checks deficiency and excess and cuts off partiality."[46] Compassion and sympathetic joy are two of the four sublime attitudes (*brahmavihāras*), which are essential to many forms of moral action.[47] Finally, we have three abstentions (that are also Path factors)—abstention from bodily misconduct, from verbal misconduct, and from wrong livelihood—that indicate that abstaining from immoral thought and action is itself a kind of positive mental factor, a "presence" of something in the mind that ceases from bad action.

The *Atthasālinī*'s additional bad factors are, besides attention: initiative, resolve, conceit, envy, avarice, rigidity, sluggishness, agitation, and worry.[48] These include what we might call emotions as well as traits or dispositions, and certain of them, as with other items among the immoral factors, occur in various groupings of defilements, depravities, and hindrances. All of them offer much that is psychologically interesting. Despite the fact that these, as *dhammas*, are irreducible events, they seem to involve complex thoughts and emotions. Envy, for example, is grumbling at others' good fortune, involving a whole set of feelings of resentment.[49] Conceit, too, is complex. Traditionally, there are several varieties of conceit, all concerned with measuring oneself in one's own estimation vis-à-vis others and thus displaying an undue preoccupation with oneself.[50]

As interesting as these additional factors are, we may also note what is *not* included here. Fear, for example, is not listed here or anywhere in the lists of immoral factors. This may be surprising, given its importance in other contexts as entangled with problematic states of mind and immoral action.[51] Indeed, the absence of fear as a motivation generally in the Abhidhamma is something of a puzzle. While it appears in the list of moral factors in the form of *ottappa* (a moral disposition to fear one's

47. The other two sublime attitudes, *mettā* and *upekkhā*, are covered by nonhatred and particular equanimity.

48. As 250: *manasikāra, chanda, adhimokkha, māna, issā, macchariya, thina, middha, uddhacca, kukkucca.*

49. As 373.

50. Vibh-a 487–89. See Heim, "The Conceit of Self-Loathing," for more on conceit.

51. Such as M.i.16; D.iii.181–82.

52. Rupert Gethin has suggested one way to see that fear may be present in a type of hate (*dosa*), that is, the hate rooted in delusion (*moha*) associated with agitation (*uddhacca*), based on Vism 454 (Gethin, "On the Nature of Dhammas," 189–90). I think that fear might be present in the feeling of pain (*dukkhavedanā*), as suggested in the *Atthasālinī*'s treatment of the 10 courses of bad action, in which theft, for example, can be accompanied by a feeling of pain described as frightened and fearful (*bhītatasita*) (As 102). As Gethin also notes, such attempts at getting fear into the picture are not unproblematic, however, for they build additional qualities into *dhammas* that are themselves supposed to be discrete or indissoluble phenomena.

own capacity for evil), there is no mention of more negative types of fear (*bhaya*) as contributing to bad thoughts.[52] We might also find the omission of fear surprising in light of recent evolutionary psychological approaches to the emotions that claim that fear is a universal emotion and an indispensable motivational factor in our biological makeup.[53]

The Work of Intention

The foregoing census of the many factors of conscious awareness, though all too briefly sketched here, provides a model of mind that depicts many complex and interrelated elements at work in moral agency. This view of the mind is very much in keeping with key Buddhist doctrines of dependent arising. But how do these many factors relate to intentions? And why is intention deemed to be the chief factor generating action when many of these seem also to play an important role in it? Here we must turn to a closer inspection of *cetanā*, examining what it is and how it constitutes action.

That intention belongs to the first five prereflective factors of consciousness, universally present in every conscious moment, means that intentions are always present in conscious experience. Also, they themselves are not morally valenced; they become good, bad, or neutral depending on which other factors occur within a thought moment. We can also see that the presence of so many factors of mental life relevant for thought and action decenters *cetanā* from being an isolated or discrete mental state that is solely responsible for the moral quality of karma.

In his commentary on the opening verse of the *Dhammasaṅgaṇī*'s listing of all 56 factors that can arise in a good thought that we reviewed, Buddhaghosa defines and elaborates on all the factors.[54] This section of commentary is particularly concerned with issues of how conscious awareness arises in relation to its object. Along with his discussion of all

53. Ekman (*Emotions Revealed*) argues that there is a set of universal human emotions deeply embedded in the species and essential to human response and agency: fear, anger, sadness, surprise, disgust, contempt, and happiness. It is striking how few of these appear as such in the Abhidhamma treatment of experience.

54. Dhs 1; As 106–7.

55. A technical definition usually includes naming four things: *lakkhaṇa* (the "characteristic" or its particular or generic nature), *rasa* (the "function," that is, its work or the accomplishment of it), *paccupaṭṭhāna* (the "manifestation," that is, its manner of service or the result), and *padaṭṭhāna* (its "proximate cause," its near condition) (As 63). Here Buddhaghosa does not mention *cetanā*'s proximate cause.

of the 56 *cetasikas*, he provides a technical definition[55] of *cetanā* that suggests a good starting place for our inquiries:

> *Cetanā* is what intends (*cetayati*), which means that it puts together (*abhisandahati*) with itself its accompanying factors as objects. Its characteristic is what is intended (*cetayita*), which means that its characteristic is its nature of intention (*cetanābhāva*).[56] Its function is accumulating (*āyūhana*).[57] Intentions in the four realms[58] are never without the characteristic of being intended. All have as their characteristic what is intended. But its function of accumulating occurs only with reference to good or bad [karma]. [When its function] obtains in accumulating good or bad karma, then there is only a partial role for the remaining associated factors. Intention is exceedingly energetic, exceedingly striving, it does double effort, double striving.[59]

There are many things going on in this brief passage. The insistence that *cetanā* be characterized either by its nature of intending or by what is intended indicates the different ways the word is used that has parallels with English intention: roughly, intention can be the result and the activity of intending. To say that intentions in all four realms will have the sense of being intended is to say that even arhats have intentions in this sense: every kind of *cetanā* (even *kiriyacetanā*) involves putting itself together with other mental factors as an object of thought and action. But the particular function of *cetanā* to accumulate is restricted only to intended

---

56. This says that *cetanā* can be what is intended and what intends (since *cetanā* is what intends, as the first sentence in the passage states). *Cetanā*, like all *dhammas*, bears its own characteristic, *sallakkhaṇa*, which defines it according to itself or its particular nature, *sabhāva* (Karunadasa, *The Dhamma Theory*, 17, referring to Vibh-a 45). The *Mūlaṭīkā* says the *cetanābhāva* is "work" (*byāpāra*) (*Dhammasaṅgaṇī-mūlaṭīkā* 87 [Myanmar edition]).

57. Recall from the last chapter (notes 18 and 44) that accumulating is a specialized sense of *āyūhana*, discussed by Bodhi in his translation of the *Saṃyuttanikāya*, 342, and supported by the textual evidence I have already described.

58. The four realms are the three worlds—that is, the sensory world, the world of form, and the world of formlessness—and the supramundane reality (stream-entry, once-return, nonreturn, and arhatship). Intentions occur in all of them.

59. As 111 (cf. Vism 463; Mil 61). The *Mūlaṭīkā* adds: "*Puts together* means connects and sends forth. The *nature of intention* is the nature of working. *Double effort* is not said to indicate the joining of two kinds of effort, but rather the extensive state of its duty of working" (*Dhammasaṅgaṇī-mūlaṭīkā* 87 [Myanmar edition]).

action that involves amassing karma (and thus excludes *kiriyacetanā* and *maggacetanā*).

The language of accumulating as *cetanā*'s chief function is by now familiar. *Cetanā* puts itself together with the other factors of conscious awareness (the universals and whatever other factors or *cetasikas* are operative) and makes them objects of thought and action. The definition also emphasizes *cetanā*'s energetic effort that is the mind's work in good and bad action. When it is present in a neutral thought moment, it coordinates the other factors, but it does not strive toward any action. Buddhaghosa goes on to offer a simile that anthropomorphizes *cetanā* in a way that makes it more accessible. He likens *cetanā* to a landowner who takes 55 strong men (i.e., the other 55 moral mental factors possible in a good thought moment) and with "exceeding energy, exceeding striving, double effort, double striving" puts the workers to their work and toils alongside them.[60] The double effort and striving indicate its own work and its way of making the other factors do their work.

Buddhaghosa also defines *cetanā* according to its manifestation. Again, similes help tremendously, not only for elaborating or ornamenting the concept but also for providing its basic content.

> [*Cetanā*'s] manifestation is arranging (*saṃvidahana*). Arranging, it occurs accomplishing its own and others' work, like the head student, the head carpenter, etc. For it is just like the head student who, seeing the teacher approach from afar, learns the lesson himself and makes the other students learn it themselves, and they resolve to learn and do so by following him. And it is just like the head carpenter who himself works and makes the other woodworkers do the woodwork, and they resolve to work and do so by following him. And it is just like the army general who himself fights and leads others in the line of battle, and they, in their resolve to fight, fight without turning back by following him. So too [*cetanā*], produces its object by its own work, and makes the other associated factors produce it with their own actions. By its undertaking its own work, those [factors] associated with it undertake [theirs]. Because of this,

60. As 111.

> it is said that "it occurs accomplishing its own and others' work, like the head student, the head carpenter, etc." Moreover, it should be understood that it is manifest as making associated [factors] energetic in such things as remembering urgent action.[61]

Considerations of a phenomenon's manifestation concern how it appears or is manifest in experience. From these illustrations, *cetanā* is a factor of the mind that coordinates, rallies, and marshals other factors to produce the objects of conscious awareness and thus generate action in the world. It is operative whenever there is energetic activity of putting the factors of mind to work on their objects. It is a dynamic activity of collecting and animating rather than a state, decision, choice, or inclination.

The similes here suggest that the mind is a complicated and manifold set of operations, in which intentions, as, say, head tutors, are assigned multiple responsibilities for their own and others' mental work; they can see what is needed and the urgency of it (the teacher is approaching), and they are driven to stimulate themselves and the others to action. *Cetanās* seem to be able to remember—they "recall important work"—which begins to show how they connect present thought and action with the past. We may note in passing that these similes are doing essential philosophical work, invoking ideas that cannot be otherwise easily communicated. In keeping with the Theravāda's affirmative stance on figurative uses of language, we can appreciate the substantive work that simile does in developing the ideas, not just in illustrating them.[62]

Perhaps most intriguingly, *cetanā* "produces its object by its own work," which means that through its activity, this property of the mind makes the objects of our experience. The term *object* (*ārammaṇa*) refers to the objects of the six senses (the five sensory faculties and the mental sense). *Cetanā* is like a carpenter who makes a house by working and getting his subcontractors to do their specialized tasks. Or just as an army general creates the reality of battle for himself and others, *cetanā* creates its object through its

61. As 111–12; cf. Vism 463. The *Mūlaṭīkā* adds: "The state of instigating is the state of respect (or carefulness, *ādara*). For it is like respect in that it respects the accompanying factors like its own self" (*Dhammasaṅgaṇī-mūlaṭīkā* 87 [Myanmar edition]).

62. Iris Murdoch argues that it is "impossible to discuss certain kinds of concepts without resort to metaphor, since the concepts are themselves deeply metaphorical and cannot be analysed into non-metaphorical components without a loss of substance" (Murdoch, *The Sovereignty of Good*, 75).

activity. This is not idealism, but it is constructivist. Our cognition does not simply mirror or represent the world out there. Rather, our experience of the world and of our own mental life is constructed and shaped by the work of our mental processes. This idea links *cetanā* with the constructive aspects of *saṅkhāra* that we explored in the previous chapter. *Cetanā* is constructing the objects of our conscious awareness, which it does by its own work and by putting other mental factors to their particular tasks. Thus, intentional action—karma—is the active rallying of mental factors as one constructs the world of experience. To put it another way, action is this very construction of experience.

To sum up, we can say that this phenomenology depicts intention as a matter of coordinating a quite large number of other mental factors, each of them an irreducible process, component, or quality of the mind. These numerous factors contribute to morally relevant thought and agency in complex ways not limited to either rational deliberation or various appetitive forces, but invoking other sensibilities, motivational roots, faculties, aptitudes, capacities, energies, and functions. Such a depiction stretches considerably beyond modern conceptions of intention construed as a combination of belief and desire and some kind of relation between them.[63] In this model, belief and desire are presented as rather self-evident discrete thoughts and wants appearing in the mind, rather than forces or factors driving it: I *believe* that the 7 P.M. plane leaves for New York, and I *desire* to go to New York, and so I *intend* to catch the plane. While this seems a plausible account of the matter at one level, it tells us little about the promptings and causes behind our beliefs and desires that the Abhidhamma considers crucial in accounting for our intentional actions. The Abhidhamma theory of action may seem to be rather cluttered compared to modern,

63. Anscombe, *Intention*; Davidson, *Essays on Actions and Events*. Even though Bratman (*Intentions, Plans, and Practical Reason*) attempts to go beyond this basic model in important ways, he still barely touches on the web of psychological causes underlying intentional action. But see Baier, *Death and Character*, in her reading of Hume's ideas of "character" in a way that presses substantially beyond desire and belief as explanatory of action.

64. Many contemporary philosophical notions of desire do little to account for intentional action, except to state what precedes it. Desire is treated as a necessary component of intentional action but is given little psychological substance. Resting on a sketch of desire drawn largely from Hume and rather circular from the perspective of accounting for intentions, contemporary philosophy "characterizes desire by the job desire does in collaborating with belief and thereby generating action" (Pettit, "Desire"). Susan James charts how 17th-century philosophy increasingly moved toward a generic conception of desire and notes that "taken generically, desires lack the inflections that would make them explanatory" (James, *Passion and Action*, 291–92).

sparer theories of action. Yet what it lacks in economy, it makes up for in psychological richness.[64]

A Theory of Action

We now have before us the conscious mental factors and the operations of intention occurring in action. But how is karma understood in this branch of Pāli thought? Although the Abhidhamma texts do not take up karma as a central category of analysis, Buddhaghosa does think it deserves special attention, and he examines it closely in part III of the *Atthasālinī*. In his treatment of karma, he begins by mentioning the *Aṅguttara* passage identifying karma with *cetanā*.[65] He also quotes from the Intention Sutta, to state that feelings subjectively experienced are caused by bodily, verbal, and mental intention,[66] and he cites a *Majjhima sutta* in which the Buddha explains that one doing an intentional action with body, speech, or mind feels pleasure, pain, or neither and goes on to describe the 20 courses of action.[67] He also mentions an *Aṅguttara* passage that refers to the 20 good and bad courses of action and how they are divided by body, speech, and mind.[68] Finally, he quotes the *sutta* on bright and dark actions to suggest that karma can be classified into four groups (bright, dark, both, and neither). From his references to these passages, with which we are also familiar, we learn which texts Buddhaghosa thought were essential for defining intentional action. We also see him underscore the idea that karma is intention.

His own definition, however, differs slightly but importantly from the equivalence of karma and *cetanā* cited in the *Aṅguttara*. He asks, "What is karma?" and replies, "It is just intention *as well as some factors associated with intention*."[69] Karma is not just intention, but additional *dhammas*

---

65. As 88; he mentions quotations found at A.iii.415 and Kv 393.

66. As 88; S.ii.39; A.ii.157. See McDermott, "The *Kathāvatthu Kamma* Debates," on the distinctiveness of the Theravādin insistence that the result of karma is a matter of subjective experience as debates about this unfolded in the *Kathāvatthu*.

67. As 88; M.iii.209.

68. As 88; A.v.264; Kv 393.

69. *Kim panetaṃ kammaṃ nāmāti? Cetanaṃ ceva, ekacce ca cetanāsampayuttakā dhammā* (As 88).

70. As 89. Jaini says that covetousness, malice, wrong view, noncovetousness, nonmalice, and right view are not, strictly speaking, roots (*mūlas*) but are "intensive states" of the six

as well. He goes on to describe 21 factors that are associated with intention: the seven factors of awakening, the eight factors of the Path, and six other factors: covetousness, malice, wrong view, noncovetousness, nonmalice, and right view.[70] These factors are not identified with *cetanā*, but are to be understood as "factors associated with *cetanā*" that constitute karma; the theory is that there are some actions that are not defined entirely by intention. The first 15 are soteriologically important factors in that they contribute to the destruction of karma and thus to freedom from the woes of *saṃsāra*. Though these factors when present in intentional action are still called karma, they in fact do not produce further karma but rather lead to the destruction of it. Soteriological actions are not defined solely by *cetanā*, but also by these Path factors that have a different logic than accumulating good and bad karma. This is very much in keeping with Buddhaghosa's views on *kiriyacetanā*, and in fact here he mentions these soteriological factors in the context of his reference to the *sutta* on bright and dark actions.

The additional factors that together with *cetanā* can constitute karma are the six good and bad mental deeds: covetousness, malice, and wrong view and noncovetousness, nonmalice, and right view.[71] These, too, are considered "factors associated with *cetanā*" rather than just *cetanās*. These six kinds of actions are intensified motivational roots (greed, hatred, delusion, and their opposites). We may recall that our earlier discussion of the 10 bad deeds defined the first seven bodily and verbal actions as *cetanās* and the last three mental actions as *cetasikas*.[72] And likewise for the 10 good deeds. These mental actions are, for Buddhaghosa, not just matters of intention but also, and perhaps principally, these mental factors. When one commits a mental action of malice, it is principally the pervasive and intensified motivation of hatred that is operative, not just the activity of accumulating and animating that *cetanā* does. Of course, intentions themselves are the assembling and energizing of other mental factors, including motivations, so we might think they can cover this specific set of things.

actual roots (*lobha, dosa, moha, alobha, adosa, amoha*). They are the grosser forms of the basic, underlying roots, which may be overcome by those advanced in moral and religious progress, while the deeper motivational roots remain (Jaini, "The Sautrāntika Theory of *Bīja*," 221).

71. As 89.

72. This distinction was already made evident in our discussion of the 20 deeds; the first seven of each set are *cetanās*, and the last three are factors associated with *cetanā*, that is, other *cetasikas*. Buddhaghosa makes this point at As 101, 104, and Vism 7.

Intentions have motivational roots, and indeed to a large degree, motivations are at the bottom of all of our constructive activity. But Buddhaghosa wanted to emphasize that these particular actions are best understood as amplifications or full manifestations of the motivational roots rather than solely intentions; some actions of our minds are principally the actions of fully realized motivations. This was an issue of some contention among the mainstream Buddhist schools, and the Sautrāntikas disagreed, preferring instead to see this type of action simply as *cetanā*.[73]

We shall return later to this matter of seeing certain karmas as *cetasikas* rather than *cetanās*, but for the moment several other issues about defining karma must occupy us. The interpretation of the Buddha's equivalence of *cetanā* with karma gave rise to different views among the mainstream Buddhist schools concerning the exact relationship of *cetanā* with karma. The Theravāda position is clear: there is no gap between intention and action. In addition, action is not material (*rūpa*) but mental (*citta, nāma*), even when it is bodily or verbal karma. The Theravādins reject language that suggests that there is a mental process of intending that results in a bodily or verbal action that can then be characterized as good or bad; instead, the intending and the acting are the same, and they are *citta*, not *rūpa*. These positions were, as we shall see in the next section, contested by the Sarvāstivāda. The *Kathāvatthu* insists that what is morally relevant in an action are mental doings—"the apprehending, the idea, the considering, the attention, the intention, the aiming, the aspiration."[74] It is this activity, not the gross physical properties of the body or the vocal activity of speech, that is deemed good or bad.

Yet as we know, there are three types of karma: mental, physical, and verbal. For Buddhaghosa, all are, first and foremost, intentions. The

---

73. For discussion of this controversy, see Jaini, "The Sautrāntika Theory of *Bīja*," 220; and Devdas, *Cetanā and the Dynamics of Volition*, 390–99.

74. *āvaṭṭanā ābhogo samannāhāro manasikāro cetanā patthanā paṇidhi* (Kv 380; Kv-a 111–12). Some of these may be little more than synonyms (the commentary equates intention, aiming, and aspiration [Kv-a 111]), but collectively they describe related elements of attention, interest, thinking, intending, and wanting. See McDermott for the debate between Theravādins and other Buddhists on this point about karma ("The *Kathāvatthu Kamma* Debates," 428–29). McDermott also argues that "the Theravādin has set himself to defend the definition of *kamma* as intentional impulse (*cetanā*) against all inroads" (430).

75. The term *doorway* means the "intimation" (*viññatti*) generated by conscious awareness. Intimation is what communicates to the body or voice or mind to act; the intimation "displays" the intention. There follow material changes, though these material (*rūpa*) properties are not, strictly speaking, karma or morally valenced (As 82–83; Cf. Vism 447–48).

language of doorways is important for Buddhaghosa in describing how intentional action works in these three locations. The mental processes of intending are located in the body, mind, or voice.[75] Buddhaghosa says that intentions are "accomplished in" the physical, verbal, or mental doorways.[76] Though sometimes I have spoken of these processes as happening "in" the mind (and they are mental rather than material), in fact, it is more appropriate to visualize them as occurring in the body and voice in the case of bodily and verbal actions. If intending is doing, then this must be so: it is not as though one thing (an intention) happens in the mind and then something else (the action) occurs in the body, but that intention *is* its very occurrence in the bodily (or verbal or mental) action. (The analogy of perceptual processes may be helpful here: perception or sensory contact, though mental, is something that happens in the bodily organs, according to this system. While there is a strong division between mental and physical phenomena, there is not such a strong division between mind and body—mental phenomena can occur in the body.) Intentions occur in the doorway, for example, of the physical body, resulting in movement in which a person "with a good, bad, or neutral thought moves forward, steps back, beholds, looks closely, bends or stretches the body."[77] When a person kills, it is said that a *cetanā* to kill occurs in the bodily doorway; when one speaks harsh speech, a *cetanā* occurs in the verbal doorway.[78] An intentional action of the mind is described the way we have already seen, as that which "accumulates, constructs, heaps up, cognizes, creates, and arranges"[79] accompanying factors. In the case of the six mental courses of action of covetousness, malice, wrong view, and their opposites, the *cetanā* occurs in the mind doorway.

Buddhaghosa gives an illustration that shows that actions can be parsed according to these different varieties.[80] A hunter decides to go and hunt deer but is unsuccessful at catching one. Does he perform an action? Yes, he performs a mental action—malice or the thought to kill—for which he is karmically accountable. But he does not fully complete a bodily action since he did not manage to kill any creature, and so he is not culpable of a physical act of killing. In this way, what we may see as a single action may actually be a matter of several actions—mental actions of malice, intended

76. As 85–87.

77. As 82.

78. As 84, 86.

79. *āyūhati abhisaṅkharoti piṇḍaṃ karoti ceteti kappeti pakappetīti* (As 87).

80. As 90.

verbal actions of declaring one's intentions, and intended bodily actions of physically performing the act. They are all intentional, but the full "course of action" (*kammapatha*) of the bodily action has not occurred.

The idea that what we might see as a single deed is in fact a series of intentional actions occurs elsewhere in Buddhaghosa's work. In a brief distinction between three types of intention, the *Sammohavinodanī* states that *cetanās* occur *prior to*, *during*, and *after* giving a gift or taking the precepts. When giving a gift, the agent has an intention to give, an intention while giving, and an intention after the gift is given.[81] Buddhaghosa says that the intention afterward is an "understanding made by giving," suggesting that one's thinking about a gift or other moral action after it is complete is a deepening of understanding about it made possible only upon completing it.[82] Other commentaries suggest that in the example of giving a gift, the gift should not be followed by a change of heart or regret, and so the ongoing intentionality surrounding what one is doing is important.[83] Giving a gift is really a matter of multiple intentional actions: planning to give, actually giving the gift, and reflecting about it afterward. Again we see a concern with time and the temporality of intention and action.

Here we notice that the definition of *cetanā* differs markedly from contemporary philosophers' definitions of intention, which generally assume that intention precedes the action or occurs simultaneously with it; modern philosophers would probably suggest that thoughts about an action after committing it are, quite simply, different thoughts that have nothing to do with intentions. We may come to regret an action or wish we had different intentions when we performed it, but we cannot change or alter the intention that led to it, and it would be odd to call subsequent feelings and thoughts about the action "intentions."

Yet in some sense Buddhaghosa is getting at something important and suggested by intuition by proposing that since intentional action is constructing activity, then how we construct our experience is something that unfolds over time. The intentions surrounding a gift can be

81. Vibh-a 412–13. He also mentions this distinction in As 159. In his translation of the *Abhidharmakośa-bhāṣya*, de La Vallée Poussin also noticed that *cetanā* can refer to a mental state following an action with which it is associated; this made him uneasy about his translation of *cetanā* as volition (*Abhidharmakośabhāṣyam*, vol. 2, 709, n. 3).

82. Vibh-a 412–13.

83. See Heim, *Theories of the Gift in South Asia*, 42–43, where I discuss the *Upāsakajanālaṅkāra*'s discussion of the three times of giving.

parsed into many separate moments of assembling our thoughts, motivations, and feelings about it. Since action is so deeply tied to intention, then how we continue to construe and construct actions in our minds remains essential to what they are. It does seem that often we become aware of our intentions and attribute importance to them only after the deed has been completed, when we go back and try to reconstruct its meaning by naming what we intended to do in committing it ("I really meant to give her something she would enjoy" or "I had no intention of harming him when I ate the last piece of his favorite cake"). In such cases, intentions become most relevant to us in how we consider them or reconstruct them after the deed has taken place. And sometimes, perhaps even often, it is this intention as it is constructed after the fact that carries the day in terms of the meaning and significance we assign to the act ("I believe her when she says she did not mean to hurt his feelings"). In addition, we sometimes continue to intend things about actions we have completed ("I hope she is still getting use out of that sweater I knitted for her last year"). But also, intentions can change over time and be reconstructed or altered in ways that change how we see the moral value of the action. The text's example of regretting one's earlier generosity does seem to take away from the value of the generosity itself and the moral quality of the action. Perhaps it even changes what the action was: now it is considered a mistake, and this shift entails that one is no longer generous. Conversely, regret over doing wrong actions can sometimes make up, at least to some extent, for a wrong action. Much legal thinking seems to concur that this sort of regret—changing one's thinking and feeling about the action—is relevant, at least in assigning punishment, and of course, many religious traditions celebrate such changes of heart in relation to one's sins in ways that redefine the nature of the action itself.

But again, why call subsequent thoughts about an act "intentions"? In the Buddhist view, action is what it is constructed to be, and *cetanā*, as we saw in the many metaphors about it, is that very constructing process (it "produces its object by its own work"). Strictly speaking, we have to suggest that in what may appear to be a single action—giving a gift—there are actually many intentional actions occurring over time. Constructing our actions and what goes into them goes on even after a deed would seem to be complete. These considerations open action up temporally—an act like giving a gift is really multiple intentional actions not confined to a discrete moment in time when the action is committed or an intention occurring shortly before. Buddhaghosa posits a theory of action that is open-ended; the meaning and value of actions continue as we construct them, literally, in our minds and conversations, a process and activity that happens over time. (Chapter 4 on narrative treats the dialogic and temporal aspects of intention as central themes.) While Buddhaghosa does not elaborate on all of the puzzles associated with the temporal aspects of moral action as it is experienced in the mind, he goes further than many contemporary treatments of action that treat it and its moral dimensions as a discrete and finite event.

Action as Abstinence

We turn now to how it is that actions that are really abstentions or restraints are to be understood. The Abhidhamma, no less than the Suttanta, has many instances of describing good actions as refraining from bad actions. The *Dhammasaṅgaṇī*, for example, says that right speech and right action are "leaving off, abstention, refraining, abstaining, not doing, not acting, not committing, not transgressing, and destroying any bridge to" the four bad speech actions and the three bad physical actions.[84] Buddhaghosa elaborates each of these synonyms with great nuance; "leaving off" is delighting in being apart from something, and "abstaining" is destroying the bad action, for example. Some of these seem to be part of an inhibitory system, others simply the presence of an absence. Above all, these good actions comprise a mental factor (*cetasika*) that prevents the committing of bad action or speech.[85]

But abstaining—that is, *not* engaging in wrong action—raises intriguing challenges for the tight focus on intentional action that is otherwise pervasive throughout the texts. Are abstentions intentions? When refraining from committing a bad action, whether out of resisting temptation or because I have taken a precept or because it does not even occur to me to do it, what is the nature of my intention? In what sense is abstaining an action? We turn first briefly to a passage in the *Vibhaṅga* that is the chief place where precept taking (and thus issues about proper action) is

84. Dhs 299–300.

85. As 218–19. Another interesting place where speech is considered to be an abstinence is in Buddhaghosa's discussion of karma where he says that speech is threefold: intention, abstinence, and sound (As 86). Sometimes not saying something is a speech act.

discussed in the canonical Abhidhamma. The *Vibhaṅga* devotes a chapter to the training precepts (*sikkhāpada*), which it lists as five abstainings (*veramaṇī*): from killing, from taking what is not given, from sexual misconduct, from false speech, and from taking intoxicating drink.[86] (These are the same as what is often understood as the five *sīla* precepts, though Buddhaghosa tends to define *sīla* as the 10 good deeds.)[87] We will also turn to the *Paṭisambhidāmagga*[88] and to Buddhaghosa's *Visuddhimagga* for a closer look at this variety of precept.

The *Vibhaṅga* discusses the five training precepts as matters of *cetanā*, abstaining (*veramaṇī*), and factors associated with both of these, though it does not offer any actual distinctions between these.[89] Buddhaghosa thought that this could be potentially confusing—is keeping a precept, say, not killing someone, a matter of abstaining or intention? He suggests that keeping precepts can be understood as *cetanās* only in a figurative sense (*pariyāya*) and that the canonical text says they are abstainings (*veramaṇī*), not *cetanās*. He argues then that since the Buddha generally "taught by referring to *cetanās*," we can say figuratively or conventionally that keeping precepts is a matter of intention. But in fact, a precept is literally (*nippariyāya*) an abstention (*virati*). So we can say that in the case of misconduct, at the moment of transgression there is a hostile intention, but in the case of good conduct, there is a moment of abstention. In addition, there are the associating factors accompanying each of these that also comprise the precepts (that is, the other relevant factors of the 52 *cetasikas* that work with a *cetanā* or a *veramaṇī*).[90]

---

86. Elsewhere, 10 *sikkhāpada* are listed, including the additional abstaining from eating at the wrong time, worldly amusements, using scents and ornaments, sleeping on high beds, and accepting gold or silver; these latter five are factors less of moral practice than monastic renunciation. For a discussion of the 10 *sikkhāpadas*, see Pj I.22–37; while these are not the same as the *dasasīla* (that is, the 10 *kusala* actions), there are similarities and overlaps in how Buddhaghosa treats the 10 *sikkhapādas* in this text and how he discusses the 10 good and 10 bad actions that we considered in chapter 1.

87. Vism 7: Buddhaghosa describes *sīla* not as the five precepts or *sikkhāpadas*, but as the 10 *kusala kammas*—abstaining from killing, taking what is not given, sexual misconduct, false speech, malicious speech, harsh speech, frivolous speech, covetousness, malice, and wrong view.

88. The *Paṭisambhidhāmagga* is really an Abhidhamma text, though it is part of the Khuddhaka Nikāya of the Suttanta. Buddhaghosa relies on it heavily in the *Visuddhimagga*.

89. Vibh 285–90.

90. Vibh-a 381–82.

We thus see a preference, at least for Buddhaghosa, for talking about the morally good activity of abstaining as a distinctive kind of action that is not identical with intention. He turns with even more detail to such questions and tangles in the treatment of *sīla*, which he describes as the 10 good deeds in the *Visuddhimagga* and his commentary on the *Paṭisambhidāmagga*. The *Paṭisambhidāmagga* offers a number of ways of classifying or dividing *sīla*. One of them is that *sīla* is fourfold: it is (1) intention (*cetanā*), (2) mental factor (*cetasika*), (3) restraint (*saṃvara*), and (4) nontransgression (*avītikkama*).[91] One and the same precept can involve combinations of these; they are not mutually exclusive. Let us take the latter two first. *Sīla* as "restraint" can be fivefold: restraint by the Vinaya rules, by mindfulness, by knowledge, by patience, and by energy.[92] *Sīla* as "nontrangression" is simply not breaking the precepts by bodily or verbal action.[93] But what is *sīla* as *cetanā* and as *cetasika*? We may recall that Buddhaghosa defines the first seven abstentions of bodily and verbal misconduct as, properly speaking, intentions, and the last three good mental actions of abstaining from covetousness, malice, and wrong view are *cetasikas*.[94] We have seen this idea before, and it seems to suggest that the mental actions are, chiefly, intensified motivations rather than intentions. But we might also posit that since they are really abstentions, they are not a matter of the accumulative work of intentions. Their logic is abandoning, not accumulating, and this makes them, above all, a kind of *cetasika*, rather than a *cetanā*.[95] (*Cetasika* is, of course, a very

91. Paṭis i.44; Vism 7.

92. Vism 7; Paṭis-a i.218; but see also Vism 11, where *sīla* is restraint in four senses: Vinaya rules, restraint of the sense faculties, of the purification of livelihood, and concerning the monastic use of requisites. In fact, it is this latter list of four that Buddhaghosa goes on to discuss at great length (Vism 15–46 and thus the bulk of his treatment of *sīla* here). The treatment of restraint in largely a monastic register suggests that restraints are best treated in our Vinaya chapter.

93. Vism 7.

94. See chapter 1, p. 103.

95. This is one place where I find my interpretation to be in substantial disagreement with that of Nalini Devdas. She suggests that mental karma is classified as *cetasika kamma* to avoid a redundancy problem. That is, since *manokamma* accomplishes much the same work as *cetanā*, there is the danger that it might appear that two intention-like processes are at work in one karmic event (*Cetanā and the Dynamics of Volition*, 399). This is plausible, but I think that, at least in the case of good mental actions, they are chiefly *cetasikas* because their main action is abandoning and abstaining, not accumulating (but they cannot be considered *kiriyakammas* because they are *kusala*). And intending and abstaining are consistently regarded by Buddhaghosa as conceptually distinct because they entail quite opposite logics.

broad category of factors that can include absences and various kinds of abandonings.)

In another listing of the varieties of *sīla*, both texts add a fifth type: abandoning (*pahāna*).[96] Buddhaghosa says that abandoning is not actually a factor (*dhamma*), so it should just be understood as the nonarising of killing and so on. And it is also the upholding of good factors in the sense of establishing them, and it is a resolution in the sense of preventing wavering.[97] The texts then go on to describe these five operations of abandoning, abstaining, intention, restraint, and nontransgression, not only with reference to the 10 bad deeds but also in higher forms of mental and spiritual development: *sīla* is abandoning, abstaining, intention, restraint, and nontransgression of the hindrances in experiencing the first *jhāna*, for example, and of applied and sustained thought in the second *jhāna*. And right up to arhatship, *sīla* is these processes of abandoning, and so forth. *Sīla* thus leads to nonremorse, joy, delight, calm, happiness, and so on, right up to *nibbāna* itself (a formula we saw in the last chapter and will see again in the next). Again we see a logic of abandoning and abstaining—that is, absences—that make possible the presence of other felicitous things. If we want to understand morality and religious development in this system, we must learn to see the precise ways that the presence of absences makes possible other processes.

A final discussion may be helpful for discerning the precise nature of precept taking and abstaining. The mainstream schools had different views on how it is that intentions might work. The issue concerns the temporal aspects of intentional action. Is the intention to refrain from violating a precept (such as killing) something one has at the moment of making a vow or precept, or does it occur when one does not in fact kill? How do we locate that particular moment of "not killing"? The Sarvāstivādins had a theory of karma and *cetanā* that posited a certain underlying intention

96. Paṭis i.46; Vism 11, 49–51. Dhammapāla's commentary to the *Visuddhimagga* deems it necessary to try to clarify this passage by mentioning that *cetanās* are present in all of the three actions—physical, verbal, and mental—but when one wants to offer a more specific treatment of the abstaining from the bad mental deeds, one says that the *sīla* is a *cetasika* to be understood separately from *sīla* as intention (even though intention is also present). He goes on to argue that either *cetanā* or the *cetasika* of abstention will be primary depending on the case, though both are present. Restraints for him are when "bad factors do not occur as though they were being concealed." Nontransgression is when mental factors occur that are opposed to the transgression (Vism-mhṭ I.24). Some of these seem to indicate functions of an inhibitory system; others are pointing simply to absences.

97. Vism 50–51.

that occurs at the moment of taking a precept and that persists over time and ensures that one does not violate it. To see how this works, it is helpful to observe that there are serious differences between the Theravādins and the Sarvāstivādins on how to interpret the Buddha's identification of intention and action. Dipping into these debates can sharpen our grasp of the Pāli position.

The Theravāda adherence to the close identification of karma and *cetanā* was rejected by the Sarvāstivādins. As we have seen, the Theravādins argue that the Buddha's statement "having intended, one acts by body, speech, and mind" means that there is only one event: the intending *is* the acting. This is against the Sarvāstivāda view that the Buddha's statement refers to two events, the intention and the action produced by the intention. Vasubandhu says: "There are two karmas: the karma of intending and the karma after having intended."[98] In this view, there is a mental action, the intention, which is the cause of bodily or verbal actions. Vasubandhu thus posits a sui generis intention, a pure intention that intends the intentional action.[99]

This move leads the Sarvāstivādins to develop a distinction that we do not see in the Pāli literature. For them, *vijñapti*, referring to the action that makes itself known to others, is introduced to name the bodily or vocal manifestation of the intention in the action.[100] Then they introduce the term *avijñapti* to refer to the intentional act in the mind (the sui generis intention) that is not known either by bodily or verbal movement. *Avijñapti* karma is a latent potential that can carry beyond a bodily action. Thus when one takes the precepts or the Prātimokṣa rules and then refrains from harming beings, there remains, beyond the formal action of taking

---

98. *Abhidhammakośa* iv. 1b–d (de La Vallée Poussin, *Abhidharmakośabhāṣyam*, vol. 2, 551–52). See also Gombrich, "Merit Detached from Volition," 429, n. 2. The Mahāyāna texts tend to follow the Sarvāstivāda position; for example, the *Prajnāptiśāstra* interprets karma as two events: volitional action and action following the intention (de La Vallée Poussin, *Abhidharmakośabhāṣyam*, vol. 1, 24), as does Asaṅga's *Abhidharmasammuccaya* (Rahula and Boin-Webb, *Abhidharmasamuccaya*, 112).

99. de La Vallée Poussin, *Abhidharmakośabhāṣyam*, vol. 2, 559. This move introduces the possibility of regress, as Gilbert Ryle (*The Concept of Mind*) would suggest, though Theravāda and Sautrāntika arguments against it do not go this route.

100. There are some similarities with this term and Pāli *viññatti*, intimation, or what communicates to the body to act (see note 76). Note also that although Vasubhandu represented and himself subscribed to much of the Vaibhāṣika view, in places he disagreed with certain aspects of it, and he argued against what follows concerning *avijñāptirūpa* (see Hayes, "The Analysis of Karma in Vasubandhu's *Abhidharmakośa-bhāṣya*").

the precepts, an intention that is not manifest in bodily or verbal action in the form of a lasting, inner restraint known only to the agent, or perhaps even the agent is not always consciously aware of it.[101] This moral intention persists even if the mind is, at moments, bad or neutral. Intriguingly, it is considered to be material (*rūpa*) in nature.[102] The *avijñapti* is the absention (*virati*) of a wrong action when one is committed to the restraint of the precepts, which is considered a "real *dhamma*."[103]

This theory of *avijñaptirūpa* karma relies on the Sarvāstivāda view of time, in which past and future are said to exist in some sense; it allows the Sarvāstivādins to posit the notion of an enduring latent intention that persists even when other actions are being carried out or other thoughts are in the mind. Dharmaśrī, an early Sarvāstivādin author, says, "If, for example, a person undertakes the precepts, his mind can then be bad or neutral: nevertheless the precepts continue."[104] The theory offers an explanation for the presence of intentions that seem to outlive the finite action with which they are associated. It also allows an explanation of moral actions of restraint that involve the absence of immoral conduct: the interpretation given here is that when one refrains from breaking the precepts (which involves no overt bodily or verbal action), an inner, uncommunicated, but nonetheless real moral intention is at work over time.

The Theravādins rejected this doctrine of *avijñapti*; it is a bit clumsy and compromises the insistence that karma is no more than intention. For them, as we have just seen, when one refrains from killing or lying, for example, discrete intentions or abstainings are at work. There is no single intention that occurred at an earlier moment of taking a precept that remains lurking underneath other mental experiences, culminating in later actions or nonaction. Rather, when one is not killing or lying, it is because any number of mental experiences we have been discussing are at work, whether they are abandoning, abstaining, intention, restraint, or

101. For thorough accounts of the meaning of these terms and the implications of these views, see McDermott, *Development in the Early Buddhist Concept of Kamma/Karma*, 132–140; Gombrich, "Merit Detached from Volition" and *How Buddhism Began*, 55; and Hayes, "The Analysis of Karma in Vasubandhu's *Abhidharmakośa-bhāṣya*."

102. Gombrich argues that this move to see it as material may have been the result of influence from the Jains ("Merit Detached from Volition," 429). Hayes charts how and why the Vaibhāṣikas argued for a form of "non-phenomenal matter" ("The Analysis of Karma in Vasubandhu's *Abhidharmakośa-bhāṣya*," 28–29).

103. de La Vallée Poussin, *Abhidharmakośabhāṣyam*, vol, 2, 562.

104. Ibid., vol. 1, 47.

nontransgression. These are situation-specific absences that are present at that moment. For them, this is a sufficient explanation of precept taking and keeping vows.

A Theory of the Unconscious?

Up until this point, we have been concerned with the irreducible factors of conscious experience (*citta*). But there are further dispositions of human psychology in addition to the irreducible factors that make up moments of thought. The *Dhammasaṅgaṇī* treats a variety of groups of dispositions that contain some of the *cetasikas* with which we are familiar, as well as additional forces we have not considered. These are understood variously in how they pervade and influence experience. For example, the *āsavas*, or "depravities"—there are four: desire, becoming, wrong view, and ignorance—"attend" good and bad factors that are themselves results of previous karma.[105] They flow or ooze and ferment our experience in *saṃsāra*, attending even good and neutral factors of mind in all three realms: sense-desire, form, and formless.[106] Arhats, also called "those rid of the depravities" (*khīṇāsava*), are the only people free of them entirely. The depravities are inherent in a beginningless way to our experience in *saṃsāra*. While all of the depravities are important, Buddhaghosa emphasizes ignorance and its pervasiveness in our condition. He quotes the Buddha: "There was no earlier point at which ignorance was not present whereby we could say that once there was no ignorance."[107] In our unawakened state, we never stand outside our condition of ignorance. In terms of our interest in intentional action, we can recall that in the doctrine of dependent origination, ignorance is a direct condition of our constructions (*saṅkhāra*), and thus intentions.

In the Abhidhamma, to classify is to define. As different dispositions and factors are grouped in diverse classifications, we learn more about their nature. A group of 10 inclinations—sensual desire, repulsion, conceit, wrong view, doubt, the rigid adherence to rule and observance, the passion for becoming, envy, avarice, and ignorance—are considered

105. Dhs 1096–1112; As 42; The *āsavas* are *kāma, bhava, diṭṭhi,* and *avijjā.*

106. As 48.

107. As 48 quoting A.v.113.

108. Dhs 1113, 1151. The fetters (*saṃyojana*), floods (*ogha*), and yokes (*yoga*) are *kāmarāga, paṭigha, māna, diṭṭhi, vicikiccha, sīlabbataparāmāsa, bhavarāga, issā, macchariya,* and *avijjā.*

variously as fetters, floods, and yokes.[108] Buddhaghosa says that fetters and yokes tie one to the round of rebirth, and floods sink and submerge one in rebirth.[109] There are four bonds that knot us to *saṃsāra*: covetousness, malice, rigid adherence to rule and observance, and an inclination to dogmatize.[110] Hindrances or blockages are six: sensual initiative, malice, stubbornness and lassitude, worry and anxiety, doubt, and ignorance.[111] And the defilements are 10: greed, hatred, delusion, conceit, wrong view, doubt, stubbornness, worry, shamelessness, and the lack of moral apprehension.[112] Most of the items on these lists are various *cetasikas*, but some are more complex tendencies of behavior, habit, and disposition, such as the inclination to dogmatize or the rigid adherence to rule and observance.

Groupings define these terms through a distinctive kind of exposition. When particular terms appear under different classifications, we can get a sense of their varied nature and influences. These different groupings of negative forces, dispositions, and inclinations, and the evocative nature of their names and descriptions, depict a corrupted and depraved anthropology. We human beings come to our experience heavily freighted with dispositions that distort our perceptions and incline us to immorality. In the context of our interest in intentional action, we can see that these various forces operate in a pervasive way on our constructions of the world as we act within it. When we reflect on these dispositions, we become aware of a sense of patiency, of being acted upon by our own inherited and entrenched dispositions and inclinations.

Although it is not easy to say how much we notice the presence of these many dispositions (since one of the chief things we are ignorant about is the nature of our own mental lives, and since it was only with extraordinary insight that the Buddha discovered and parsed all of them), the factors among them are, by definition, matters of conscious awareness (*citta*). It is noteworthy that the Abhidhamma mapping of mind does not attribute much weight to unconscious drives or motives as such. But the idea of *anusayas*, that is, biases or latent tendencies, was taken by some

109. As 48–49.

110. Dhs 1135. The *gantha* are *abhijjhā, vyāpāda, sīlabbataparāmāsa*, and *saccābhinesa*.

111. Dhs 1152. The *nīvaraṇa* are *kāmacchanda, vyāpāda, thinamiddha, uddhaccakukkucca, vicikicchā*, and *avijjā*.

112. Dhs 1229. The *kilesa* are *lobha, dosa, moha, māna, diṭṭhi, vicikicchā, thīna, uddhacca, ahirika*, and *anottappa*.

Buddhist thinkers to indicate forces that lie below the level of conscious thought. The list of seven biases consists of items we have just seen: sensual desire, repulsion, conceit, wrong view, doubt, desire for existence, and ignorance.[113] The word *anusaya* is not mentioned in the *Dhammasaṅgaṇī* and appears just once in the *Vibhaṅga*. It is not a category that was central to the Abhidhammikas. This may be noticed in contrast to the Sarvāstivāda Abhidharma traditions that foreground the *anuśayas*' (in Sanskrit) role in action much more directly than the Pāli Abhidhamma.[114] Vasubandhu features the *anuśayas* prominently as underlying prompts of action:

> We said that the world, in all its variety, arises from action. Now it is by reason of the *anuśayas*, or latent defilements, that actions accumulate: in the absence of *anuśayas* actions are not capable of producing a new existence. Consequently the roots of existence, that is, of rebirth or action, are the *anuśayas*.[115]

Vasubandhu makes a very clear link between action and the latent or inherent biases or defilements that drive it. This direct framing of action in terms of the *anusayas* is not evident in the Abhidhamma sources; where *anusaya* is mentioned, it is usually in reference to abandoning them in the quest for arhatship and to make the point that arhats are free of them.

For the Pāli Abhidhammikas, the trouble with the biases is that they suggest a latent presence or quality in the mind that does not arise in a moment of consciousness; since Abhidhamma is concerned with conscious experience (*citta*), it does not offer a theory of an unconscious mind. There is also the problem of momentariness, as Nalini Devdas points out. If all experience is momentary, how can there be enduring tendencies lying inactive in the mind?[116] The *Kathāvatthu* rejects the idea that other Buddhist schools propose, namely, that there could be a nonmanifest motive in the mind, or that a person could have a moral or neutral thought under which lurks an immoral latent defilement.[117] Thus, the latent

---

113. Vibh 383. These are *kāmarāga, paṭighā, māna diṭṭhi, vicikiccha, bhavarāga*, and *avijjā*.

114. In addition to Vasubandhu's treatment of the *anuśayas*, Dharmaśrī's *Abhidharmasāra* has an extended and quite innovative discussion of them (Frauwallner, *Studies in Abhidharma Literature*, 153f.).

115. de La Vallée Poussin, *Abhidharmakośabhāṣyam*, vol. 3, 767.

116. Devdas, *Cetanā and the Dynamics of Volition*, 146–49.

117. Kv xiv.5–6.

defilement is no different from the manifestation of it (*pariyuṭṭhāna*), a position that appears to reject a notion of dormant or unconscious motivations altogether.[118] This would seem to have important implications for agency: we are not, in fact, driven by unconscious tendencies to which we cannot have access.

Yet this stance is moderated to some degree in other Abhidhamma texts, and the texts are not conclusive on this matter. The *Vibhaṅga* mentions the biases and emphasizes their tenacity. Buddhaghosa suggests that, like robbers on the road who beset travelers, the manifested latent tendency for ignorance besets moral consciousness, seizes and plunders it.[119] Another passage connects them with habit.[120] He also notes, interestingly, that there are no equivalent good latent tendencies (*kalyāṇānusaya*).[121] The *Yamaka*, which discusses the *anusayas* more than any other book of the Abhidhamma, does not address the question of their relationship to action directly, but it does consider where the *anusayas* are said to adhere (*anuseti*). Sensual desire, repulsion, and conceit adhere to feelings, and wrong view, doubt, and ignorance adhere to all the factors associated with persons; that is, they are intrinsic to the unawakened human condition. Finally, the desire for existence adheres to experience in both the realms of form and formlessness, gripping beings even beyond the realm of sense desire.[122] Here, the latent tendencies are posited not so much as a matter of conscious or unconscious mental factors but as proclivities inherent to our experience in *saṃsāra* in fundamental ways, much like the other groupings of dispositions.

---

118. A readiness to see *anusayas* as truly latent or unmanifested tendencies may be more apparent in the Suttas than the Abhidhamma, which is concerned with conscious experience. For example, the Mahā-Māluṅkāya Sutta suggests that even a young and tender infant possesses the five lower fetters, such as greed and malice, which are described as underlying tendencies (*anusaya*) (M.i.433). See Jaini, "The Sautrāntika Theory of Bīja," 223–26; and Devdas, *Cetanā and the Dynamics of Volition*, 146–49 and 455–56, for good treatments of the Theravāda inconsistencies on this doctrine.

119. Vibh-a 141.

120. Vibh-a 40.

121. Vibh-a 461.

122. Yam vii.

Promptings and Spontaneous Actions

When the *Dhammasaṅgaṇī* asks, at the very start of its treatise, "Which factors are good?" it is referring to a particular type of thought—one that arises in the realm of sense desire that is "accompanied by joy," "associated with knowledge," and directed to an object of the six senses.[123] The text goes on to list good thoughts that arise in the realm of sense desire that are not accompanied by joy or associated with knowledge, as well as the various kinds of possibilities of different combinations of these. It later mentions good thoughts that occur "with prompting," introducing a new variety of thought.[124] It then treats bad and neutral thoughts, and then the kinds of thoughts that occur in the realm of form and the realm of formlessness.

We need not work through all of these variants, and in particular we may set aside the consciousness that those experiencing the form and formless realms enjoy. But we do need to turn to Buddhaghosa's treatment of the *Dhammasaṅgaṇī*'s distinctions concerning thoughts that arise with or without knowledge, with or without joy, and what is meant by "prompting." Buddhaghosa thought these were very important distinctions, and he dilated on them at some length. Although we cannot treat all of the intricacies of this fascinating commentary, discussion of the different ways that morally good thoughts come about demonstrates a very nuanced appreciation of internal and external conditions for our thoughts and actions that has not yet surfaced.

Buddhaghosa, in his treatment of these different kinds of distinctions, discusses the fact that thoughts are always connected to objects. The color that the eye falls upon or the sound that greets the ear stimulates the sensory contact that makes possible conscious awareness. He is particularly interested in what is experienced by the sixth sense, that is, the mind, because this is the mind's way of representing to itself objects that need not be present to the five sensory organs. What the mind calls up and attends to is shaped by previous sensory and mental experience. It is here that, in the case of a good thought, we can see important factors of moral and religious development shape and influence thoughts. Buddhaghosa—and here he mentions that this particular view is not mentioned by the earlier commentators—says that at least four things can influence the emergence

123. Dhs 1.

124. Dhs 146.

125. As 74.

of a thought that occurs at the doorway of the mind (i.e., a thought that arises with a mental action). These are faith, preference, thoughtful reflection, and patience with wrong views.[125] So what one represents to oneself in a thought will be in part determined by these other processes of faith, reflection, and so on.

He goes on to suggest that even what occurs to the other five senses is experienced in a good thought in a way that is inflected by what we might refer to as virtues or habits. That is to say, when one experiences a beautiful color, one may be moved to a good thought (*kusalacitta*) if one's consciousness has been "trained, inclined, practiced, and turned toward" the good. Otherwise, the sight of a beautiful thing could lead to greed.[126] He elaborates:

> For one who says "I should do something good," the mind is trained on good actions, turned away from the bad, inclined towards only good actions, and practiced only with good practices through repeated action; thus, an appropriate idea occurs through relying upon living in a suitable place, associating with good people, listening to the Good Dhamma, having done good deeds before, and so on. For such a [person] that which is called good arises through being trained, inclined, practiced, and turned in these ways.[127]

Buddhaghosa is highly sensitive to the larger conditions for moral development, quite external to the constituents of good thought, that make possible the ways we attend to our senses and thus the very nature of the thoughts that occur to us.

When he considers the kind of good thought that is "accompanied by joy," Buddhaghosa sees additional influences at work. When one sees the Buddha, unless one has faith and is free of wrong views, joy will not arise. But for those with faith and right view and who can see the advantage of merit, immense joy will spring up in seeing the Buddha.[128] Similarly, for a good thought to be "associated with knowledge" is also a matter of how our present experience is shaped by the past: we get knowledge from the nature of our previous karma, our past births, the maturity of our faculties,

---

126. As 75.

127. As 75. Jayasuriya refers to living in a suitable place and so on as "predisposing causes" of moral action (Jayasuriya, *The Psychology and Philosophy of Buddhism*, 55).

128. As 75.

and our distance from the defilements. These will influence the nature of our current thoughts. On this topic, Buddhaghosa sees fit to mention the seven awakening factors associated with inquiry into the Dhamma: frequent questioning, making clear fundamental things, bringing the faculties into equilibrium, avoiding foolish people, frequenting wise people, reflecting on deep matters, and inclining the mind toward this.[129] If one wants to have thoughts that are endowed with knowledge, one can adopt these intellectual practices.

Then Buddhaghosa makes a distinction that he argues is present even if unmentioned by the *Dhammasaṅgaṇī* passage he is working on. He says that the text will later offer a class of good thoughts that are, among all of these other variants, said to be "prompted" (*sasaṅkhārena*). This implies, he argues, that though these first kinds of good thought do not explicitly say so, they are spontaneous (*asaṅkhārena*). Of course, we are familiar with the language of *saṅkhāra*, but this is a specialized and technical sense appearing in the Abhidhamma that was developed in the commentaries into a distinction between prompted (*sasaṅkhārena, sasaṅkhārika*) and unprompted (*asaṅkhārena, asaṅkhārika*) thought.[130] Buddhaghosa mentions this distinction in his commentary on a Sutta passage in which he says that there can be intentions that are "not instigated by others which one does with an unprompted mind, and there are those which are generated by others which one does with a prompted mind," such as when one is inspired to act when told that karma has results.[131] This distinction returns us to intersubjectivity and the ways that our intentions can be influenced by others.

Prompted good thoughts are those that take some prodding to come into being, either by one's own moral thinking or by the impact others' words can have on us. Buddhaghosa defines *prompted* as occurring "by a means, by an expedient, by a collection of causes" and provides this helpful illustration:

When the time came to sweep in front of the *stūpa*, attend to an

129. As 76.

130. For example, Dhs 146, 402.

131. Spk.ii.57. Bodhi, *The Connected Discourses of the Buddha*, 749, n. 78, suggests that "this text may be the original basis for the Abhidhamma distinction between *sasaṅkhārikacitta* and *asaṅkhārikacitta*." For more on this distinction, see Nārada and Bodhi (*A Comprehensive Manual of Abhidhamma*, 36) and Rhys Davids (*A Buddhist Manual of Psychological Ethics*, 34–35, n. 1).

> elder, or listen to the Dhamma, a certain monk living in a neighboring monastery would think, "it will be too far for me to go and return, so I will not go." But then he would consider, "it is not fitting for a monk not to go to the *stūpa,* to attend an elder, or to listen to the Dhamma, so I will go after all." Whether it is through his own means, or whether others have admonished him showing him the benefits of doing his duty and the dangers of not doing it, or whether they have rebuked him saying "come and do it," his moral consciousness arises by being prompted, that is, it arises by a collection of causes.[132]

These promptings are not mental factors (*dhammas* or *cetasikas*), but rather internal or external instigators of action. They can be either thoughts that occur to oneself or the suggestions or rebukes of others. Buddhaghosa additionally describes prompted good thoughts of those who lack knowledge as the experiences of young boys whose parents grab them by the head and make them pay homage to a shrine. The children then worship excitedly and happily, even if it was not their own aim.[133] Such proddings show yet another way that our actions do not spring solely from the combinations of mental factors discussed previously, but that they are subject to either outside influences and admonishments or to our own inner voices that tell us what we should and should not do.

But what about unprompted thoughts? Where do these come from? Buddhaghosa says that we can have good thoughts that are unprompted or spontaneous in the sense that they arise without any such means. These are good thoughts that occur to people that consist of either generosity (*dāna*), habit (*sīla*), or mental cultivation (*bhāvanā*). When one sees something beautiful and then spontaneously (because one is generous) wants to give it to the Saṅgha, then we have an instance of the first kind. Spontaneous gifts that are given out of habit (*sīla*) are done when one acts according to one's family customs and traditions. The things we regularly do out of habit do not take much additional prodding to make us continue them. And thoughts that occur due to mental cultivation arise when, for

132. As 156. But in fact, as is apparent in the lists of these kinds of thoughts, prompted thoughts do not differ in content from unprompted thoughts.

133. As 156.

134. As 77–79.

example, one is moved to give a gift by reflecting on the impermanence of things (which, presumably, dislodges greed and attachment to the gift object).[134] A deep awareness of the fundamental transience of reality can make us act reflexively in certain ways. The category of unprompted thought shows the many ways Buddhaghosa sees whereby we can be spontaneously inspired to act either out of a sense of beauty and generosity or because of a deeper awareness through meditation of the fleetingness of things.

This carving out of the spontaneous from prompted intentional action suggests how certain domains of action are assigned to the realms of disposition, habit, custom, or religious awareness. Spontaneous action is not unintentional, but it does not require the full repertoire of moral psychological factors to interpret. Roy Wagner has argued that "what we call 'culture' thus has much to do with how different peoples in different parts of the world figure spontaneity within an intentional field—how they may deny it, claim it, impute it."[135] Buddhaghosa is recognizing, among other things here, the role of what we would call culture—the habits, traditions, and customs that produce so much of what we do. Much good thought and action are simply the results of habit, of doing what one's family or community has always done, and no further explanation of it need be sought. The category of the spontaneous also functions as shorthand for accounting for why people do what they do due to disposition or character, which is thought to produce action in something like an automatic fashion: "Why did she give that gift? Oh, because she is a generous person." No further account of the deed is required. Finally, we see a particular emphasis on how religious awareness works on people to make them act reflexively or automatically.

Conclusions

We have spent the preceding pages in an intricate dissection of conscious experience, both the discrete factors that comprise thoughts and the various dispositions and influences that shape them. As complex and manifold as this psychology is and his probing into the nuances of it, Buddhaghosa still marvels at how the mind produces the great range of effects that it does. He suggests that the mind is like a painter who paints a great work

135. Wagner, "Hazarding Intent," 164.

of art that is the product of many artistic skills and designs. He says that the Buddha once mentioned a particularly beautiful masterpiece that was the result of diverse artistic mastery and said that the mind is even more diverse in its arts than that painting.[136] The mind is even greater than the greatest artist in its creativity and design of the world of experience through action. The mind creates our good and bad actions and through them our current experience and our future destinies. We are reminded, too, that the Abhidhammikas and Buddhaghosa described human experience in a manner resistant to closure, as an artist somehow not bound by the borders of the canvas.

Intention is the primary agent of constructing reality in present and future existence through marshaling and constructing the mental and material experiences we will have. Its creativity is likened here to that of an artist, elsewhere to that of a carpenter, a tutor, a landowner, and an army general, all of whom, in their own distinctive and complex ways, fashion their objects.

One of the striking things about this entire account is that as fundamental as intention is in action and world construction, the texts never tell us how to change our intentions, as such. Although the Buddha pointed to *cetanā* as the key element in moral agency (karma), he never directly or explicitly instructed how one might go about correctly ordering or developing one's *cetanās*. How then does one do moral work? Intentions themselves are not directly managed; rather, programs of meditation and moral development work at the level of uprooting immoral motivations and enhancing and developing the many moral motivations, sentiments, and capacities that are operative in moral consciousness. A close look at *cetanā* reveals a complex network of conditioned and changing causal factors that are assembled and galvanized into action through *cetanā*'s activity. The Buddha's emphasis on intention did not lead to any programs aimed directly at *cetanā* as we might expect if *cetanā* was a matter of will or choice, which could, presumably, lend themselves to programs of will formation or to instructions on how to make the right choices. Rather, *cetanā* is, at least in the Abhidhamma treatment of it, a rather elementary, though

136. As 64–65. Buddhaghosa quotes here from S.iii.151. There are numerous puns in this passage and in Buddhaghosa's development of it, based mostly on the word *citta*, which can be either "picture" or "thought" (i.e., mind), that we cannot hope to render adequately in English. Bhikkhu Bodhi is also drawn to this passage and how it expresses the fundamental artistry and creativity of "the will" (Bodhi, *Nourishing the Roots*, 20–21).

crucial, operation of the mind in garnering and propelling the many other mental factors that come together in action.

From a modern Western perspective, perhaps the most conspicuous feature of the model of mind advanced in the Abhidhamma is that it does not turn to "reasons" for its explanations of moral or immoral action. By reasons, I refer to those "representational mental states (desires, beliefs, valuings) that the agent combines in a (sometimes rudimentary) process of reasoning that leads to an intention."[137] This domain for explaining actions is perhaps the dominant mode of describing intention in modern Western thought, whether in folk, philosophical, or psychological discourse. In this view, the concept of intentional action is seen to involve two minimal reasons for an action to be considered intentional: "that an agent have a desire for an outcome and that the agent have a belief that the intended action leads to that outcome." On the "causal history of these reasons," however, modern accounts usually remain silent.[138] The Abhidhamma and, for the most part, the Pāli literature as a whole do not treat intention in these terms. Intentional action is not boiled down to discrete desires and beliefs that may be said to precede and generate it in a process of practical reasoning, but rather is located in a complex web of causal factors that come together in ever-changing moments in almost infinitely diverse combinations. Given how entrenched the desire-belief model is in contemporary thinking about intentions, this style of interpreting intentional action represents a significant departure from our modern expectations of what intentional action is about.

We might also underscore that neither the Abhidhamma treatment of mind nor Buddhaghosa's work emphasizes rationality or deliberative choice in their depiction of intentional action. Elements of cognition and thinking are present, to be sure, in initial and sustained thought. However, these are never described as rational processes of means-ends calculations or other kinds of rational decision making.[139] Nor is the act of intending a matter of balancing and negotiating competing claims by the affective

---

137. Malle, "Folk Explanations of Intentional Action," 267–68.

138. Ibid., 267.

139. Certain discourses in the Sutta literature stress reflection on action through processes of reasoning about ends as important for moral agency; see, for example, M.i.415–16, where the Buddha instructs his son Rahula to think about what actions lead to before committing them. So while reflection and reasoning are important to some Pāli thinking on action, they are not central to the tradition's thinking about *cetanā*.

and rational components of the mind. What is clear is that the presence of *cetanā* in every conscious moment places intentional processes at the heart of conscious experience; it directs one's mind and action in a constant intentional engagement with the world. The constancy of intention's work in conscious experience suggests that intention does not get featured primarily in a kind of problems and arguments approach, where it gets wheeled out to make choices in moral dilemmas.[140] In fact, there is no term in the Abhidhamma texts that does the work of this modern conception of choice.

Perhaps because the Theravāda's formal thinking on morality is more interested in causes, that is, in moral psychology or phenomenology, we do not get branches of systematic ethical thinking, such as we have in the West, that are focused on the rationalities of ethical decision making.[141] Although many modern scholars have been keen to determine which of the three families of Western ethics—consequentialism, virtue ethics, or deontology—best fit Buddhist ways of thinking, they are met with some resistance to the project by the Buddhist sources themselves, at least in the case of the Theravāda. This is because Theravādin thinkers trained their energies on phenomena that for the most part fly below the radar of these Western systems, that is, on the deep, complicated, and nitty-gritty psychological factors and their interrelationships that lie beneath choice and virtue.[142]

Other genres—most notably Vinaya, to which we turn next—make more of decision, choice, or consent in their interpretations of karma and cast different light on the notion of intention than the moral psychology sketched here. This examination of the Abhidhamma account of karma shows that intention is the fundamental mechanism by means of which

---

140. See Kapstein's Introduction to his *Reason's Traces*, on the limits of a problems and arguments approach to understanding Buddhist philosophy. On the pervasiveness of "choice" as the trademark of modernity, see Rosenthal, *The Era of Choice*. It could be argued that the modern emphasis on choice heavily influences our styles of thinking about how to do philosophical ethics.

141. See also Garfield, "What Is It Like to Be a Bodhisattva? Moral Phenomenology in Śāntideva's *Bodhicaryāvatāra*," where he argues against assimilating Buddhist ethics to consequentialism or to virtue ethics and characterizes it as a moral phenomenology.

142. In this regard, as I have suggested elsewhere, I think these Buddhist thinkers might be more usefully brought into conversation with Western moral psychological theories, such as the British moral sense theorists and those influenced by them, or with the traditions of Christian moral anthropology, such as Jonathan Edwards. See Heim, "Toward a 'Wider and Juster Initiative.'"

the mind organizes mental factors and engages with the world through action. We have seen just how many and how complex those factors are and the dynamic and shifting ways they may come together in constructing action and, through action, our experience of the world. This is an essential truth about karma, in their view, and locates our intentional activity at a very fundamental level indeed.

A final feature of the moral psychology we have explored here concerns the role of abstentions in the moral and religious life. Buddhaghosa sees abstentions as distinctive actions that do not follow the same logic of accumulation that ordinary *cetanā* involves. Many of the most important moral and religious actions advanced by this system—the five precepts, the 10 good deeds, the Eightfold Path—are described, in large measure, as abstentions and restraints. Much of the moral life consists chiefly of *ceasing* habitual and problematic actions. With this in mind, we turn to the Vinaya, a body of practical guidance on the technologies of restraint.

3

Culpability and Disciplinary Culture in the Vinaya

AS HE INTRODUCES the Vinaya, Buddhaghosa tells a story that mentions the *Aṅguttara* linking of karma and intention and affirms the importance of intention in action.[1] He tells of an incident regarding the Indian emperor Ashoka, who offered royal support and prestige to the Buddhist Saṅgha. Under Ashoka's reign, the Saṅgha, due to its wealth and status, swells with the ranks of pretender monks and heretics who refuse to participate in the Uposatha ceremonies that monks are obliged to perform. The Saṅgha does not seem able to handle this "tumor, stain, and thorn" in the community and appeals to King Ashoka for help. He sends a minister to force them to settle the problem and revive the Uposatha. The minister interprets these instructions to mean that he should kill the wayward monks and beheads many. When King Ashoka hears that this is what the minister is doing, he is filled with anguish and remorse, and he immediately worries that the evil (*pāpa*) from this slaughter is his. Some of his advisors say that since the minister acted at his command, the evil is Ashoka's, while others say that since his aim was good (*kusalādhippaya*)—that is, since he merely commanded that the Uposatha be restored—he bears no fault.

Wracked by doubt, he consults the great elder Moggaliputta Tissa about his remorse. Elder Tissa insists on the importance of Ashoka's thoughts, what Ashoka *thought* the minister would do. Since he had not thought the minister would kill anyone, he bears no evil. And here Buddhaghosa quotes from the *Aṅguttara Nikāya*: "Monks, I say that karma is intention; intending, one acts in body, speech, and mind." For additional support, the elder mentions a *jātaka* story that describes a similar case where "it is the thought that counts."[2]

1. The story is in Sp i.53–61.

2. This is Jātaka No. 319, Ja.iii.64ff. (Tittira Jātaka). In this story, a decoy pigeon is forced to call out and attract other birds, whereupon they are killed. Since the pigeon is coerced, he bears no evil for his action.

We thus have in Buddhaghosa's introductory presentation and contextualization of the Vinaya a move similar to that in the Kālāma Sutta we observed in our study of the Suttanta. Evil may follow from an action we perform, but if it was not intended, we may be assured that we are not touched by that evil. We find once again that part of the work that the close identity of intention and karma does in the tradition is to determine matters of culpability. In assessing culpability in moral transgression, intention is central. That Buddhaghosa frames the Vinaya with this story and with this assurance helps us to see that the element of intention will be crucial to much of the Vinaya literature's reflection on culpability and transgression.

But questions about culpability are not our only entry point into intention in this literature, and the Ashoka story presents several other themes helpful for understanding intentions and agency. The story introduces remorse and shows how it prompts inquiry into actions; we will need to attend to remorse and the work that it does. The story also indicates the importance of the Uposatha, the ritual recitation of the rules and confession of transgressions required of monastics every fortnight. The Uposatha is just one of the disciplinary practices—here it is helpful to invoke Michel Foucault's language of the "technologies of the self"—that the Vinaya advances for the constitution and formation of a certain type of moral person. This moral person is shaped by the rituals, norms, and ideals of the monastic community in a manner that makes possible self-examination and restraint. Charting these processes will allow us to see how intentions are often constituted and constructed *prior* to intentional action.

A Shift in Terminology

We recall that while Buddhaghosa suggests that the Suttanta and the Abhidhamma concern questions of meaning, he claims that the Vinaya is about actions, training, and matters of restraint. Vinaya is a teaching brought about by transgression and is centered on the Buddha's commands about physical and verbal actions.[3] Moreover, in several places, Buddhaghosa asserts that Vinaya governs acts of body and speech but not acts of mind.[4] Up until now, the texts have been interested in all three types

3. Sp.i.17–23; As 19–24; Sv.i.17–22.

4. Sp.i.19, 103; As 19, 93. A possible exception to this is the *pācittiya* offense of holding fast to a heretical doctrine (which might appear to be a mental event). But it comes to be classed as a verbal offense since it requires verbally espousing the doctrine (Vin.iv.135; see Dhirasekera, *Buddhist Monastic Discipline*, 108–9).

of action—bodily, verbal, and mental. But he recognizes that the rules of the community do not legislate mental actions; they govern only visible acts of body and speech. We shift here to thinking about how action, as experienced by others, may be represented, controlled, and mastered.

Although the Vinaya *legislates* only bodily and verbal actions, it is still very concerned with the intentionality of these actions, and intention is a primarily factor in discerning culpability. But we will notice an important shift in the language used to talk about intention. Buddhaghosa states that where the Abhidhamma parses the discrete psychological factors that go into experience—perception, feeling, intention, and the like—in the Vinaya it is enough to talk simply and more vaguely of thought or mind (*citta*)[5] without assuming one has to analyze the intricacies of the interior conditions of action.

> When the Buddha arrived at an explanation according to the Vinaya, he did not ask [an offending monk] "what is your sensory contact, what is your feeling, what is your perception, what is your intention?" Rather, he primarily asked simply about his thought (*citta*): "monk, what was your thought?" And when the reply is "I had the thought to steal, Bhagavan," the Buddha does not say "the offence of stealing is of sensory contact, etc.," but rather that "the offence, monk, is in the thought to steal." And not only is this so of Vinaya teaching, but in other worldly teachings also he teaches primarily simply about thoughts.[6]

While Abhidhamma takes mind and thought to its deepest level of analysis, much of the time when we try to understand our intentional actions, we do not need to engage in such technical and reductive moral phenomenology. This has important bearings for *cetanā*, which has been until now our central category. *Cetanā*, like many of the other philosophical and psychological terms that have been with us throughout our discussions of Suttanta and Abhidhamma discourse, can be a very technical term. Like English "intention," *cetanā* is used differently in different contexts, from

---

5. As we have seen, mind and thought are identical: *yaṃ cittaṃ taṃ mano, yaṃ mano taṃ cittaṃ* (Vin.iii.74; Sp.ii.442). On the other hand, Devdas shows the subtle differences between them (and the concept of *viññāṇa* as well) as the terms are used in the Suttas and Abhidhamma (Devdas, *Cetanā and the Dynamics of Volition*, 104–10).

6. As 68.

legal and philosophical discourse to everyday folk conversation about actions. Despite occurring in many contexts, however, *cetanā* is not a term ordinary people (as we find them in the story literature, for example) use often, and even the rules of the monastic code, while highly attuned to issues concerning intentions, do not usually invoke intention with this level of precision. Instead, we will see the language of thought or mind (*citta*) throughout Vinaya discussions, just as Elder Tissa queried King Ashoka about his thoughts, rather than his *cetanā*.

This variance in terminology is very much in keeping with Buddhaghosa's sensitivity to how language is used and to the distinctive qualities of the different genres of the Buddha's teaching. As we have seen, the Buddha made use of conventional or absolute language depending on the circumstances, context, and capacities of those hearing the teaching. Technical or absolute language, such as talking about the aggregates, invoked to dismantle the self (appropriate to Abhidhamma discourse) is not going to be helpful to those who need to hear about everyday moral actions such as those that cause us shame and embarrassment, that embody different kinds of love for others, or that involve knowing appropriate gifts to give. For these purposes, the Buddha teaches in a conventional fashion.[7] Since *cetanā* is a foremost factor in the aggregate *saṅkhāra*, it bears the hallmarks of the absolute or ultimate language that befuddles people in everyday conversation.

In most instances in the Vinaya where intention comes up, the word used is *thought* (*citta*) or some variant of it rather than *intention* (*cetanā*). To provide just a few representative examples of this usage, when discussing the element of intention in the offense of stealing, the question concerns whether the offender had the "thought to steal" (*theyyacitta*).[8] When determining whether an action might have been committed accidentally or unknowingly, the Buddha asks an offender, "Monk, what was your thought?" or, more colloquially, "Monk, what were you thinking?"[9] The answer that often works to clear the monk or nun of wrongdoing is "Sir, I didn't know" what I was doing. In related terms, monks and nuns are said to commit faults deliberately (*sañcicca*), purposefully (*cittasaṅkappa*),

7. Ps.i.137–39; Mp.i.95–96. See Hallisey, "In Defense of Rather Fragile and Local Achievement," 125–28, on conventional and absolute teachings.

8. For example, Vin.iii.48; Vin.iii.59.

9. *kiṃ citto tvaṃ, bhikkhu?* (Vin.iii.60).

purposely (*cittamana*), and knowingly (*jānanta, sañjānanta*).[10] The texts are also interested in whether an action was done willingly (*adhiṭṭhāya*) and what can be said about one's aim or wish (*adhippāya*) in performing it.[11] The language of "aim" can, though rarely, also cover motivation, as in the case of a monk who released a pig from a hunter's trap: since his aim or motivation was compassion, he is not at fault.[12] Finally, the language of consent (*sādiyati*) is invoked, particularly in matters of sexual infractions. For the most part, the Vinaya's language of intention is concerned with whether an action was done knowingly, willingly, with consent, and, more rarely, what may be said of its aim.

I think that this movement to a more general description of awareness of one's action is akin to a shift we would see in our own English usages of *intention*. Intention is going to be treated as an identifiable mental state in certain philosophical treatments of it, but in criminal jurisprudence, it is enough to point to an intentional element in an action without having to identify its psychological complexities. The intentional element in law can be an omission of an action, or amount to recklessness; in other contexts, it is framed as consent. To be sure, as Buddhaghosa puts it, in the worldly or workaday morality (*lokiyadhamma*) of the Vinaya, mind or thought is still chief, but one does not have to get into a reductionist description of its workings, as one does in Abhidhamma.[13]

Buddhaghosa's Vinaya

Before we press on to issues of intention and culpability, we need to look more closely at what the Vinaya does, in keeping with the idea that meaning is always closely connected to the nature of discourse. As we have just seen, Vinaya discourse is quite different than Abhidhamma or Sutta material, with quite different purposes. Modern scholars have read the

---

10. Vin.iii.73, 79–80. In an example of the *pārājika* offense of killing, Vin.iii.74 glosses *cittasaṅkappa* as being aware of killing, having the intention to kill, having the aim to kill (*maraṇasaññī maraṇacetano maraṇādhippāyo*). We will consider in more depth how Buddhaghosa understands all of the terms mentioned in this paragraph, but here he sees that elements of awareness, intention, and aim are being brought together (*saṃvidahana*) in the term *cittasaṅkappa* (Sp.ii.442).

11. Vin.iii.74, 79.

12. *Anāpatti, bhikkhu, kāruññādhippāyassa* (Vin.iii.62).

13. As 68.

Pāli Vinaya in various different ways—as legal literature, as ethics, for its institutional concerns, and how it depicts an ideal religious life and contributes to Buddhist soteriology.[14] All of these are quite appropriate, and often these concerns overlap. But how did Buddhaghosa understand Vinaya? What did he think the purpose of this *piṭaka* is?

In the introductory chapter (literally the "external context" [*bāhiranidāna*] of the *Samantapāsādikā*), Buddhaghosa does several things to locate and contextualize the Vinaya. In addition to providing several narrative contexts in which the text is to be located—providing an account of the three councils and of Buddhism's arrival and presence in Sri Lanka, a history of kings and teachers, and the account of Ashoka's angst with which we began—he mentions the benefits of studying and learning the Vinaya. This part of the introduction emphasizes, as Buddhaghosa often does, the pragmatic context of the root text, that is, the ideal context in which the text is to be received. The Vinaya, he suggests, should be an object of study. Those who study it accrue several benefits: they come to be looked on as mother and father by those with faith in the Buddha's dispensation, and people will come to rely on them for their ordinations, for their practice of duties, and for ensuring the goodness of their conduct (*ācāra*) and alms gathering. Quoting a passage from the *Parivāra*, he says that those who study the Vinaya, whom he calls "*vinaya* experts," enjoy five benefits: their body of moral precepts (*sīlakkhandha*) is well guarded and well protected, they become a refuge for monks who are by nature scrupulous, they live confidently in the midst of the Saṅgha, they firmly restrain their adversaries with the Dhamma, and they practice in a way that prolongs the Dhamma.[15] This suggests that for Buddhaghosa studying the Vinaya served to advance a moral education. This education results not simply in

14. Von Hinüber ("Buddhist Law According to the Theravāda Vinaya) and Huxley ("Buddhism and Law" and "Buddhist Case Law on Theft") are good treatments of the legalistic nature of Vinaya; Dhirasekera (*Buddhist Monastic Discipline*) is probably the best text on the ethical dimensions and their role in the religious life the Vinaya promotes; Gregory Schopen's voluminous work focuses primarily on the social, economic, and institutional aspects of the Vinaya literatures; and Thanissaro (*The Buddhist Monastic Code)*, Wijayaratna (*Buddhist Monastic Life*), and Holt (*Discipline*) are very helpful accounts of the religious life and values articulated in Vinaya texts.

15. The next several paragraphs are drawing from Sp.i.104–5. The "Bāhiranidāna" is the only part of the Pāli *Samantapāsādikā* that is translated into English (Jayawickrama, *The Inception of Discipline*; see pp. 92–93 for this passage). We also have an English translation of a Chinese version of the *Samantapāsādikā*, the *Shan-Chien-P'i-P'o-Sha* (Bapat and Hirakawa), which is a very helpful guide to the text. All translations from the *Samantapāsādikā* are my own and are drawn from the Pāli edition.

expertise in judging ethical and legal cases but also, ideally, transforms a person into a moral exemplar. This offers a useful clue for us in learning how to read Vinaya: we will attend closely to how Buddhaghosa shapes his own reading of the *vinayapāli* (that is, the canonical material) into a certain type of moral instruction.

Using the language of good factors (*kusaladhammas*) already familiar to us, Buddhaghosa says, "The *vinaya* expert becomes heir to the good factors described by the Buddha as having their roots in restraint." In other words, one who studies the Vinaya makes himself the beneficiary of the good factors, as we know them from the Abhidhamma, that are caused by restraint. And then we see a formula with which we are already familiar from chapter 1, with an important emendation. Buddhaghosa says (again quoting the *Parivāra*) that "*vinaya* (here the concept of discipline rather than the *piṭaka*) leads to restraint, restraint leads to nonremorse, nonremorse leads to joy, joy leads to delight, delight leads to calm, calm to happiness," and so on all the way to *nibbāna*.[16] But in the *Aṅguttara* passage that we considered earlier, the foundation of these processes is *sīla*, the precepts. Here the foundation is *vinaya*, which leads to restraint, and from restraint nonremorse kicks in, making possible the other links of the chain.

In our first reading of the *Aṅguttara* formulation, when we considered it in the "No Need for an Intention Sutta," we were interested in how these processes are said to flow one from the other naturally without the need for intention, and we were also interested in nonremorse as a state of mind. Our interest here is the way that Buddhaghosa sees *vinaya* and restraint, which replace *sīla* in this version, at the foundation of the soteriological process this passage elucidates. This move locates *vinaya* in the larger system: it lies at the foundation of the soteriological path.

The connections and overlaps of *vinaya* and *sīla* are many, and Buddhaghosa's commentary on the *Parivāra* passage says that *vinaya* is the foundation (*upanissaya*), the condition (*paccaya*), of *sīla* that has as its end the purification of livelihood.[17] At the heart of both is restraint from wrongdoing, in other words, nonactions. Jotiya Dhirasekera has shown the many ways that the Pāṭimokkha rules (the formal strictures for monks

16. Vin.v.164; the *Aṅguttara* passage we looked at in chapter 1 is A.v.2.

17. Sp.vii.1365. As we have seen in these last few paragraphs and will continue to see, Buddhaghosa relies heavily on the *Parivāra*, a text that modern scholars often neglect.

and nuns) are identified with or considered *sīla* par excellence, and he argues that "Buddhaghosa is conscious of the paramount importance of the Pāṭimokkha as a body of *sīla*."[18] In this conception, then, Buddhaghosa is telling us what *vinaya* is—it is the ethical foundation of restraint that lies at the foundation of the whole soteriological project that leads to highest freedom. It does not instruct on meditation or reflect on the highest echelons of religious awareness, but it is the entry point to a path that can go to them. The *Mahāvagga* says this of the Pāṭimokkha, the rule code: "The Pāṭimokkha is the entrance, the beginning of the good factors."[19]

As he works through the Vinaya texts, Buddhaghosa is ever conscious of the larger whole of which the Vinaya is a part, a whole that he both sees and helps create through his systematization of the material. As he begins to work through the beginning of the *Suttavibhaṅga*, Buddhaghosa spends a huge amount of time on the context that the Vinaya itself opens with, which is a conversation that the Buddha has with a brahman. There is much that he sees going on here that would take us too far from our present concerns to begin to explore, but one thing we can say is that he uses the opening passages of his *Samantapāsādikā* to discuss many topics, including Buddhist cosmology, the nature and knowledge of the Buddha, dependent origination, the intricacies of the *jhānas*, and the extraordinary pliability of the mind when disciplined. At one point in this discussion, he tries to rein himself in, saying that "the sense of mental cultivation should be understood by looking at the *Visuddhimagga*. While mentioning it here, the Vinaya context is also quite serious and so I need to stick just to illuminating the meaning of the root text of the Vinaya."[20] Indeed, he often presumes and refers to the *Visuddhimagga* throughout his commentarial work. Here, as elsewhere, he assumes the reader will have access to the *Visuddhimagga* and the systematic whole—that is, morality (*sīla*), concentration (*samādhi*), and wisdom (*paññā*)—it espouses and represents. The Vinaya is to be understood in the context of its role in this larger path, that is, as the foundation that is *sīla* from which one can develop the mind.

One way to talk about this whole is suggested by Dhirasekera's discussion of *sikkhā*, the "culture, training, discipline, and also study" of the monastic life. This training is said to be threefold: training in higher *sīla*

18. Dhirasekera, *Buddhist Monastic Discipline*, 3.

19. Vin.i.103; see also Sp.iv.787; it is also echoed at the beginning of the *Kaṅkhāvitaraṇī*.

20. Sp.i.146.

(*adhisīlasikkhā*), training in higher conscious awareness (*adhicittasikkhā*), and training in higher wisdom (*adhipaññāsikkhā*), with Vinaya as the first.[21] These are successive stages of practice that culminate in the elimination of the deep motivational roots of lust, hatred, and delusion.[22] They also describe the three *piṭakas*: Vinaya is training in higher morality, Suttanta is training in higher conscious awareness, and Abhidhamma is training in higher wisdom.[23] Buddhaghosa also says that ordinary *sīla* can be established by people without a Buddha present in the world, but higher *sīla*, that is, the restraint of the Pāṭimokkha, can be known only when a Buddha teaches it.

Dhirasekera also shows how *sīla*, *sikkhā*, and *sikkhāpada* (the Vinaya precepts) are the foundations of this holy life. They are "perfectly coordinated but at times almost identified with one another."[24] They are different aspects of restraint, which in turn allows the elimination of the hindrances that block religious development. The basic logic is that it is only through restraint of the senses and of bodily and verbal action that the religious life can be lived and joy can be found.

We can also understand something of Buddhaghosa's treatment of Vinaya discourse by looking at the contexts in which the first rules were given and the reasons the Buddha gave for the rules. The *Suttavibhaṅga* mentions that at one time Sāriputta requested that the Buddha give the community rules by which to live. But the Buddha refused, saying that the rules are not to be given until conditions causing the depravities appear in the community, and these unfold only over time. The Buddha does not assign the community rules just for the sake of having rules, but only when prompted by problems that come up.[25] At least initially, rules are pragmatic matters provoked by the actual circumstances that call them forth.

Buddhaghosa adds several interesting points here. He says that the Buddha did not prescribe rules while the community was still pure, that is, free of bad actions, because he was concerned about what people would say. How would it look to people for the Buddha to pester men from good

21. Vin.iii.24; A.i.235; Ps.ii.313.

22. Dhirasekera, *Buddhist Monastic Discipline*, 43; A.i.230.

23. Sp.i.22; 243.

24. Dhirasekera, *Buddhist Monastic Discipline*, 53.

25. Vin.iii.8–9.

families who renounce great wealth for this life of austerity? Would not laying down rules that appear unnecessary look like he underestimated them, that he failed to discern the quality of these men? It would be like a bad doctor who pops a patient's boil, though it had only begun to swell, and makes it bleed painfully, leaving the patient worse off.[26] The imagery is appropriate: only when the depravities ooze to the surface to make themselves known can they be treated with the medicine of rules. The skillful physician knows how to treat skin diseases appropriately and only when they present symptoms. The Buddha knows that depravities lie beneath the surface, but monastic rules can treat them only when they erupt into actions. Here again, we see that the rules treat actions that are present and visible, not underlying dispositions or mental actions.

Eventually the presence of impurity does emerge, however, 20 years into the Buddha's teaching career, in the actions of the monk Sudinna. We will look more closely in the pages ahead at his violation of what then becomes the rule against monks engaging in sexual intercourse, as it raises several fascinating issues about intention, but here we can say that it is on this occasion that the Buddha realized that laying down the first rule is now necessary, and he offers up 10 reasons for the Vinaya rules. These reasons, and Buddhaghosa's treatment of them, suggest the many purposes that the rules serve. The 10 reasons for the rules and Buddhaghosa's interpretations of them are:

1. "For the excellence of the Saṅgha." Buddhaghosa says this means that the rules support the community's joy and happiness for a long time. The monastic life is meant to be joyful.
2. "For the comfort of the Saṅgha." The rules make it possible for the monks and nuns to live together in happiness.
3. "For subduing bad people." The rules subdue people with bad moral habits (*dussīla*), who are shameless, or who commit transgressions.
4. "For the comfort of well-behaved monks." Buddhaghosa says that well-behaved monks who care about good practice whether or not they know all the boundaries of what should be done or not done and what is blameworthy or not, should not be wearied or exhausted as they strive to purify their practice. Additionally, there is the very practical matter that the monastic rituals, the Uposatha, the Pavāraṇā, and so

26. Sp. i.191.

on, cannot be held in the presence of impure monks, so for these reasons the rules allow good monks to meet their monastic obligations and thereby live comfortably.

5. "For restraint of depravities in this visible life." Buddhaghosa elaborates to say that the rules fend off various forms of suffering one might experience in this life as the result of immoral action, such as blows by the fist or rod, cutting off of hands and feet, dishonor, defamation, and regret.
6. "For warding off depravities that lead to results in future lives." The rules keep one from committing bad actions that lead to the hells.
7. "For gladdening those lacking faith." Buddhaghosa elaborates to say that the rules attract the notice of learned people who will see the monks living in austerity and who will also be impressed that they have a book by which they live just like the heretic, three-Veda brahmans.
8. "For increasing faith." This means that people of good families will see the monks and they will increase their faith.[27]
9. "For supporting the Good Dhamma." Buddhaghosa divides the Good Dhamma into three parts: study of the scriptures, practice, and the attainment of the goal, all of which the rules help to preserve for a long time.
10. "For the sake of aiding *vinaya*." Buddhaghosa says *vinaya* (discipline) is fourfold: the discipline of restraint, the discipline of abandoning, the discipline of calming meditation, and the discipline of the established rules.[28]

We can see multiple concerns at once in the reasons themselves and in the ways that Buddhaghosa is interpreting them. Right on the surface, we see both the Buddha and Buddhaghosa thinking institutionally in terms of how to hold together an organization with very different kinds of people, to provide for the harmonious workings of its community and their rituals, and to make it go into the future. These reasons show how the rules keep monks out of trouble with the public and with secular authorities who wield the rod, attract people of good families, and put Buddhist monks on par with or above the social status of brahmans. But beyond practical and institutional concerns, they show ethical and religious commitments,

---

27. *Pasanna* and *pasīdati* are more complex than "faith," of course, and also indicate brightness, gladness, and calmness.

28. Vin.iii.21; Sp.i.223–24.

creating the conditions for a good life lived with others in happiness and joy, helping people restrain their depravities that will bear consequences in this and their next lives, and supporting the Dhamma and its goals. In fact, the texts do not separate the institutional from the ethical (these are our distinctions); instead, what benefits the community practically is of a piece with its ethical and religious ideals.

Buddhaghosa goes on to quote the *Parivāra* to develop the idea that these reasons (*atthavasa*) can be considered conditions (*paṭicca*) that build on one another, a logic of conditionality with which we are by now quite familiar. That is, when the first condition is present, then the following one also can occur, and when that one is present, it leads to the next. So when there is the excellence of the Saṅgha, then people can live comfortably; and when the community is living comfortably, bad monks can be subdued, and so on.[29] The various concerns that these conditions reflect are mutually supportive: securing the institutional health of the community makes possible the ethical and religious goals, and vice versa.

Because Buddhaghosa's treatment of the purpose of the Vinaya rules interprets the concept of *vinaya* (discipline), the 10th reason bears additional consideration.[30] *Vinaya* can be used in the sense of absence, restraint, calming, and the established rules themselves. Since absence and restraint, along with intention (*cetanā*), figure prominently in Sutta and Abhidhamma thinking as forms of *sīla*, we are particularly sensitive to their appearance here as forms of *vinaya*. *Vinaya* can be the absence of wrong conduct and the restraint of the depravities and other problematic urges. If we stay within this logic, we see that much of what is true of *sīla*—that only some forms of it are, strictly speaking, matters of intention, and much of it is the presence of absences and restraints—is also true of *vinaya*. But how are these four kinds of disciplines related? Buddhaghosa does not say, but a later subcommentator says that the discipline of the established rules is for the sake of the discipline of calming meditation, calming meditation is for the sake of restraint, and restraint is for abandoning.[31] The rules allow a calm mind, which helps people restrain themselves so that they can enjoy the absence of bad factors.

---

29. Sp.224; Vin.v.143.

30. Since "Vinaya" can mean the *piṭaka* or the concept, I clarify the first as "Vinaya-piṭaka" and leave the concept in lower case. Additionally, I later refer to *vinayapāli* when I want to make a clear distinction between the canonical material and the *aṭṭhakathā*.

31. *Vajirabuddhiṭīkā* 72.

Finally, in our brief exploration of how Buddhaghosa understood Vinaya, we turn to a short passage that opens the *Parivāra*. (The *Parivāra*, though canonical, is an Abhidhamma-like expository handbook on the Vinaya that proceeds through a kind of commentary through classification and listing that is familiar to us from the Abhidhamma. Because it is working on a second-order level, it is quite helpful for us to see how *vinaya-piṭaka* and *vinaya* discipline more generally are being theorized, and this is why Buddhaghosa, who is also attempting this kind of theorization, relies so heavily on it.) In its opening passage, it raises and answers questions concerning the meanings of key terms we have already begun to consider, including:

> What is *vinaya*? What is *adhivinaya*? *Vinaya* is the established rules (*paññatti*), and *adhivinaya* is analysis. What is *pāṭimokkha*? What is *adhipāṭimokkha*? *Pāṭimokkha* is the established rules, and *adhipāṭimokkha* is analysis. What is falling away? Falling away is nonrestraint. What is success? Success is restraint. What is practice? Practice is [saying] "I won't do such and such anymore," as one trains in the training precepts, having undertaken them for as long as one lives until one's last breath.[32]

Here we get distinction between the rules laid down and the analysis or division of them (*vibhatti*, which Buddhaghosa takes as "analysis," *vibhaṅga*), a second-order expository treatment through classification. In his comments, Buddhaghosa defines *nonrestraint* as transgression and *restraint* as nontransgression; restraint is simply not breaking the rules. Most interesting for our purposes is how the *Parivāra* treats practice with an insertion of the very thought a person would have who has undertaken these rules: "I won't do such and such anymore." The text makes explicit that practice is having certain intentions or thoughts: "I won't do this anymore." The practice of *vinaya* creates certain identifiable thoughts in a person's head, creating, as it were, a distinct intention. Our task then, throughout this chapter, is to look at the processes whereby a person comes to have the restraint to say, "I won't do this anymore."

---

32. Vin.v.2; Sp.vii.1303.

Kinds of Rules

Buddhaghosa draws several distinctions that can guide us to how intention figures in the different classes of rules in the Pāṭimokkha. Well known, of course, is that there are 227 rules for monks and 311 for nuns[33] and that there are seven different classes of rules divided according to penalty: *pārājika*, violations entailing "defeat," that is, disrobing; *saṅghadisesa*, violations that involve formal acts of the Saṅgha; *aniyata*, rules with undetermined penalties; *nissaggiya pācittiya*, rules that involve confessing and forfeiting a wrongly acquired article; *pācittiya*, rules requiring confession; *pātidesaniya*, rules entailing acknowledgment; and *sekhiya*, training in decorum. These violations are also classified into grave offenses (*thullaccaya*) and mere wrongdoings (*dukkata*); violations of *pārājikas* and *saṅghadisesas* are usually grave unless they do not reach full completion or there is some mitigating factor making them only wrongdoings, and violations of the remaining classes of rules are almost all considered wrongdoings.

Buddhaghosa draws a distinction among these classes of rules, distinguishing between the first two, which are matters of *sīla*, and the latter five, which are matters of *ācāra*.[34] Both these terms can mean moral conduct and habit, but *sīla* means not violating at the very least the five precepts. *Ācāra*, on the other hand, is a more general term for good conduct that can also mean etiquette, good manners, and customary practice, and it may be considered in some sense as the external representation of an idealized inner morality.[35] Since the first two classes of rules entail forbidding sex, theft, killing, and lying, they are very much matters of *sīla*, four of the five precepts. The remaining rules are either lesser infractions or matters of decorum and etiquette. Thanissaro Bhikkhu says they concern social relationships, and "social relationships are defined by seemingly minor points."[36] Buddhaghosa also says that the first two are heavy and wicked and the other five are light and not wicked.[37]

---

33. Technically, there are 220 rules for monks and 304 rules for nuns according to Buddhaghosa in Sv.i.13, because the seven *adhikaraṇasamatha* (rules for settling cases) are not disciplinary rules (*sikkhāpadas*) (Dhirasekera, *Buddhist Monastic Discipline*, 155–56).

34. Sp.vii.1303, 1414.

35. Collins shows how *ācāra* is concerned with demonstrating empirically the virtue lying within, citing *Visuddhimagga* 19 on what a monk's bodily decorum looks like ("The Body in Theravāda Buddhist Monasticism," 198–99).

36. Thanissaro, *The Buddhist Monastic Code*, 26.

37. Sp.vi.1279, vii.1319. Buddhaghosa is using classificatory terms in the *Parivāra* (Vin.v.115).

Another important distinction suggested by the *Parivāra* and developed by Buddhaghosa is the difference among classes of offenses that are prescribed as blameworthy and those that are blameless. Buddhaghosa interprets blameworthy offenses to be "blamable for the world" (*lokavajja*), while blameless offenses are "blamable because of the rules" (*paṇṇattivajja*).[38] The first are actions that are universally condemned, such as killing and so on, that are blameworthy no matter who commits them, and the second are actions proscribed only for monastics. Interestingly, the *Milindapañho* picks up this distinction and says that the 10 bad actions (*akusalakammapatha*) are blameworthy universally, but actions like eating at the wrong time or playing in water are blameworthy only for monastics.[39] Buddhaghosa elsewhere goes further with the distinction to say that actions that are universally blameworthy are matters of a bad thought (*akusalacitta*) involving conscious awareness (*sacittaka*).[40] That is, one cannot commit them unintentionally or unknowingly, and given the context in which this distinction first occurs, in which a monk has had sex with a monkey, it is easy to see that the perpetrator is conscious and full of bad thoughts at the time of the action (how could it be otherwise?). Certain minor violations that are blameworthy only for monks and nuns, on the other hand, can be done unwittingly or even unknowingly and still warrant a penalty, and the *Milindapañho* argues that even arhats, who cannot know everything, may commit them.

We thus gain a distinction that is helpful to us and quite in keeping with what we know about intentional actions so far. A person may commit certain relatively minor monastic infractions unintentionally, but it is

---

38. Vin.v.115; Sp vii.1319.

39. Mil 266. See von Hinüber on the presence of this distinction in the *Milindapañho* and how it differs from the interpretation in both the *Parivāra* and the *Samantapāsādikā* ("The Arising of an Offense: *āpattisamuṭṭhāna*," 66–68).

40. Sp. i.227–28; i.270. Here he is using a distinction between *sacittaka* and *acittaka*, which occurs only in the *Parivāra* (Vin.v.125, 206–7; see Horner, *The Book of the Discipline*, vol. 1, xv). Buddhaghosa glosses *acittaka* as "one commits [an action that is] blamable because of the rules not deliberately (*asañcicca*), as in the case of [a violation of] lying down together," which refers to a monk inadvertently sleeping in the same building as a woman (Sp.vi.1379). Again, the idea is that one can commit relatively minor breaches of monastic rule unknowingly but not a universally condemned moral practice. Thanissaro Bhikkhu has a different interpretation of this, however: "The concepts would seem to have been developed originally to deal with the exceptional cases in which a bhikkhu would be led by mature consideration to break a rule—e.g., where another person's life was at stake. Under such circumstances, the world at large would not criticize his actions, although the rules would impose a penalty" (*The Buddhist Monastic Code*, 25).

not possible to commit a universally condemned immoral action without awareness of what one is doing (since karmic action itself is the constructing of it intentionally). Otherwise, the action has simply not been committed, or there is some mitigating factor that downgrades it to a wrongdoing. But a lesser violation can be committed unwittingly and still warrant a penalty, such as when a monk intending to sleep alone falls asleep and is later joined by a woman sleeping elsewhere in the same building. Buddhaghosa says that milder offenses can result from even good or neutral thoughts, but universally condemnable offenses are always matters of bad thoughts.[41] Thus, intention broadly construed is not always relevant, particularly when the issue concerns relatively minor matters of institutional reputation or appearance, where it does not really matter whether one deliberately committed an embarrassment for it to still count as an offense. Breaching minor rules or etiquette is not always a matter of bad intent but is still important in various ways to monastic practice and must be regulated.

Intention and Other Factors of Culpability: The First Four Rules

As Thanissaro Bhikkhu analyzes the *Suttavibhaṅga*, there are five factors of action that can come into play to determine whether a violation has occurred, what kind of violation it is, and what sort of penalty it incurs: the object of the action, the perception, the intention (literally, the "thought"), the effort, and the result. The object of an action concerns the person the action affects, such as in a sexual violation or murder, or, say, in the case of theft, the object stolen. The perception refers to a general awareness of the facts of the case: when one steals, one is actually aware that the object belongs to someone else. The thought means that one knows what one is doing as one steals; that is, one acts deliberately rather than accidentally. The arising of thoughts alone, without a concomitant action, are never offenses in the Vinaya sense (though they might incur karmic results, as we saw in the case of the hunter in the last chapter).[42] This can be a

41. Sp. i.270. Here he is attempting to map different types of offenses onto the classification of good, bad, and neutral thoughts that we are familiar with from the last chapter. He also mentions a distinction, mentioned only rarely in the *vinayapāli*, of the "origin" of offenses, whether they emerge from body, speech, or mind. See von Hinüber about this classificatory scheme ("The Arising of an Offense").

42. Vin.iii.56.

somewhat elastic category and sometimes can slip into the area of motivation. The effort refers to the commission or omission of the act and the lengths the monk or nun goes to in order to carry out the action. Finally, the result of the action must come to completion for the act to rise to the level of a full violation: an attempted murder in which the victim does not die will not entail a full *pārājika* (though it incurs a lesser penalty).[43]

Generally speaking, the graver rules require all or most of the five factors to be present, but the more minor rules may involve only several of them. As we have just seen, intention or thought usually has to be present for the action to count as an offense, but not always, such as in minor rules like lying down on the wrong sort of bed. Because the working out of these criteria is done on a case-by-case basis in the canonical text (the *vinayapāli*), to know how each of these factors may be weighed and interpreted in each of the many rules, one would need to go through each of them to see how the texts treat them in their particulars. Thanissaro Bhikkhu has done this work with admirable clarity and thoroughness, and there is no need to duplicate his work here (even if space permitted such an exhaustive analysis).[44]

My approach will not attempt to parse each rule for its various factors of culpability but rather to spend time with just four rules, considering closely the ways that intention is treated in the different layers of each rule. The *Suttavibhaṅga* embeds each rule in several expository layers. First is the story in which the first violation of the rule occurs, which is a narration of the circumstances in which the first offender does something that makes the Buddha lay down the rule. Then the rule is laid down, and the *vinayapāli* supplies a word gloss on it, clarifying the most important terms in the rule. Then the text provides various amendments and extenuating circumstances whereby a monk or nun would be exempt from the penalty or that would alter the judgment of the case up or down. Finally, for the major rules, there is the *vinītavatthu*, related case law that describes similar cases and how they are to be judged. Although many monks and nuns memorize just the rules themselves and recite them in the Pāṭimokkha, *vinaya* experts study the *Suttavibhaṅga* and the commentaries on it as part of a complex ethical and legal education. The expository

43. Thanissaro Bhikkhu, *The Buddhist Monastic Code.*

44. Ibid. Also very helpful is Harvey ("Vinaya Principles for Assigning Degrees of Culpability"), which attempts to provide an account of the general principles of culpability in the Vinaya.

matter surrounding the rules is considered canonical and essential to know and study.

At the next level of textual material we have, of course, the commentarial exposition of Buddhaghosa in his *Samantapāsādikā*, and again, Buddhaghosa's work with the canonical material is of central interest. Buddhaghosa's treatment of the rules is, as we must expect by now, expansive. He picks up and adds to details in the many layers of the *vinayapāli* and offers more word commentary, additional stories that add to the settings of the rule, and, often, supplemental narrative details that make the cases even more complex and nuanced. Part of our interest here, as throughout the book, is learning to see how Buddhaghosa approaches this material and how he guides us to a distinctive kind of interpretation.

The importance of the *vinayapāli*'s narrative particulars and extensive use of case law has been studied by legal scholar Andrew Huxley. Huxley has pushed back against Max Weber's scorn of casuistic legal reasoning and has suggested that while Vinaya case law is less succinct than, say, modern English law, it communicates a rational legal education. Case law makes use of far fewer abstract nouns to convey its legal principles, preferring instead to describe complex legal content in narratives of particular cases.[45] Huxley argues that casuistry is no less rational than nominalized conceptual analysis. He also suggests that the *vinayapāli*'s style of using case law was chiefly for purposes of education. By exploring particular cases in detail, a *vinaya* expert could convey to his students complicated legal instruction, which Huxley begins to demonstrate by taking up several cases regarding the treatment of theft.

Gregory Schopen has also considered the role of narrative particulars in *vinaya* texts. Discussing the *Mūlasarvāstivāda-vinaya*, he argues that "*vinaya* cases are neither fables nor historical accounts but rather the forms that *vinaya*-masters chose narratively to frame the issues that concerned them."[46] He argues that *vinaya* cases are embedded in a much larger body of accumulated cases that collectively provide general principles whereby the particularities of each case may be examined and debated. Where Huxley is interested primarily in the legal knowledge *vinaya* cases explore,

45. Huxley, "Buddhist Case Law on Theft," 313–19. Jonson and Toulmin, in *The Abuse of Casuistry*, offer a persuasive philosophical defense of casuistry as a case-based, bottom-up method of moral reasoning.

46. Schopen, "Ritual Rites and Bones of Contention," 311.

Schopen is interested mostly in sociopolitical concerns, how "power, access, and economics" are negotiated in these texts.[47]

I, too, am interested in how these narratives frame the issues that the *vinaya* experts were concerned with. But while I find both the legalistic knowledge and the glimpses of the social, political, and economic negotiations they afford us fascinating, my interest is chiefly in the *ethical* concerns evident in the treatment of particular cases. I want to show how the complex circumstances and narrative particulars convey a sophisticated ethical education, even while they exemplify the Buddha's pragmatic and particularist approach to the rules. Buddhaghosa has already told us that the *vinayapāli* is to be an object of study and that many benefits flow from the education it provides. My interest in this section as I take up each of the four defeats (*pārājikas*) in some detail is twofold. First, I am interested in what the *vinayapāli* and Buddhaghosa teach us about matters of intention, motivation, and reasons for action and how they identify the factors of culpability in action. Second, I suggest (as I have throughout the book) that explorations of these matters cannot be analyzed separately from the styles of discourse in which they occur. The fact that these discourses are highly contextual and particularized should not be taken as a matter of inconvenience for us, in which we must sift out the particulars to get to the bare facts or general principles of the rule, but rather as constituting the very subject of our inquiries. Our maxim that "no detail is unimportant," here as elsewhere, requires an openness to the possibilities for reading and interpreting that can lead us into many varied directions. Instead of reading in a way to close off certain of these directions (and thus the moral education they provide), I try to follow some of them, at least as Buddhaghosa points the way.

But of course, as we have seen elsewhere, the idea that no detail is unimportant, means that we must be selective in other ways, else we will begin to write a book that can never be finished. I have chosen to focus on just four rules, a tiny fraction of the overall Vinaya corpus, and even within them, I have not tried to treat exhaustively all of the *vinītivatthu* or even all of the matters pertaining to intention that the many extenuating circumstances suggest. Instead, I focus on the origin story and particularly the narrative settings that introduce each rule which the tradition regarded as important to understanding the rules themselves. Buddhaghosa, here as

47. Ibid., 310.

throughout the book, is treated as both a model for learning how to read the canonical texts and as a fascinating thinker in his own right.

In this way, I offer a style of reading the Vinaya texts as a kind of moral instruction. This entails trying to determine how factors of culpability work and how intentions are treated in this legal-ethical discourse. But it also suggests that more is going on in these cases than merely determining a judgment in a legal case. I see, additionally, that an ethical sensitivity is being cultivated, one that is attentive to an array of human concerns in the context of people finding themselves in difficult and challenging predicaments.

The Case of Sudinna

The rules begin, we have already seen, when Sudinna has sex with his former wife. The *vinayapāli* goes to some length to describe the circumstances of Sudinna's fall, beginning with his story prior to his ordination when by renouncing he has to defy his parents' wishes for him to maintain the family and its wealth. He is an only child, and his leaving the household will be catastrophic for them. After pleading with his parents three times to let him become a monk, he goes on a hunger strike to force them to consent to his decision. Realizing they will lose their son either way, they relent and he goes forth. After some time has passed (eight years, according to Buddhaghosa) and Sudinna has become particularly well established in the more austere practices of a forest-dwelling monk, he returns to their home to seek alms. When he returns, his parents and former wife beseech him to return to lay life. Even after much persistence on their part, he refuses to return to the household, but he does agree to have sex with his former wife so that the family will at least have an heir.

As it stands, the story in the *vinayapāli* presents Sudinna quite sympathetically. This is not a depraved monk who has fallen due to uncontrollable lust, but a committed and sincere monk who relents to his parents' pressure. The dictum that a child has to secure his parents' consent before ordaining stems from the acknowledgment that a child's decision to leave the family in this manner is often devastating. This acknowledgment came when the Buddha's own son Rāhula renounces the world (an episode to which Buddhaghosa eludes in his treatment of Sudinna).[48] When

48. Sp.i.204.

Rāhula renounces the world, his grandfather, the Buddha's own father, tells the Buddha of the pain that it causes parents when their sons leave them in this way (which is itself a quite arresting rebuke to the Buddha). Since "affection for sons pierces the skin, cuts the flesh, pierces the sinews, pierces the bone, and stays there pressing into the marrow," the loss of sons through renunciation causes "not a little sorrow" to parents.[49] The context for Sudinna's lapse is thus complex and multivocal: Sudinna is a sincere renunciant who is burdened by parents who have very genuine and sympathetic claims on him. It is not easy to condemn him.

If the story in the canonical account contextualizes the events in ways that are sympathetic to Sudinna's predicament, Buddhaghosa's treatment of the matter goes even further. Buddhaghosa refuses to allow us to see Sudinna's commitment to the monastic life as anything but resolute. Yet, the anguish of the parents, who view the loss of their only son to the monastic life as akin to death, is palpable. No detail in the *Suttavibhaṅga* is too small to garner additional emotional weight by Buddhaghosa. Why do the parents mention to Sudinna that he is their "only son"? It is emphasized, Buddhaghosa tells us, because they sought to stimulate his compassion.[50] We see their grief also in their initial refusal to allow him to ordain, relenting only after he forces them to: you will lose me either to the monkhood or to death through a hunger strike. Their reaction at this point is to relent, and they do so quite graciously, helping him to restore his strength with good food and drink; they bathe and massage his body and honor him as tears stream down their faces.[51]

We may look closely at a small later encounter between Sudinna and his father to see some of the emotional weight that Buddhaghosa sees in the original story. Sudinna has arrived for alms and is lingering outside the house where the maidservant, not recognizing him at first, has given him last night's leftovers. Upon recognizing him, she reports to the parents that Sudinna has come home. His father approaches him and is horrified to see him out by the wall eating leftover gruel; he is so shaken that all he can do is exclaim that his son is eating leftovers outside when he should be in his own house. He is so overwhelmed by his grief that he cannot say more, so he takes Sudinna by the arm and leads him into the

49. Vin.i.82–83.

50. Vin.iii.13; Sp. i.204.

51. Sp. i.206.

house. Why, Buddhaghosa asks, does Sudinna allow himself to be led by the arm into the house? Sudinna "becomes compliant by his father's affection," and out of compassion he agrees to take a meal there the following day since otherwise his father's sorrow will be extreme.[52] Buddhaghosa takes small, tangible details in the text and finds them fraught with the claims of a parent's love. And we can begin to see what Sudinna is up against even as he tries to pursue monastic austerity.

Picking up on a small phrase in the text that says that Sudinna saw no danger in having sex with his wife because the rules had not yet been laid down, Buddhaghosa insists that Sudinna had no idea that his having sex was forbidden. Had he known that it was not to be done, he never would have done the very thing that would "ruin his life."[53] Moreover, his thought in agreeing to it was that otherwise his family would never let up pestering him to rejoin lay life and he would never be able to practice the Dhamma in ease. But if they were given a child from him he could meet his obligations as a son, and they would leave him to practice in peace.[54] Ironically, *he commits the act in order to continue as a monk.*

These fine aspirations notwithstanding, Sudinna is riddled with anxiety and remorse after the deed is done, and he becomes "emaciated, discolored, pale, veins popping out, depressed, sluggish, suffering, miserable, remorseful, and oppressed," as the canonical text puts it, thereby hinting that at some level he was quite aware that what he did was wrong.[55] The deities witness the whole affair and, realizing that impurity has now entered the community of monks, give a big shout that there is no longer any place in the world free from evil actions. Sudinna realizes that his deed has gained him nothing because he is so remorseful that he cannot practice the holy life of the threefold training, that is, morality, concentration, and wisdom. Buddhaghosa depicts Sudinna's condition of remorse

52. Vin.iii.16; Sp.i.209.

53. Vin.iii.19; Sp.i.213.

54. Sp.i.212.

55. Vin.iii.19. Curiously, Buddhaghosa describes Sudinna's very first encounter with the Buddha's teaching when he decides to become a monk as his realization that the holy life entails the threefold *brahmacariya* (morality, concentration, and wisdom), which are incompatible with living in a household, and that lapsing even once imperils them (Sp i.203). This makes it difficult to see how later he would not have seen danger in having sex with his wife. Dhirasekera is quite skeptical of Buddhaghosa's view that Sudinna did not know he was doing wrong (*Buddhist Monastic Discipline*, 47), which is a point well taken, but I think Buddhaghosa wants to play up Sudinna's good intentions. He does not want to make it easy for us to condemn him.

quite vividly: sluggish, his mind is so withdrawn and lethargic that he can do nothing; he is oppressed, burdened, like an ass.[56] He discovers directly and empirically that the religious life is incompatible with the remorse that follows from sex.

In this last point, we see at work the idea that the rules of defeat indicate standards that are constitutive of the monastic life. To violate them means, simply, that one is no longer a monk; one has tried but has been defeated in wearing the robes and the practice of the religious life that they represent. The defeats are not punitive—there is no outside actor such as the Buddha punishing a monk by excommunication; even before the Buddha enters the scene to establish a rule, we see that to be defeated is to act in a manner so opposed to what monasticism is that one is simply no longer a monk thereafter. This is why there are no rituals or procedures for excommunication; in doing the action, one is leaving the monkhood, as Sudinna discovers for himself.[57] We also see how remorse follows naturally from a breach of *vinaya/sīla*, the reverse of the natural progression of nonremorse following from *sila/vinaya* that we explored earlier. Here we see a natural process of remorse following a violation of moral conduct that then cuts off further religious progress.

His fellow monks admonish Sudinna that the Buddha taught the destruction of the passions and the absence of desire, and they promptly report on him to the Buddha. Their scolding is nothing compared to the Buddha's, however, who calls him a "foolish man" and says that surely Sudinna should have known from the teachings against desire that sex is completely inappropriate for a monk. He accuses him of indolence, discontent, lust, and for making himself hard to sustain and support. Sudinna has fallen into low ways, "village Dhamma," lewd and wicked things. The Buddha rebukes him so harshly that Buddhaghosa feels moved to say that the Buddha scolded him out of compassion, just as parents sometimes need to scold their children harshly, even with terrible words (something we know about from chapter 1).[58] In the end, one is left with no ambiguity about the wrongfulness of this action and its incompatibility with the monastic life.

---

56. Vin.iii.19; Sp. i.215. Buddhaghosa frequently says that remorse from violating the precepts makes concentration impossible, as, for example, Sp. i.237.

57. Dhirasekera, *Buddhist Monastic Discipline*, 10.

58. Vin.iii.20; Sp. i.220.

What can we say about intention from this account? Janet Gyatso has noted that Sudinna's motivations do not seem to be terribly problematic. He is not interested in passion, and he has sex purely for instrumental reasons to help his parents and to free himself of their entreaties. It is his *behavior* that is problematic—the doing of the action—rather than the motivation underlying it or reason behind it. She says, "It is still incumbent upon Sudinna, who in his earlier days had been particularly struck by the impossibility of leading the holy life as a householder, to confront the brute fact that *he performed householder activity*—no matter what the mitigating circumstances, and no matter what his particular intention or subjective state."[59] In Gyatso's reading, sex with women is the worst violation because of its "practical upshot: marriage, children, the householder's life; in short, *saṃsāra*."[60] His action is simply incompatible with monasticism, regardless of why he did it. Intentionality is narrowly construed in the Sudinna case—he consented to it, and he knew what he was doing (even if he did not know it was a violation, he most certainly knew he was having sex). Issues of motivation or the reasons given for actions, here as elsewhere in the rules, are largely irrelevant for determining culpability.[61]

The Buddha's censure demonstrates that Sudinna is culpable and that his action is contrary in every way to the monastic life, and thus his condemnation is strong. The Sudinna story precedes the account of the 10 reasons for the rules, and the Buddha shows how his act is counter to the institutional, moral, and religious values of monasticism. In terms of establishing a clear precedent for what constitutes a violation, the Buddha's harsh condemnation of Sudinna is apt. But why does the story itself, and particularly Buddhaghosa's development of it, take pains to present Sudinna's situation in such a sympathetic and multivocal light? If the message of this rule is simply that sexual intercourse with women is

---

59. Gyatso, "Sex," 281. Holt, in contrast, takes a dimmer view of Sudinna's motivations, arguing that his act means that he retained a passion (*rāga*) for riches so he sought an heir for his family (Holt, *Discipline*, 90).

60. Gyatso, "Sex," 280.

61. An interesting exception to this is the case of the monk who released a pig from a trap. He is not culpable of theft because his aim was compassion (*kāruññādhippāya*) (Vin.iii.62). The motive of compassion does not work, however, in the case of the monks who praise the beauty of death (that is, encourage suicide) to a gravely ill monk out of compassion for him; they are guilty of a *pārājika* for murder (Vin.iii.80). One of the key differences in the two accounts is that in the latter case, the monks have remorse. Remorse is a clue that one has acted wrongly.

prohibited, then there are more expedient ways of saying so than telling Sudinna's sad tale with the rich detail and feeling that the *vinayapāli* suggests and Buddhaghosa embellishes.

Both the *vinayapāli* and Buddhaghosa are not concerned merely with fastening onto an ethical or legal judgment of a case, but with the cultivation of a broader moral education. We can see some of this moral education in noticing how Buddhaghosa trains us to attend to the emotions of the main players, such as the parents' anguish and loss, Sudinna's yielding to them out of compassion, and his visceral grief and remorse following his action. We see also complex treatments of motivation and the reasons offered for Sudinna's action and their ultimate irrelevance from the standpoint of his culpability. We also observe a humaneness in Buddhaghosa's treatment of the complex ties between parents and children and how they are explored in small, almost imperceptible moments, such as in the nature of the encounter between Sudinna and his father when words fail the father and a small gesture of taking his son by the arm to bring him into his home is explored with great tenderness. The training one is gaining by this exposition is a moral sensitivity and a deep and nuanced moral anthropology. One suspects that a monk trained in the particular details of such cases will greet human affairs with a wiser eye.[62]

Even in the few details we have had the space to explore, we see that Buddhaghosa is deeply interested in questions of motivation, not because a transgressor's motivations will determine the outcome of the case, but because trying to discern people's motivations requires a closer look at them and the predicaments, conflicts, and confusions they face. Buddhaghosa does not want *vinaya* experts to rush to hasty and uncharitable judgments in human affairs. The moral stature he attributes to them that we considered earlier in this chapter is earned by a careful and generous study of human beings. He picks up on the fact that the other monks reported Sudinna's act to the Buddha. Why did they do so? They reported on him neither because they wanted to ingratiate themselves with the Buddha nor because they wanted to get Sudinna expelled. Rather, they

62. Rebecca French describes a legal anthropology in pre-1959 Tibet that is similar in some respects to what we see here, in which the legal system is infused with moral values, and a proper legal education involves standards of moral self-regulation, discernment of emotion and motivation, and close and careful considerations of character (*The Golden Yoke*, see especially ch. 6).

simply realized that an impurity had occurred in the community, and they were eager that the Buddha now lay down the rules.[63]

Lest a reader of the rule be quick to condemn Sudinna's parents, Buddhaghosa fills out their predicament with detail. Their worry is that with their only child gone to the monastery, they will be heirless and upon their death their property will go to the Licchavi rulers, presumably leaving the extended family and their childless daughter-in-law in penury.[64] These are not craven people trying to lure back Sudinna to a life of wantonness, but ordinary laypeople whose loss of their son is heartfelt and whose concern for the continuation of their household and property is entirely legitimate for them. The larger implication of Buddhaghosa's treatment of people's motivations here is to suggest that it is possible for someone to break even the most important monastic rules without being entirely condemnable. And the people involved in the narrative are complex human beings, vulnerable and dependent in their relationships with others—in other words, real human beings in very real and often not fully resolvable predicaments.

Before leaving Sudinna's case, we may use this first instance of sexual lapse to explore briefly the distinctive dimensions of intentions in cases of sexual transgression. It is in the context of sexual transgressions, the intricacies of which were a topic of meticulous attention at both the *vinayapāli* and commentarial levels, that we see the notion of consent (*sādiyati*) emerge.[65] While having good motives or reasons is not exculpatory when a person knowingly engages in sexual acts, the lack of consent is: the nun Uppalavaṇṇā, raped in her forest hut, is not culpable of a violation.[66] Buddhaghosa defines consent to sexual activity as the presence of a thought of sex (*sevanacitta*) and agreeing or giving in to it (*adhivāseti*) during the act.[67] These two dimensions of having the thought and putting it

63. Sp. i.218.

64. Sp. i.212.

65. There are numerous instances of the word *consent* in the case law of *pārājika* 1 concerning a variety of sexual infractions of men and women, such as rape and monks being forced by their enemies to have sex with women (Vin.iii.29–30). While consent is an important idea particularly in sexual contexts, it is sometimes used in other areas, as when monastics are said to consent to accepting money, for example.

66. Vin.iii.35.

67. Sp. i.261.

into action are the "bridge moment," as Gyatso puts it, that conjoins desire and physical realization.[68] Neither one taken separately—merely having unrealized desires or the body acting entirely reflexively—constitutes a violation, as the many cases she explores demonstrate.[69] She also suggests that much of the discussion of sexual transgressions in the *Suttavibhaṅga* "is exactly about trying to determine what functions as such a bridge," exploring how to determine precisely where intention is put into action in a domain of human behavior that often admits of great subtlety. Moreover, what is at stake in the moment of decision, consent, or refusal is membership in the monastic community itself, that is, how one is defining or constituting oneself.

Consent is particularly relevant in many of the rules for nuns. Often it is a man initiating sexual contact, rather than the nun, and at issue is whether she consented.[70] As is well known, the nuns' rules are much stricter and harsher in this regard than the monks' rules: nuns, unlike monks, may be defeated due to the presence of sexual contact (short of intercourse) that is perceived to involve their consent (though not necessarily their instigation). How is their consent established? Often it is determined to occur if pleasure is thought to be present, as we see in the first of the nun's additional defeats.[71] The idea of consent, as in our own legal discourse, is fraught with gender politics and demonstrates how opaque (and suspicious) women's sexual desire and intentions were to the male authors who sought to regulate them through these texts.[72]

---

68. Gyatso, "Sex," especially 285–88. In a certain sense, this is restating the identity of intention and karma; what is relevant morally is the intention reaching the doorway of action, in the idiom of the last chapter.

69. Cases of nocturnal emissions of semen while dreaming are particularly challenging according to this criteria. They involve both intention (*cetanā*) and a physical act but do not rise to the level of transgression because they occur in dreams, which are not, in some very important sense, *real*. The commentary says that dreams are a matter to be dealt with in Abhidhamma, not Vinaya, as they are, it seems, mental phenomena (Vin.iii.111–12; Sp.iii.520).

70. For instance, among the four additional defeats for nuns, the first is a case of a nun who consents to inappropriate sexual activity (literally, physical contact between the collarbone and the kneecaps) with a man (Vin.iv.211–15; Sp.iv.900–2). See Shih (*Controversies over Buddhist Nuns*) on the extra rules for nuns and how female desire and consent are construed in these texts.

71. Vin.iv.213–15; Sp.iv.901. See Shih, *Controversies over Buddhist Nuns*, 32–63.

72. This is an area for further exploration, but see Shih, *Controversies over Buddhist Nuns*; Horner, *Women under Primitive Buddhism*; Collins, "The Body in Theravāda Buddhist Monasticism," 190, and "Remarks on the Third Precept," 269; Gyatso, "One Plus One

Dhaniya Builds a Hut

The second case of defeat concerns a monk who, like Sudinna, is not an obviously wicked character. The monk Dhaniya violates what becomes the prohibition of theft by taking building materials that do not properly belong to him. Huxley says: "If the word 'thief' conjures up images of a pickpocket or shoplifter, think again: Dhaniya's offence was to build his meditation hut using some government material that hadn't been cleared through the appropriate bureaucratic channels."[73] He comes to take these materials after a run of misfortune in acquiring a meditation hut. He first made himself a grass hut, but it was dismantled three times by women gathering grass. Then he made himself a mud hut, which, since he had been a potter's son and could work with clay, turned out to be quite lovely. The Buddha chastised him for this, though, since using mud destroys tiny creatures, and anyone who makes such a hut cannot be compassionate, kind, or merciful. It is at this point that Dhaniya goes in search of wood materials and asks the overseer in a lumberyard for extra wood, claiming that the king desires to give such things to recluses.

Later this overseer is brought before the king on charges of theft, and Dhaniya intervenes and assumes responsibility. The king, unwilling to flog a monk even though he regards him as shameless and unscrupulous, lets him off with a stern warning not to do it again. But people are annoyed, vexed, and angry at the monks, whom they call "shameless, immoral liars," because of Dhaniya's action; they are piqued because he has been pardoned only because he is a monk, even while his actions were not in accordance with what they deem to be monastic propriety.[74] A group of "well-behaved monks"—whose scruples and discomfiture with other monks' failings are assigned great weight throughout this literature—also becomes angry at Dhaniya for damaging the reputation of the Saṅgha.

When the Buddha confirmed with Dhaniya that these events had occurred, he rebuked him, citing some of the reasons we have already seen for the rules—his action does nothing to increase the faith of the faithful

Makes Three" and "Sex." Some discussion of a difficult case of a false accusation of rape made by a nun against a monk (a kind of he-said-she-said case), though not dealing centrally with the issue of intention, can be found in von Hinüber, "Buddhist Law According to the Theravāda Vinaya II" and Hüsken, "The Application of the Vinaya Term *nāsanā*."

73. Huxley, "Buddhist Case Law on Theft," 314.

74. Vin.iii.44.

or gladden nonbelievers. The Buddha lays down the rule: "Whatever monk having taken by theft what is not given in such a way that kings seize this thief for stealing, and flog, jail, or exile him, denouncing him 'you are a thief, fool, rascal, robber,' then that monk, taking what has not been given, is defeated, no longer in communion."[75]

The case of Dhaniya illustrates how important the image of the monastic ideal is and how the rules are designed to protect it. We might at first think that the paradigmatic case against theft would involve a culprit who is driven by greed, just as we might assume at first that Sudinna's failing was a matter of lust. But in Dhaniya's case, the considerations are rather that he has gotten in trouble with the king, stirred up ire against the Saṅgha, and made well-behaved monks uncomfortable. At worst, we can say that there is a shamelessness in his pursuit of a meditation hut that leads him first to damage creatures in making one of mud (which then becomes a lesser offense) and then to acquire building materials inappropriately.

Even so, he is hardly without scruples. The *vinayapāli* mentions and Buddhaghosa expands that when his fellow monks tore down his mud hut at the denunciation of mud huts by the Buddha, Dhaniya readily acquiesced once he learned that the dismantling was ordered by the Buddha. And the moment he heard that the overseer was in danger because of his own action of taking the wood, Dhaniya is filled with horror that someone else should be harmed by his own wood-seeking gambit, and he immediately comes forward to accept responsibility.[76]

Both the *vinayapāli* and Buddhaghosa are constantly interested in how people in the future will interpret the rules. One thing that the cases of Dhaniya and Sudinna suggest is that these flawed but still decent characters deliver the rules with particular clarity and force, making it difficult for future monks to say that they have good reasons or motives for having sex or taking something not explicitly given. There are plenty of bad monks about, most notably the notorious "band of six," who violate rules out of the crassest and lowest motives. Such monks could easily be made the paradigmatic cases of wrongdoing. But the problem with bad people doing bad things is that they are easily condemned, and good people do not see their own motivations, rationales, and reasons in the bad actions

75. Vin.iii.45.

76. Sp. ii.294.

of bad people. Sudinna and Dhaniya, because they have flawed but still sympathetic rationales for their actions, provide a more complex moral education.

As Huxley has shown, the case law that follows this first rule on theft has a kind of expository function that works variously to inspire confidence in the rulings, to establish precedent, to illustrate legal reasoning, and to clarify the nature of ownership, all of which are trainings in a legal education.[77] Thanissaro Bhikkhu has argued that the working out of all the nuances on theft is so complex because there are so many forms that ownership and theft can take, including what is meant by taking something, to what extent the value of the object is relevant, and what is the nature of ownership of things belonging to the Saṅgha collectively. These matters, while interesting, are largely matters of legal instruction that have been amply discussed by Thanissaro and Huxley, and we can leave them here.

The Case of the Murderous and Suicidal Monks

This case, the third rule of defeat prohibiting killing human beings, was initiated by a rather bizarre set of circumstances. The account begins in the *vinayapāli* with the Buddha teaching the monks at Vesāli about meditations on the disgusting, that is, how to counter lust and attachment by contemplating the repulsiveness of the body. He then goes into retreat for two weeks. The monks have been so convinced of the frailty of the body that they become disgusted by their bodies and filled with loathing for them, and they begin to kill one another to be rid of life and their attachments to *saṃsāra*. Some also approach the false monk Migalaṇḍaka and beseech him to end their lives. He does so with a large knife and then, while he is washing the knife in the river, feels remorse. He realizes that no benefit or goodness can come from such killing (again we see that remorse frequently kicks in and offers an affective guide to identifying wrongness of actions). But one of Māra's wicked minions approaches him and dissuades him from his remorse, arguing that he has in fact helped the slain monks attain release from *saṃsāra*. Migalaṇḍaka then decides that what he has done is highly meritorious, and he goes from monastery to monastery slaughtering monks.

77. Huxley, "Buddhist Case Law on Theft," 319.

When the Buddha returns from retreat, he notices that the ranks of the monks are depleted and asks Ānanda why. Upon hearing the full explanation, the Buddha assembles the Saṅgha and teaches contemplation of the breath. He then prohibits monks from taking life: "Whatever monk should deliberately (*sañcicca*) destroy the life of a human being or, seeking [death], bring a weapon [for another to do so], is defeated, no longer in communion."[78]

Buddhaghosa does several things with this account that change and deepen our understanding of what is going on here. He first emphasizes the advantages that accrue from meditations on the disgusting, since they are an entrance to *samādhi* and lead to the *jhānas.* He contextualizes these meditations because, if they are wrongly understood, they may lead to calamitous results. He then provides a backstory of the monks of Vesāli. In a previous life, they were 500 hunters who killed deer. Though they had been reborn in bad births for this violent karma, they had also done good things, and they now enjoyed human births as monks. But their karmic retribution had not been fully exhausted, and their murders in this account are attributed ultimately to their bad karma from hunting deer. Buddhaghosa says that the Buddha knew that this was the case, foresaw their impending deaths, and was also aware that he would be powerless to prevent them. He taught meditations on the disgusting to them not because he wanted to commend death, but to free their minds from attachment prior to their deaths so that they would have a good rebirth. And then he went on retreat so that when they were killing one another, people would not accuse the Buddha of claiming to be omniscient even while knowing and allowing his monks to kill and be killed. If he is in deep meditation away from these events, he cannot be blamed.[79]

These are extraordinary revelations. First, we learn that 500 monks are involved, raising this incident to the level of a massacre. Second, we learn that there is a karmic inevitability to the proceedings that the Buddha is aware of but unable to prevent. As much as the monastic life is premised on self-mastery and control, the inexorable grip of karma overrides the Buddha's own powers, not to speak of the agency of the well-meaning monks themselves (some of whom, we learn, are streamwinners, once-returners,

78. Vin.iii.71. The account of this case is Vin.iii.68–71; Sp.ii.392–446.

79. Sp.ii.397.

nonreturners and even arhats!)[80] under the sway of their own karmic past. And third, while the Buddha cannot stop this suicidal massacre from occurring, he does orchestrate the particulars of the grisly affair in a manner that will ensure that he appears unaware of the slaughter of 500 of his followers.

Buddhaghosa also has a substantial amount to say on the meditation teachings the Buddha offers here, both the meditations on the disgusting and on the breath. He describes how breathing contemplations work to bring the mind to calmness. One of the things he mentions is that development of breathing contemplation allows a monk to accomplish several things: such a monk does not violate the rules, he confesses if he does violate them, and he is not oppressed with defilements.[81] This shows how breathing exercises support morality; it is not just that *sīla* and *vinaya* make concentration possible, as we have already observed, but that meditation makes *sīla* and *vinaya*—that is, the nonviolation of moral rules—possible. He also emphasizes the nature of meditations on loving-kindness to the Saṅgha, which seem particularly pertinent to this case. In this section, he is pointing to the whole system, outlined at even greater length in the *Visuddhimagga*, of the 40 meditation practices that calm the mind (*samatha*) and make possible insight meditation (*vipassana*). In other words, what might appear like a digression on meditation is rather part of a larger teaching on the whole—the entire ethical and soteriological path of which discipline is the foundation (even as discipline itself is supported by meditation).

Buddhaghosa spends a bit of time parsing the word *deliberately* in the statement of the defeat, and here we get a quite nuanced language of intentionality. He follows a gloss by the word commentary in the *vinayapāli* that defines *deliberately* (*sañcicca*) as "knowingly (*jānanta*), fully knowing (*sañjānanta*), purposely (*cecca*), going through with it (*abhivitaritvā*), transgressing (*vītikkama*)." He adds several touches to this indicating that

---

80. Ibid. We must assume that the more advanced among the monks did not engage in killing or beseeching Migalaṇḍaka to kill; they were slaughtered in their huts when Migalaṇḍaka went on his killing spree. But generally and, I think, importantly, the account itself does not make much of a distinction between the victims and perpetrators of this massacre. Mills ("The Case of the Murdered Monks") describes, but does not resolve, some of the many challenges and oddities of this case. One possible interpretation is that Migalaṇḍaka and perhaps some of the other monks were suffering deleterious psychological effects of the meditation, which may be a rare reaction to meditation practice, but one that is anecdotally mentioned in the sources and in meditation contexts today.

81. Sp.ii.415. The section on meditation forms a large part of Buddhaghosa's treatment of this case: Spii. 404–35.

intention and knowledge of one's action admit of fine degrees or stages. He sees the verbal form *intend* (*ceteti*) in *sañcicca* and an added prefix of *sa* that adds an element of eagerness to the intention. *Knowingly* means that one knows that life is present, and "fully knowing" is that one has the thought "I will take life." *Purposely* means "intending with the intention (*cetanā*) to kill, planning." "Going through with it" means one commits it or orders it to be done, crushing any hesitation.[82] He also parses the language of "thought and intention" (*cittasaṅkappa*) in the *vinayapāli* as bringing together perception (*saññā*), intention (*cetanā*), and aim (*adhippāya*).[83] A full intention, then, would require that one be aware that life is present and will be destroyed, one intends to destroy it, and one aims at the person's death.

Also of interest for us are the mitigating factors described as the *Suttavibhaṅga* works through other cases of killing. Here a standard formula is given (with small variations) in most of the rules: "there is no offense if it was done not deliberately, unknowingly, by one not aiming at death, by one who is mad, and by the first offender."[84] Buddhaghosa clarifies: someone has been killed, but it is not done deliberately means that one does not intend "I am killing someone by this attack." "Not knowing" means that one does not realize that "by this I will kill someone." "Not aiming at death" means that one does not want the person to die. And those who are mad or are the first offenders never incur a penalty. We see in this language (and similar language throughout the rules) that intentions are of paramount importance in assigning culpability and that they are a matter of several factors of knowledge and perception, desire or aim, and soundness of mind. Both the *vinayapāli* and Buddhaghosa provide examples of cases that demonstrate how these factors work in practice, considering cases of euthanasia and assisted suicide, accidental killings, cases of mistaken identity (as when a monk intends to kill a human but kills an animal instead), and verbal acts urging others to kill or describing how they might do so.[85]

---

82. Sp.ii.436–37; Vin.iii.72–73.

83. Sp.ii.442; Vin.iii.73.

84. Vin.iii.78; Sp.ii.463.

85. Thanissaro, *The Buddhist Monastic Code*, 66–78. Harvey, "Vinaya Principles for Assigning Degrees of Culpability."

The most intriguing dimension of the defeat against killing is situating it within a story, particularly the strange backstory of these monks' karmic past. If we take the larger karmic context that Buddhaghosa provides together with these fine distinctions about intention, we are confronted by a fascinating juxtaposition of agency and patiency. The monks act as a consequence of a karmic heritage of which nobody is aware except the Buddha and that makes their actions inevitable. Yet they are culpable and accountable for such inevitable, causally determined actions. And within this larger context of karmic determinacy, we see a highly nuanced parsing of agents acting deliberately, with knowledge of what they are doing, and apparently (to themselves and others) acting freely. For Buddhaghosa, these two accounts of the action are allowed to exist side-by-side, neither undermining the force of the other.

The Case of the Boastful Monks

The fourth defeat concerns a group of monks who during a famine plot among themselves strategies to increase their take of alms. They decide on a plan to praise their religious achievements to the laity—some lay claim to have attained the fourth *jhāna*, others to have become streamwinners, still others claim to be arhats—so that people will be inspired to give ample alms to them, and they can spend the rains retreat in comfort. And it works! At the end of the rains, they visit the Buddha, who asks them why they look so robust when other monks are thin and weak from want. They report to the Buddha their strategy with its lies and deception. The Buddha rebukes them strongly and likens them to thieves: to take almsfood on the pretext of being spiritually advanced is to acquire it by stealing. The fourth defeat is laid down:

> Whatever monk claiming for himself a transcendent state free of covetousness that consists of knowing and seeing truly the noble wisdom, saying "thus I know, thus I see," so that later, he, whether or not he is questioned carefully by others, is miserable and seeking purification, says "friends, not knowing, I said I know, not seeing, I said I see—vainly, falsely, carelessly," is defeated, no longer in communion.[86]

86. Vin.iii.90.

The rather convoluted articulation of this rule builds a sense of remorse or misery into the rule itself. Whether or not he is found out, a monk in violation of this rule will find himself in a state of misery and will wish to come clean and confess to his fellows. The *vinayapāli* glosses the sense of *miserable* or, more literally, *fallen* as "having evil wishes, he claims a transcendent state that is not real or true because of those evil wishes."[87] Buddhaghosa works this in the direction of a rather complicated psychological state by quoting from the Abhidhamma *Vibhaṅga*: "a certain monk though immoral wants people to know him as virtuous," and he becomes "defeated, overwhelmed, undone because of those evil wishes."[88] Buddhaghosa is also interested in the mental state of the monk who might be closely questioned by others: if he is truly an arhat, he has nothing to fear, but the hypocrite would be terrified—"frozen in fear with hair standing on end"—at the prospect of his claims being investigated.[89]

As in all of the four defeats, the presence of remorse or some element of anguish is a key indicator of the wrongness of the action that occurs, even before the perpetrator is rebuked by the Buddha and the rule laid down. Consider Sudinna's wasting away, Dhaniya's horror at learning that the overseer is in danger, and Migalaṇḍaka's initial remorse at the river. Their anguish demonstrates a moral empiricism—people know when they have committed something gravely wrong quite independently of rules, and they know this through their emotions. The remorse can be overridden (and often is, as in the case of Migalaṇḍaka), and it can be absent (particularly in the lesser infractions) among the shameless.[90] Its presence in the defeats (which are, of course, violations of four of the *sīla* precepts) indicates that a moral order has been violated and there is a deeper awareness of this affectively. But while remorse can be said to be useful here in indicating the presence of an immoral action, it does not have any particularly redemptive or reformative value. Remorse (*kukkucca, vippaṭisāra*) is a problematic condition of mind of worrying and fretting that cuts off religious progress. In Abhidhamma terms, *kukkucca* is

87. Vin.iii.92.

88. Sp.ii.492; quoting from Vibh 351.

89. Sp.ii.492.

90. A shameless person (*alajjī*) is someone who commits offenses deliberately (*sañcicca*), hides his or her offenses, and follows the wrong course (Vin.v.158). Minoru Hara has shown the linkages in broader South Asian discourse between *vinaya* and shame ("A Note on Vinaya").

a "bad factor" (*akusaladhamma*) and one of the five hindrances (*nīvaraṇa*) of the mind.[91] In his Abhidhamma commentary, Buddhaghosa says that "since one cannot undo a bad deed nor do a good deed that was neglected, returning again to it in remorse is ugly" and, more viscerally, "it scratches the mind like the point of an awl on a metal bowl."[92]

The moral instruction developed in the four cases encourages us to attend to the subjectivity of remorse as an acute experience of one's patiency, the ways one is subject to previous conditions of one's own making, something one cannot undo. In remorse, we also observe the theme of time: remorse, and the anticipation of remorse, is the work time does in bringing to the surface the subjective reality and experience of one's past actions and omissions. If intended wicked actions were not experienced as painful at the time of committing them, time will ensure that their pain will arrive. Remorse thus enforces the dictum that we experience subjectively and internally the quality of our actions. We see in and through time the unfolding of conditions, and so in remorse we see patiency writ large. But while it can lead to self-disclosure and to awareness of that very patiency, remorse is not an edifying moral factor (as Abhidhamma discourse depicts morally good factors) and does not constitute or lead to reform or self-transformation (important to Vinaya); it is not a key component of agency because it entails merely a crippling awareness of past wrongdoing, marked most poignantly in these four cases with the affective and legal experience of defeat.

What makes this particular violation of the boasting monks rise to the level of a defeat—other lies are considered lesser infractions—is that it, like the other defeats, strikes at the heart of the ethical and institutional foundations of the Saṅgha. For a monk to claim arhatship, thereby secure the esteem of others, and then be observed backsliding is to bring the entire monastic project into question. To earn alms by making extravagant claims about one's attainments is, in effect, to steal them. To falsely claim higher wisdom because one wishes to fill the belly is to cheapen

91. I have been treating both *vippaṭisāra* and *kukkucca* interchangeably as "remorse," as in fact they are often treated in the texts. More technically, *kukkucca* has as its characteristic regretting, its function is sorrow at what has been done, its manifestation is remorse (*vippaṭisāra*), and its proximate cause is what has been done, according the Buddhaghosa's Abhidhamma commentary (As 258). For more on this mental experience, see Heim, "Shame and Apprehension."

92. As 384.

the achievements of the Buddha, which, Buddhaghosa reminds us, were acquired only after four incalculable eras and 100,000 eons of earnest spiritual growth.[93] This is an action, according to Buddhaghosa, that is clearly "blamable for the world"; it is done with full awareness and with an *akusalacitta*.[94]

There are several amendments to the rule. There is no offense if claims are made "due to the conceit of overestimation, without aiming to boast, or by one who is mad, deranged, in pain, or by the first offender."[95] One not "aiming to boast" is someone pursuing vigorously the holy life in front of others but not intending to boast or be hypocritical about it.[96] And we have seen that first offenders, mad people, and now here, those deranged or in pain, are not culpable. Those guilty merely of conceit are not culpable. There are several varieties of conceit, but what makes this particular conceit, "overestimation," relevant here is that it involves a false and prideful construal of one's spiritual achievements. One thinks one is more advanced than one is. This conceit, though problematic, is not the same as making false claims of one's spiritual advancement to acquire alms. Rather, it involves a false perception of one's accomplishments and an attendant pride in them, but it is not the falsehood of a truly immoral person.[97]

Both the *vinayapāli* and Buddhaghosa describe cases in which monks may misrepresent themselves in ways that do not rise to the level of a full offense. If one allows others to suspect one's high achievement but does not make explicit claims, one is not defeated. If a monk makes claims and no one believes him or understands what he is saying, then the action has not reached completion, and he is not culpable. The *vinayapāli* says that the violation concerns "deliberate lies" (*sampajānamusā*), which means

93. Sp.ii.483.

94. Sp.ii.502.

95. Vin.iii.100.

96. Sp.ii.502.

97. In his commentary on the *Vibhaṅga*'s treatment of the conceit of overestimation (Vibh 355), Buddhaghosa says that it does not occur to noble disciples, people of bad conduct (since they are not eager to attain noble qualities anyway), or virtuous monks who are just lazy. Rather, it occurs to virtuous monks who are sincere in their meditation practice but reckon they have accomplished more than they have (Vibh-a 488; Ñāṇamoli, *The Dispeller of Delusion*, vol. 2, 245–46). For more on this and other kinds of conceit, see Heim, "The Conceit of Self-Loathing."

that one knows one is lying before one speaks, while lying, and afterward. To elaborate on this, Buddhaghosa says that it is possible that one can plan to lie, but when one opens the mouth, the truth pops out.[98] In bringing out a lie, we can be conflicted against ourselves, planning one thing while doing another. The emphasis is on fully aware lies from start to finish.

This case thus allows a deeper examination of the moral psychology of lies, which is most penetrating in the case of self-deception. As we learn how to read the canonical and commentarial narrative settings for each of the four defeats, we not only discern the rich complexities of case law but also learn to seek deeper psychological meaning in the fundamental concerns of human life: sorting out the irreconcilable demands of family life and monasticism in the case of Sudinna, the psychology of acquisitiveness in Dhaniya, the long and inexorable reach of karma and its violence into the present intentions of the murderous monks, the intricacies of conceit and deception in the boastful monks. Never far removed from these moral and psychological concerns are institutional matters, as the Buddha is forever pragmatic in establishing a community that can survive the moral frailties of its members and go into the future. Reading the rules with Buddhaghosa suggests that proper legal and moral education begins not so much with rules but the contextual and narrative particulars in which they emerge.

Disciplinary Culture: Techniques of Admonishment and Confession

We may sum up what we have learned so far about intentions in Vinaya texts in the following way. When arriving at ethical and legal judgments of culpability in serious moral cases, it is the intention or thought in acting that matters. To count as a serious transgression, an action must be done knowingly, with consent, deliberately. A person's motivation for committing an infraction is usually not relevant to the judgment of the case. But motivations and the reasons why people do what they do are not unimportant to the larger body of moral instruction offered by both the *Suttavibhaṅga* and Buddhaghosa, an instruction that goes substantially beyond learning the criteria that decide legal cases. Instead, it is important to know the circumstances in which a violation is committed, and a

98. Sp. ii.499; Vin.iii.93.

vinaya expert will track the motivations and emotions that prompt people to do what they do. This training in moral psychology in Vinaya goes in a different direction than the reductive and analytical phenomenology of Abhidhamma. In the Vinaya cases, narrative and biography provide the content and context for examining human character and disposition and the nature of our entanglements with others.

There remains one further arena to look for agency and its conditions, and it lies anterior to the operations of all of these processes of intention and motivation. That is, the Vinaya is concerned not only with arriving at judgments of discrete cases but also with a larger way of life or disciplinary culture that, ideally, comes to constitute in an essential way the practitioners who adhere to it. That is, well before we decide, consent, or agree to do things, and before we marshal our reasons and rationales for doing them, we are constituted or disposed to be and to act in certain ways by the institutions we are a part of, by the traditions and cultures that circumscribe us, and by the people with whom we are in contact. We have seen Buddhaghosa's recognition of these diverse conditions before, in the previous chapter when he considers in a broad way the habits, traditions, and varied external promptings that can go into a good or bad thought. He recognizes that we are shaped by many forces prior to our engaging in particular intentional actions.

Vinaya discourse is a particularly useful body of material for tracking these forces because it is quite explicit about how its disciplinary culture works. The Vinaya literature identifies the forms of subjectivity that it encourages and the techniques it uses to shape monastic identity. Recall, for example, the *Parivāra* passage defining disciplinary practice in terms of the actual thoughts one will come to have: "I won't do this anymore." In this final section, I turn to technologies or techniques of self-formation that we can discern in these texts, borrowing language and ideas from Michel Foucault. This strategy can help us to see more clearly how the Vinaya literature provides additional supports for monastic life beyond simply its prohibitions. These supports or techniques make possible certain kinds of subjectivity that in turn shape intentions. Community processes—the expectations and watchful eyes of others, admonishment, public confession, and the ritual practices that formalize these—discipline subjectivity in ways prior to, and in certain ways, constitutive of intentional action.

One of the firmest impressions one gets in reading the Vinaya is of the distinctively communal nature of this way of life. Only the most advanced monks may live independently of other monks.[99] Silent retreats are prohibited.[100] Relationships and duties between teachers and students are matters of utmost importance.[101] The constant presence and watchful gaze of "well-behaved monks" is ever before the monastic subject, who learns to become alert to their considerations and sensibilities; their uprightness stands in sharp contrast to the instructive folly and wickedness of, for example, the notorious gang of six. Monks are enjoined to imitate admired monks,[102] to train under teachers, to become admired teachers themselves, to admonish others, and to be admonished. Formal legal actions such as determining verdicts, ordination, meting out penalties, and rehabilitating offenders are corporate matters involving the assembly of monks.[103] And the rhetoric of communal purity is at work throughout.

One particularly striking example of this rhetoric is an incident in the *Cullavagga* in which the Buddha is beseeched by Ānanda late into the night on the occasion of the twice-monthly Uposatha ceremony to recite with the monks the Pāṭimokkha. The Buddha remains silent through three entreaties until finally he says, simply, "Ānanda, the assembly is not pure." Moggallāna, who can read minds, immediately casts about to discover the guilty presence among them. He approaches the miscreant and instructs him to leave. Ignored, Moggallāna is ultimately forced to toss him out bodily. The Buddha observes that there are "strange and marvelous things" about the great ocean that make it similar to the Dhamma-Vinaya. The great ocean deepens gradually without sharp precipices as one enters it; it is stable and does not overflow its borders; it does not tolerate a corpse, casting it from its body at first opportunity; all rivers flowing into it lose their individuality; though rivers and rain flow into it, its fullness is not affected; it has one taste throughout; and it is brimming with treasures and great beings. So, too, the Dhamma-Vinaya: the practice is gradual, its rules are stable, and it does not tolerate a transgressor, casting him out at first opportunity. Monks and nuns joining it lose their individual social identities, and the Saṅgha has "one taste." Though

---

99. Vin.i.80.

100. Vin.i.159.

101. The *Mahāvagga* goes to great length describing duties of teachers and students, Vin.i.60–67, for example.

102. Vin.i.98: "The good follows through imitating."

103. Horner, *The Book of the Discipline*, vol. 4, xix.

many join and many within it attain final *nibbāna*, the Dhamma-Vinaya becomes neither fuller nor emptier. And of course, many treasures and great beings are found within. Thereupon the Buddha states that he will no longer observe the Uposatha with the monks and that they are to do so without him. This first instance of an impure community on the occasion of the Uposatha makes it inappropriate for the Buddha to be present. Hereafter, the monks must do what they can to regulate themselves through the communal recitation.[104]

There is much here to observe in the imagery of this collective: its uniformity and stability, its effacement of individual identity, its tossing out of transgressors. (We may also recall how the Abhidhamma was likened to the ocean as an expression of its endlessness in the previous chapter.) Moreover, that the Buddha is hereafter not present at the Uposatha reinforces the way the community regulates itself. While he lays down the rules as they come up, he does not enforce them (leaving to Moggallāna the unpleasant duty of ferreting out the miscreant and driving him off). The status of a Buddha situates him far above a tribunal context of meting out justice or enforcing the rules. Since the rules govern but, more importantly, *constitute* the community, the Buddha may remain in dignified aloofness from the business of purifying the assembly, and he treats the Dhamma-Vinaya like a natural phenomenon, constituted with the same "strange and marvelous" qualities as the ocean. This is simultaneously a highly cultivated and contrived community that yet operates through processes likened to natural phenomena.

Turning to Foucault can offer a way to understand how a disciplinary culture of restraint, tied to institutional forces with their rules, laws, and constraints, may be understood as enhancing, rather than inhibiting, agency. Foucault defined "technologies of the self" as permitting "individuals by their own means or with the help of others a certain number of operations on their own bodies and souls, thoughts, conduct, and way of being, so as to transform themselves in order to attain a certain state of happiness, purity, wisdom, perfection, or immortality."[105] In addition to the rules concerning the violations of immoral actions that we have been considering, we can identify several other technologies made possible only through the communal

104. Vin.ii.235–41.

105. Foucault, "Technologies of the Self," 18. I have also learned much on the role of disciplinary practices and ethical formation from Asad, *Genealogies of Religion*, and Mahmood, *Politics of Piety*.

disciplinary and pedagogical practices of the Saṅgha that, the texts suggest, allow people to transform themselves as subjects and as agents.

The Vinaya rituals of admonishment and confession are disciplinary practices crucial for ethical formation. Formally built into the monastic rules is the construction of a community of people that can function best through the mutual correction of its members. The regulations stipulate that monks and nuns make themselves "easy to speak to" and that they in turn be ready to admonish their fellows.[106] One easy to speak to is able to endure admonishment (*ovāda*) and is malleable rather than obdurate.[107] Admonishment can lead to confession, another technology oriented, in a manner similar to what Foucault describes for certain Christian practices of confession, toward "the discovery and the formulation of the truth concerning oneself."[108]

The *Parivāra* offers several reflections on how the technology of admonishment may be brought to bear on individuals' capacities for restraint. The text reads:

> For what purpose is there admonishment? For what reason is there remembering?
> For what purpose is there the Saṅgha? For what reason is there mental action?
> Reproving is for the sake of remembering; remembering is for the sake of constraining.
> The Saṅgha is for the sake of examining, but a mental act occurs individually.[109]

There is much going on here. Admonishment is a matter of jogging the memory: our readiness to forget our failings must be met by the presence

---

106. This is *saṅghadisesa* 12 (Vin.iii.178). Dhirasekera is helpful on the many passages in Sutta and Vinaya literatures on the importance of being easily corrected (*Buddhist Monastic Discipline*, 129–31). Particularly notable is how *ovāda* establishes and reinforces patriarchal structures; seeking out admonishment from monks is incumbent on nuns according to the third *garudhamma*.

107. Sp.iii.613.

108. Foucault, "About the Beginning of the Hermeneutics of the Self," 163.

109. Vin.v.158. The word *matikamma*, translated here as "mental act," is, as Horner notes in her translation, not found elsewhere. As she notes, Buddhaghosa glosses it as "*mantaggahaṇa*," learning mantras, even as he goes on to describe it as a matter of individual discrimination and conviction by *vinaya* and *sutta* experts (Horner, *Book of the Discipline*, vol. 6, 255, n. 2).

of attentive others to call them to mind. Remembering—a far more affectively neutral experience of past wrongdoing than remorse and its scratching—can then allow for redress and transformation. It is only when faults are remembered that can they be constrained (*niggaha*), a word encapsulating both rebuke and restraint and thereby suggesting how others can invoke one's own restraint.

I read this passage as an exploration of the play between the community's role in shaping a person and a person's own mental space—you need the community to admonish you in order to remember your faults, and the Saṅgha to come together to deliberate on your faults, as Buddhaghosa explains.[110] The *Parivāra* goes on to explore how shame (or bashfulness, *lajjā*) works, as one is keenly aware of the eyes of the community upon him. Still, "a mental act occurs individually"—there remains space for an individual mind to make its own determinations within these processes. The passage is exploring how the processes of discipline and community create the conditions for inner examination and restraint, even while those processes will not fully pervade or determine that interiority.

Admonishing works both ways: those admonished are reshaped, and those who do the admonishing are expected to engage in self-examination before they take to the task of reproving others. In fact, the *vinayapāli* is particularly concerned with the motives of those wishing to admonish others. The *Cullavagga* requires that those willing to admonish others must examine their own bodily, verbal, and mental conduct, asking themselves, for example, if they are filled with lovingkindness and free of ill will before seeking to reprove others. An admonisher should turn inward and contemplate his state of learning: "have I heard much?" "Have I studied enough Dhamma, which is lovely in the beginning, lovely in the middle, and lovely at the end?" The admonisher should consider his state of understanding and mastery of the rules before jumping to reproach another. Admonishers should look for evidence of their own compassion, good wishes, tenderness, forgiveness of offenses, and devotion to discipline. They must consider the appropriate time for admonishing another, have full command of the facts of the case, be gentle, reprove in a manner that leads to the right goal, and be motivated by lovingkindness. Failing in any of these areas, a reproving monk will himself be a victim of remorse.[111]

---

110. Sp.vii.1359.

111. Vin.ii.248–50. (Much of this is also in the *Parivāra*, Vin.v.158–62.). Buddhaghosa's exposition does not add substantially to the *pāli*.

The *Parivāra* takes these considerations in a more formal and procedural direction, asserting that an admonisher be overseen by an adjudicator and that adjudicator, admonisher, and admonished are overseen by the Saṅgha as a whole. All parties must be assessed, and all involved in a dispute are to examine themselves and others. Commenting on a line in the *Parivāra* that states that both self and other must be assessed as they deal with a conflict, Buddahghosa says that one must ask oneself: "am I able to judge this case and bring it to resolution?" Moreover, "the measure of oneself must be known." When assessing others, one considers whether the case is being taken up by an assembly possessing shame, whether they are people with whom one may effectively remonstrate.[112] In this context, the Parivāra mentions monastic rituals and formal procedures.

> For what purpose is there Uposatha? For what reason is there Pavāraṇā?
> For what purpose is there probation? For what reason is there starting over?
> For what purpose is there penance? For what reason is there rehabilitation?
> Uposatha is for the sake of coming together; Pavāraṇā is for the sake of purifying.
> Probation is for the sake of penance; starting over is for the sake of constraining.
> Penance is for the sake of rehabilitation; rehabilitation is for the sake of purifying.[113]

Here we have a concise description of what the monastic rituals of Uposatha and Pavāraṇā do. All of these penalties require a monk to make known to his fellows his penitent status.[114] The coming together of the community in Uposatha makes possible the scrutiny of conduct necessary for regulating it, and the sense of purifying the community as a whole is emphasized for the Pavāraṇā (the annual purification ceremony at the end of the monsoon retreat). Penance is a six-day period of forfeiting one's

112. Sp.vii.1364 on Vin.v.164 (Horner, *Book of the Discipline*, vol. 6, 265).

113. Vin.v.161.

114. Thanissaro, *The Buddhist Monastic Code*, 154–56; Dhirasekera, *Buddhist Monastic Discipline*, ch. 10.

seniority and abiding by additional strictures that one incurs from committing *saṅghadisesas*. Probation is an additional penalty and status one incurs for committing and then hiding a *saṅghadisesa*. Rehabilitation is the act of readmittance to the community that penance makes possible. Perhaps most interesting is the language of "starting over" or "drawing back to the beginning" (*mūlāyapaṭikassana*), as though the violation can be erased, time can be tampered with, and one can begin afresh with restraint through these rituals.

The tone throughout these considerations is pragmatic. Even conscientious monks and nuns will forget their faults, and they will need others to reprove them. They cannot restrain their conduct without awareness of it. But admonishers must be especially wise to their own motivations, and there are very important considerations as to how to go about the business of reproving—one would need to do it at an appropriate time, for example, and only with the gentlest motives. The monastic rituals of the culmination of the monsoon retreat and of fortnightly meeting and confession are experiences of communal reflection and cleansing. Penalties are useful where needed for rehabilitating and purifying serious infractions and for making possible the agency of a fresh start.

Admonishment as a technique suggests that attaining monastic ideals requires the presence of watchful and helpful others. The texts dilate on the importance of various kinds of teachers a monk must seek out to fully engage in self-interpretation.[115] While it is difficult to overstate the importance of the "voice of another," in the processes of self-cultivation in the Vinaya literature, the monastic texts, unlike their Christian counterparts, do not exalt the importance of obedience. Rather, as we see in the *Parivāra* passage, people have a propensity to forget their faults and need reminders of them. Monks and nuns need the watchful eyes of others constantly upon them and should themselves turn gentle but steady eyes on others. And of course, the shameless need to be called out. But Christian obedience—the sacrifice or subordination of the will[116] —as a religious value in and of itself is not in evidence here. A more apt term is *malleability*: a

115. Dhirasekera offers a most thorough explication of the role of the two principal types of teachers in the Vinaya, the *ācariya* and the *upajjhāya*, their duties and qualities, and the reciprocal relationships they have with their students (*Buddhist Monastic Discipline*, ch. 12).

116. On Christian obedience as the "sacrifice of the will," see Foucault, "Technologies of the Self"; for a slightly different but still complementary view on how obedience works to reorganize the soul, see Asad, *Genealogies of Religion*, especially 139–47.

person should be malleable, pliable, easily guided and shaped by admired others, and never obstinate and disconnected.

Also in contrast to certain Christian hermeneutics of the self described by Foucault, wherein the self is anticipated to be clouded by dark and depraved intentions lurking within, the subject of Vinaya discourse is not particular opaque, his intentions are not masked, and his motivations may be discerned by careful contemplation (rather than by public performances of disclosure and exposé). We see throughout the texts monks and nuns at the first pangs of remorse turning promptly to their fellows or the Buddha and confessing all. With some exceptions, when asked about their infractions, they readily confess and speak with clarity and honesty about their intentions.[117] Monks do not begin this life in a place of bad conscience, as it were, searching for the sinner within and eagerly seeking out technologies of humility. Although there is an essential element of social exposure in the penalties (but only before other monastics, never the laity), and the texts are keenly aware of the power of communal censure, monastic rituals of confession and penance are not particularly designed to humiliate the penitent, nor is there anything quite like the notion of bearing public witness against oneself. We do not find penitent monks and nuns smeared in ashes and wearing hair shirts.

The rituals of confession occur prior to the recitation of the Pāṭimokkha during the Uposatha ceremonies twice a month. All monks must gather together apart from nuns and laypeople, and nuns must gather together also in the presence of monks. The Uposatha ceremony requires that monastics declare their misdeeds before the recitation of the rules (the Pāṭimokkha) and that all (unless ill and properly excused) be present. The purity of all (even absentees) must be declared, or if there are offenders, their offenses revealed. Revealing or confessing offenses, according to the *Mahāvagga*, allows one to be comforted in a manner that will allow progress in meditation. Silence means one is not guilty of an offense, or, if guilty, one's silence is to be regarded a fully conscious lie. It is through

117. Mentioning the "inordinate amount of trust" put into the accounts of offending monks and the "extraordinary" willingness monks have to confess their faults to the Buddha, Holt suggests a paradox: how can the very monks who are undisciplined enough to commit these offenses so readily and truthfully confess all? (*Discipline*, 92–93). One possible "resolution" to this paradox that Holt does not consider but may be supported by evidence in the cases we have explored here is that the burden of remorse weighs heavily upon them, generating an impulse to come clean. The *Cullavagga* says that monks concealing offenses experience pain (Vin.ii.65).

this ritual that the community affirms to itself its own purity on a regular basis.[118]

Monks may also be permitted to confess in private to another monk prior to or during the ceremonies, and there is a ritual formula for doing so wherein the offender crouches down with palms together, acknowledges the offense, confirms to his friend that he sees what he has done, and then is told to restrain himself in the future.[119] Such confessions, described in the *Cullavagga*, are legal remedies sufficient to purify the offender of certain classes of lesser offenses. Graver offenses require accepting additional penalties in an assembly, as we have mentioned. Both Dhirasekera and Thanissaro Bhikkhu have suggested that as some of these ritual procedures became mere formalities, their ethical possibilities were hollowed out, but we can see in the way the texts describe them that they are intended to foster self-examination, disclosure, and reform.[120]

The Pavāraṇā is an annual rite at the end of the monsoon retreat before receiving an annual gift of requisites from laypeople, with certain elements of purification similar to those of the Uposatha but involving also a communal rite of each monk formally inviting other monks to judge his conduct. Each monk assumes a bodily posture of crouching down with palms together and invites his fellows to come forward with anything they have seen, heard, or suspected with regard to his conduct and to mention it out of compassion. Seeing it, he can then redress it.[121] Again, the language of seeing appears; people need to see their infractions to restrain themselves in the future and can be brought to see them when others expose them. The bodily posture of crouching low is also considered important, for immediately following this instruction from the Buddha, the group of six shameless monks is observed remaining sitting on their seats and are then commanded to crouch—all must participate in this ritual. The text goes on to say that bringing charges against another monk in this context

118. Vin.i.103. Holt, *Discipline*, offers a helpful account of these rituals.

119. Vin.ii.103.

120. In particular, Thanissaro Bhikkhu says that when the formula of confession is recited by rote by every monk before the Pāṭimokkha, it becomes "little more than a formality" (*The Buddhist Monastic Code*, 543). Dhirasekera charts how the rites evolved to a "ritualistic purge from guilt" at the start of the ceremonies and that confession to a single person was permitted, so that, evidently even in the *vinayapāli*, "the Pāṭimokkha recital thereafter ceases to be a powerful instrument in the proper maintenance of monastic discipline" (*Buddhist Monastic Discipline*, 105).

121. Vin.i.159.

is not to be taken lightly, for if an accusation is unwarranted, the accuser is guilty of a wrongdoing himself.

These measures formalize and structure the requirements of admonishment. They depend on the honesty and integrity of the participants, though, as the *vinayapāli* itself shows, they are not without loopholes that shameless monks and nuns will try to exploit. Regardless, they demonstrate the way this community, as imagined by these texts, regulates itself legally and morally through requiring its members to watch others and learn to be watched. These rituals, at once legal and ethical, have a gentle and civil tone—monks are "invited" to come forward and should make accusations only "out of compassion." Although quite serious matters are taken up, the texts do not suggest a spectacle of public shaming or humiliation.

The theoretical importance of intersubjectivity that we have seen in the Sutta and Abhidhamma contexts is developed here in practical terms: monks and nuns are ideally constituted to be open to their fellows in ways that comprise who they are and how they act. These processes are both subtle (a general awareness of watchful eyes) and overt (being called to account in an assembly). They operate on a person in a manner that inclines and disposes, though does not determine, what one does.

Conclusions

The *Mahāvagga* says that even if the Abhidhamma and the Suttanta were to be destroyed, the Buddhist dispensation could continue so long as the Vinaya was present.[122] Vinaya, through both its overt prohibitions and its techniques of self-formation, is restraint, which in turn fends off the remorse that obstructs joy and spiritual progress. According to the neat divisions of labor Buddhaghosa attributes to the three *piṭakas*, Vinaya makes possible the practice and realization of the teachings found in the other two.

Let us now draw together the lessons to be learned from the Vinaya's approach to intentional agency. From both the ethical and legal standpoints, intention and action are so closely bound up with one another (once again) that to do an act means that one has intended it. What Foucault referred to as "ethical substance," the element of one's behavior or conduct that

122. Vin.i.98–99.

is the domain for ethical judgment, is here the very conscious awareness one has while constructing and performing an action.[123] It is this element that is generally identified with culpability, not the motivation or reason for acting. If a monk or nun has unwittingly done something immoral, then in some sense the action has not been done, a principle consistent with the close linking of karma and intention and with notions of karma we have seen elsewhere.

The Vinaya's anthropology is a pragmatic one. The community is initially pure, but, human nature being what it is, its members will eventually and inevitably fall and must be regulated by rules. The Vinaya's focus on physical and verbal actions (rather than mental actions and factors) indicates an awareness of its own limitations; the law cannot effectively reach into and govern people's minds and thoughts. In addition to curbing action, the rules come also to constitute the people in it, displaying who they are to themselves and to others. Intentional agency is inflected by others and by the institutions and practices by which one lives. Within its vision of ideal action, we discern the formation of persons with certain dispositions: one becomes alert to the gaze of others, easily chastened by admonishment, sensitive to remorse. Moreover, study of these texts results in a moral education whereby, if we may borrow a line from Buddhaghosa, "the measure of oneself can be known."

---

123. Foucault identified four main aspects of ethics: the "ethical substance," the part of our conduct most relevant for morality (e.g., feelings in our present society, desire in medieval Christianity, intention for Kantian ethics); the "mode of subjection," that is, the way people are invited or incited to recognize their moral obligations; the "self-forming activity," how one works on one's ethical substance, how one changes to become an ethical subject; and the *telos*, the kind of being one aims to become in acting morally (Foucault, "On the Genealogy of Ethics," 352–59).

4

Making Actions Intelligible

INTENTION AND MIND IN STORIES

THE OPENING STANZA of the *Dhammapada* famously asserts:

> Mind is the forerunner of all things. Mind is chief, and they are mind-made. If one speaks or acts with a wicked mind, suffering follows even as the cartwheel follows the hoof of an ox.[1]

The mind is the source and creator of all experiences, a theme with which we are, by this point, quite familiar. The stanza suggests that actions are inseparable from what is occurring in the mind, echoing in its own idiom our formula that karma is intention. The stories in the *Dhammapada Commentary* flowing from this first stanza explore and elaborate this idea.

Mind, Buddhaghosa has suggested, can be a conventional and everyday term for intention widely construed, appropriate for Vinaya teachings and, we may extrapolate, narrative teachings also. We are also familiar with the idea that Buddhaghosa saw *jātaka* as a distinct method of teaching

1. Dhp 1. The translation of *dhamma* as "things" is imprecise, according to the Dhammapada commentaries on this verse; it should be translated as *cetasikas*, mental factors. The interpretation of this verse is complicated, and the commentaries on it disagree with one another on what it means to say that mind precedes mental factors (Dhp-a 21–24; Mp.i.73; and the commentary on Nett 129), as explored thoroughly by Palihawadana, "Dhammapada 1 and 2 and Their Commentaries." My reading, in contrast, is operating at a conventional level in interpreting this stanza as it speaks to the story in which it occurs. The narrative commentary concerns a blind arhat who accidentally squashes bugs. The stanza is taken to comment on how suffering inexorably follows wicked deeds produced by bad thoughts: the arhat's blindness is the result of his greed as a physician in a previous birth who gave a woman eye ointment that caused her blindness because she was reluctant to pay his fee (which involved her slavery and that of her children). In taking "mind" conventionally here (rather than by parsing it by an Abhidhammic method), I have the precedent of Buddhaghosa, who in the *Atthasālinī* treats this stanza as a worldly teaching, like the Vinaya, in which analytical dismantling of mental experience is not appropriate (As 68).

(*pariyāya*), at least for some purposes, though of course it is not considered a *piṭaka*. Buddhaghosa had good reason to see the distinctive exegetical potential of stories. The story collections that comprise the *Dhammapada* and *Jātaka* commentaries that we explore in this final chapter provide an exegetical movement from the general to the particular and from the abstract to the concrete that serves to develop a specific kind of knowledge that the texts prize highly.

These commentaries are, in effect, large story collections attached, sometimes apparently tenuously, to the aphoristic stanzas of two collections of canonical verses; the *Dhammapada* also circulated as its own collection of aphorisms, but the *Jātaka* stanzas are seldom (if ever) known without their attending stories that expand and frame them. Scholars have sometimes doubted that the *Dhammapadaṭṭhakathā* and *Jātakatthavaṇṇanā* are commentaries at all. Eugene Watson Burlingame suggests that their exegetical purpose has receded to such a degree that "what was once a commentary has become nothing more or less than a huge collection of legends and folk-tales."[2] While it is certainly the case that these stories take on a life of their own quite apart from the root texts on which they are commenting, it is worth considering the tradition's defining them as commentary (*aṭṭhakathā*) so that we might expand our notion of what commentary is and what it can do. Commentary as narrative has its own techniques for developing meaning, shaping our interpretative capacities, and providing moral education.

We have already seen how the Vinaya treats narrative context as essential to the interpretation of general rules. The rules are grounded in and predicated upon the particular narrative settings in which the need for them arose. The stories in which the rules are nested in both Vinaya canon and commentary are not expendable garnishes to the rules but guides for interpreting and practicing them. They tether Vinaya knowledge to the everyday, quotidian circumstances in which particular monks and nuns learn how to live the monastic life. The *Dhammapada* and *Jātaka* are part of the Sutta *piṭaka*, and within this genre, they exemplify Buddhaghosa's expectations that Suttanta knowledge embodies "conventional teachings," in keeping with the popular understanding of the world. Unlike the Vinaya, which is geared to monastics, the Suttanta is said to be taught "according to circumstances" appropriate to beings of "diverse dispositions, biases, practices, and inclinations."[3] It has a wider application and

2. Burlingame, *Buddhist Legends*, vol. 1, 26.

3. As 21.

audience and thus makes use of a more widely accessible range of idioms and registers, which stories, and especially the great variety of stories that these collections offer, can do particularly well.

Perhaps the most essential way narratives may be said to develop our understanding of intentional action is that they render actions *intelligible*. They do this by first selecting out what is to count as an action from a stream of movement or behavior. As Alasdair MacIntyre has argued, even selecting and naming an action as an action requires a narrative that provides it a setting and history. Consider, for example, the various ways the question "What is he doing?" might be answered in the example he provides: the replies "digging," "gardening," "taking exercise," "preparing for winter," or "pleasing his wife" may all be truthfully offered even while they each identify the action differently. These various replies signify quite different, though possibly overlapping, intentions as they identify the primary action a person is engaged in. MacIntyre says that we cannot "characterize behavior independently of intentions and we cannot characterize intentions independently of the settings which make those intentions intelligible to agents themselves and others."[4] Moreover, the histories behind those settings may be framed differently, and as they are, the identity of the intentional action is renegotiated.

These considerations suggest that narratives are the settings and histories that identify intentions and actions and begin to render them intelligible. But narratives differ according to who is telling them and toward what end, suggesting that actions and intentions are products of eminently social and dialogic processes. Intentions and actions exist in and through narratives in the ways that narrators choose to select and organize experience. Narratives are also temporal in character, requiring that selected actions be identified through a chosen arrangement of time. For example, narratives are often after-the-fact reconstructions of an event that identify the relevant action or intention only post hoc. Such a construction of an

4. MacIntyre, *After Virtue*, 206–7. The insights in this section are indebted to MacIntyre's ch. 15 and to other scholars who have written helpfully on narratives, including Nussbaum, *Love's Knowledge*; Schofer, *The Making of a Sage*, 12–15; and in relation to Buddhism, Hansen and Hallisey, "Narrative, Sub-ethics, and the Moral Life"; Hansen, "Story and World"; and Lang, *Four Illusions*. The importance of storytelling in giving an account of other people's actions is also helpfully treated in Daniel Hutto's work. He argues, synthesizing work from a range of fields, that folk psychological accounts of others' intentions and actions are not a matter of reading others' minds or offering mentalistic explanations or predictions, but are conditioned by narrative practices and tailored to the exigencies of everyday encounters (Hutto, *Folk Psychological Narratives*).

action depends on events that run downstream of the action it attempts to render intelligible.

If narratives are essential for behavior to be intelligible as intentional action, much of what has been kept at the margins of the more abstract and generalized discourses of the Abhidhamma and Suttanta analyses of intentional actions is, in fact, indispensable. Insofar as these other genres assume that for purposes of analysis actions may be lifted from the very narratives that constitute them, they ignore how actions are identified to begin with. From this perspective, narratives are not expendable but rather essential to a full understanding of intentional action.

Buddhaghosa provides a helpful clue in the *Atthasālinī* about how we might begin to interpret the relationship of the abstract inner workings of the mind offered by the Abhidhamma with the particular narrative accounts in the story collections. In a section in which he is working out the nature and history of the Abhidhamma within the biography of the Buddha, he asks, "Where did Abhidhamma originate? Where did it mature? When, where, and by whom was it mastered?" It originated, he continues, in the Bodhisatta's confidence in the aspiration for enlightenment (the vow of the Bodhisatta). It matured in the 550 *jātakas,* and it was mastered, of course, by the Buddha on the full moon day of the month of Visākhā under the Bo Tree.[5] More details follow, to which we need not attend, but we might linger on the idea that the "maturing" (literally, the "ripening" [*paripācita*]) of the Abhidhamma occurred in the *jātaka* stories. This is a biographical reference referring to the narrative of the Buddha's past lives when he, as a person named Sumedha, first made the aspiration for awakening under the Buddha Dīpaṅkara and then, in his many subsequent lifetimes, developed his character and insight as the Bodhisatta (some of these lifetimes comprise the *jātaka* tales). Thus the idea that the knowledge of the Abhidhamma (the ultimate truth of the Dhamma), originates (is first glimpsed?) in the encounter with Dīpaṅkara but comes to maturity in the *jātakas* is a biographical or historical truth about the development of the knowledge of the Dhamma in the Buddha's life. But it might also work at another level as well. Abhidhamma insights—that is, the most abstract distillation of the truths about mind and reality that we have—are matured in the concrete and particular narratives of the Bodhisatta's life.

5. As 31.

This notion of the ripening or maturing of abstract truth in concrete stories of life as it is lived suggests how Buddhaghosa read narratives. It is not, as scholars sometimes assume, that stories provide simple moral instruction for the unlettered or unsophisticated, but rather that they are the location and condition in which general insights reach maturity. This movement from the general and abstract to the particular and concrete is not a move from the complex to the simple but rather an expansion and growth of general teachings in and through the contingent realities of actual circumstances. In this sense, the *Jātaka* and *Dhammapada* commentaries are exegeses very much in Buddhaghosa's expansive sense of "commentary": commentaries grow the teachings and expand them in almost infinite directions, and they do this by caring tremendously for details. Recall that Buddhaghosa wrote the 850-page *Visuddhimagga* on just two verses: the brilliance of the text lies in the concrete working out of the details and implications. And the particular details to which narrative exegesis attends are the pragmatic, messy, often prosaic, but stubbornly unavoidable details of living a life.

If we allow ourselves to see how narratives *develop* and *mature* the Dhamma rather than simply exemplify or illustrate it, we can better appreciate the ethical knowledge they offer. One way that stories might be said to develop or mature more abstract formulations of the teachings is in their capacity to produce affective experience. The stories model valued emotional experiences in the characters and promote them in readers and listeners. We find characters experiencing shame, joy, and energy, prized experiences in moral consciousness as *cetasikas* in the Abhidhamma lists. But the stories can *create* such morally good experiences in ways that, say, the analysis provided in a Abhidhamma list might not. In this genre, such experiences are *inhabited* rather than observed, by characters and audience alike. The sting of remorse does its work in these tales, and a certain feeling of sadness or sorrow teaches its own particular lessons about *saṃsāra*. Charting the affective work these tales do begins to show a further ethical dimension of the development and expansion of the teachings.

Points of View and Shifting Frames of Reference

The *Dhammapadaṭṭhakathā* and *Jātakatthavaṇṇanā* as we have them consist of several layers: the root stanzas, commentarial glosses of those stanzas, and the stories that frame them. These layers are likely the products of different hands at different points in time.[6] We are not entirely clear how the attaching of the stanzas with the stories came about. In many stories, the stanzas appear at the end of the tale as a sort of moral of the story, where they seem to comment on the tale (rather than the tale commenting on the stanza). The stanzas are short epigrammatic verses that provide general moral exhortations and principles; they often mention characters and events but are opaque without the attending commentary (particularly in the *Jātaka* collection). The stories involve a character (usually the Buddha) uttering the stanza and offering it in the context of a conversation where it is deployed to provide a general maxim, an ethical argument, or a pithy statement of key events in the plot. The *Dhammapada* stanzas are usually self-contained enough to stand as general maxims free of a larger narrative (and sometimes their insertion into the narrative is far from seamless), but the *Jātaka* stanzas, though likely to be older than the prose narratives that we now have, are themselves kernels of the tales.

The stories report their author as the Buddha, who alternates between first-person and third-person point of view in the frame stories and nested stories in both texts. In the *Jātaka* stories, which are stories of the Buddha's own previous lives as the Bodhisatta, he is a central character in all the tales; in the *Dhammapada* stories, he is not usually a main character in the narratives beyond his role as teacher and interpreter of the events. In this sense, these stories are Buddha's words quite regardless of how we

6. The translator and redactor of both collections is considered by the traditional sources to be Buddhaghosa; more so than his involvement with the other commentaries we have been considering, modern scholarship has called this claim into question. The colophon of the *Dhammapadaṭṭhakathā* names Buddhaghosa as the author, but the rest of the text does not mention him. On the authorship of the *Jātakatthavaṇṇanā* (which he refers to as the *Jātakaṭṭhakathā*), see Jayawickrama, *The Story of Gotama Buddha*, xiii–xiv; Cowell, *The Jātaka*, vol. 1, x–xi; T. W. Rhys Davids, "Translator's Introduction," lxii–lxvii; Malalasekera, *The Pāli Literature of Ceylon*, 117–22; and von Hinüber, *A Handbook of Pāli Literature*, 131–32. On the authorship of the *Dhammapadaṭṭhakathā*, see Burlingame, *Buddhist Legends*, vol. 1, 45–60; Law, *The Life and Work of Buddhaghosa*, 80–83; von Hinüber, *A Handbook of Pāli Literature*, 132–35; and Palihawadana, "*Dhammapada* 1 and 2 and Their Commentaries." The *Dhammapada* Commentary is thought to be later than Buddhaghosa's commentaries and the *Jātaka* collection it frequently mentions. But both collections are large and layered; while some versions of the *Dhammapada* stories differ significantly in style from the same stories told in Buddhaghosa's commentaries on the Nikāyas, others bear almost word-for-word similarities to them. There are also some tales in the *Dhammapada* collection that suggest that Dhammapāla had a hand in them. We find a great deal of material shared across both collections and shared with other texts, such as the Vinaya, the *Therīgāthā*, the *Udāna*, and the Nikāya commentaries. Burlingame provides synoptic tables of these versions (49–15).

understand the chronological layering of the texts we now have or the precise distinctions in this genre between "canon" and "commentary."

The structure of the stories in both texts follows a standardized pattern wherein the particulars of time and occasion are given (for example, "the Teacher told this tale in Jetavana concerning a certain monk") and the "story of the present" or frame story is related. Its events lead the characters to ask the Buddha to fill in further background of the present case, prompting the Buddha to tell the "story of the past," which reveals a previous life of the present characters and their relationships. This backstory casts light on the events and characters of the present. The story of the past usually ends with the Buddha identifying who was who in both stories ("In those days, monks, Ānanda was the king, Sāriputta was the minister, and I myself the wise stag"). He also often identifies, particularly in the *Dhammapada* tales, the fate of the main characters, the sequel to the events in the present story ("At the conclusion of the stanza, the executioner attained stream-entry and upon departing this life went to Tusita heaven"). This overall pattern is flexible: sometimes the story of the past precedes the story of the present; sometimes additional stories are nested in either tale; sometimes more than one story of the past is given.

What might we observe so far about what the structure of the stories can teach us to interpret them? The importance of the use of time to frame events cannot be overstated. Past and future render present events intelligible; they give them meaning and interpretability. Moral teachings and the stories in which they are embedded have backstories to which the Buddha has direct access and which he shares with us for any number of purposes. Often scholars have seen the purpose of the rebirth story motif as principally rendering explicit the operations of karma, how *tit* follows *tat* in the inexorable fruition of karmic action.[7] But other possibilities are at work in the use of past and future to interpret the present in ways that have direct bearing on our investigations into intentional agency. We can read them not only to glimpse the workings of karmic justice but also to interpret human psychology. We can begin to see, for example, how intentionality in the present has roots through habit or causes from the past. The stories insist that nearly every event has a prequel, and that prequel is the key to unlocking the meaning of the present. A longer perspective on time also gives us access to the concrete workings of intersubjectivity

7. Burlingame (*Buddhist Legends*, vol. 1, 29–34) provides a helpful discussion of how this motif works to teach the fruit of past deeds.

in the lives these stories tell; people are involved in intricate relationships with others in the past that continue in the present. These relationships shape what people do and why they do it.

"Only the Buddha," the Tittha Jātaka informs us, fully "knows the intentions and inclinations" of others.[8] His omniscience takes several concrete forms. In some stories, he knows minds because he is an astute observer of beings and infers what they are thinking, such as in the story from the Tittha Jātaka, wherein the Bodhisatta infers the thoughts and bruised feelings of a vain and pampered horse. In other stories, he reaches directly into a character's head and reports what they are thinking. Finally, he knows what is going on in a character's mind because his own thoughts traverse time; knowing the past, he knows what drives one's thoughts now, and knowing the future, he knows where one's thoughts tend. This recourse to past and future is in and of itself a teaching about how to think about intentions and minds: they never exist in an isolated present. By providing a much longer timescape in which to locate and interpret the present, the Buddha provides access to the long view of cause and effect and the shaping of disposition.[9]

The Buddha's insistence that actions have prequels that, once revealed, give them meaning and significance demonstrates that the true meaning of the action is unavailable to those who see merely the present. Many tales employ a group of bystander monks who discuss, debate, register astonishment at, query, and generally scrutinize the doings of the main protagonists in the tale. The Buddha comes upon these bystanders, learns their conjectures, and then sets them right about what has just happened by telling them the story of the past. This device teaches that actions are penetrated by the past: their meaning, their significance, and their nature cannot be discerned by observers acquainted solely with the present facts. Intentionality *is* biography, and what a person does now is a product of the things they have done in the distant past.

Shifting narrations of actions indicate the degree to which intentions emerge through conversation and dialogue: the act of narrating itself constitutes intentionality in an important way. Attributions of intentions are negotiated dialogically and are thus socially constituted. Intentions are posited and revealed in the conversations of bystanders and the Buddha

8. Ja.i.182. Cowell, *The Jātaka*, vol. 1, 64.

9. See Hansen, "Story and World," 61, for a similar point about how the *Gatilok* works.

and, more rarely, in the first-person report of the characters themselves. Anthropologist Lawrence Rosen has suggested that intention, while long treated as the "preserve of philosophical abstraction, psychological theorizing, and religious dictate," is "above all, a social and cultural phenomenon." Leaving the attribution of inner states "at the level of the universal and analytically abstract does injustice to their varied roles in human relationships." What might at first appear to be a "wholly ideational phenomenon" is in fact entwined with cultural and social life. He suggests a host of questions that a turn to the social and cultural context can raise:

> Who controls the way in which inner states will be attributed to others? How do different sectors of a population—or the state itself—characterize the intentions of those who fall within the ambit of their power? Why, in some cases, has the language of intent developed as a predominant vehicle for characterizing persons and their conduct, and what is the relationship of this emergent discourse to the rise of new social groupings? Are the interests of a religious and political elite, for example, served when they characterize others' inner states in a way that justifies the elite as intercessors, managers, or rulers?[10]

If intention is a dialogical phenomenon negotiated in the ways we tell stories about ourselves and others, then those negotiations invite scrutiny. When we pay attention to the processes of ascribing intentions in our narratives, we begin to notice that certain people attribute certain intentions and motivations to others and can begin to ask what leads them to do so in the way that they do.

The Buddhist stories before us are particularly inviting for questions about the ascription of intentions because they so often involve people, usually bystander monks, debating and discussing people's actions and what lies behind them. These monks, even as they so often get things wrong, model a lively curiosity about why people do what they do as they construct folk theories of mind. We also have an extraordinary omniscient narrator always on hand—the Buddha—to fill in the blanks about what a given action means. His selecting of what is even to count as the relevant events, as well as his reframing the interpretative scope of time and

10. Rosen, *Other Intentions*, 3.

biography, constructs the intentions of the main protagonists in the tales. The stories thus show what it is to read the intentions of others naively as well as omnisciently.

The insights of cultural psychology can take us deeper into the ways that intentions and social life make up each other. Richard Shweder argues:

> No sociocultural environment exists or has identity independently of the way human beings seize meaning and resources from it, while, on the other hand, every human being's subjectivity and mental life are altered through the process of seizing meanings and resources from some sociocultural environment and using them.[11]

This dialectical model for interpreting intentions moves back and forth between cultural forms and a posited inner space or psyche of a person, suggesting finally that they mutually constitute one another. People attribute intentions for diverse purposes from assigning moral or legal culpability or responsibility, to selecting and idealizing certain pious modes of being, to selecting other dispositions and motivations for censure and reproach. These ascriptions, in turn, shape people's intentions and how they experience them. Shweder posits the idea of "intentional worlds" that gets at how "subjects and objects, practitioners and practices, human beings and sociocultural environments, interpenetrate each others' identity and cannot be analyzed into independent and dependent variables." Nothing real "just is," but "instead realities are the product of the way things get re-presented, embedded, implemented, and reacted to in various taxonomic or narrative contexts."[12] Focusing explicitly on discourses about particular characters' intentions allows us to examine how and why actions and motives are described, framed, selected, and put forward in the way that they are.

Cognitive scientists are also increasingly resisting a conception of intentions as private mental states residing in the minds of individuals by not only paying more attention to folk constructions of intentions (how observers describe and locate intentions) but also seeing intentions themselves as irreducibly a complex unity of self in action with others. As

---

11. Shweder, *Thinking through Cultures*, 74.

12. Ibid., 74, 76.

they shift to recognizing the "dynamic, interactive nature of intentional action," they see intentions as "emergent products of social interactions."[13] Not only are *ascriptions* of intentions matters of collaborative and negotiated narrative effort but also intentional actions themselves are very often collaborative. Consider where the intentions lie in a couple ballroom dancing or in an interaction between a mother and her baby—they emerge in an irreducible way in the interplay of self and other.[14]

The story collections offer an enormously heterogeneous body of causes, reasons, and explanations for why people do what they do. Often the reason people do what they do is simply because they are inveterately foolish, greedy, miserly, lustful, angry, or abusive in past lives as well as present. Such stories reveal little more than the intransigence of vice and the horrors of repeated folly. Other stories involve dramatic transformation in which the past is prologue to a stunning reversal in disposition and insight. Still other stories reveal a long and interwoven history with others to show how our entanglements with other people across time shape present intention. This chapter begins to inventory—though neither systematically nor exhaustively—the sheer variety of the sources and shapers of human intentions as they are constructed through narratives. Intentions as social processes can now be given full play.

In the next three sections, we consider several contrasting depictions of intentions and how they work in time. In the first, we find a story (representative of many stories in this literature) of a character whose intentions are not easily held apart from her entanglements with others in present and past lives; past lives shape and explain present intention. In sharp contrast to this kind of account, we find in the section following the intentions of arhats and other highly advanced practitioners treated as quite insulated and remote from the messy circumstances in which they occur; unlike those of ordinary people, arhats' intentions are not conditioned by past or present entanglements in *saṃsāra*. We then turn from how the past shapes and interprets the present to how the future might do so. The final two sections in the chapter carry forward these concerns about time but shift to stories that explore the subjectivities such understandings—or better, the lack of understanding—produce in narrative characters about the nature and moral value of their intentions.

13. Gibbs, "Intentions as Emergent Products of Social Interactions," 105–9.

14. Ibid., 113, 120. See Malle, Moses and Baldwin (*Intentions and Intentionality*) for an excellent collection on recent cognitive science on intention.

A Game of Cat and Mouse

In our first story, told in both collections, a young married woman named Kāṇā returns home for a visit with her mother and is about to return to her husband when her mother insists she not go back empty-handed and instead take him a cake.[15] She bakes a cake and is about to leave when a monk happens by for alms, and she gives him the cake. But again her mother requires her to bake a cake for her husband, and again a monk drops by for alms. The same events happen yet again, and then a fourth time. Finally, the husband, unwilling to wait for her, takes another wife. Kāṇā is so distressed that she weeps and takes to reviling any and all monks who come near, to such a degree that they learn to avoid going near the street on which she lives. The Buddha, knowing what has happened, pays Kāṇā and her mother a visit to investigate the matter. He suggests that the monks only took what she had offered and were not to blame and that she is blameworthy for abusing them, whereupon Kāṇā begs his forgiveness. He teaches the Dhamma to her, and she attains the fruit of stream-entry (that is, a highly advanced conversion wherein she will attain *nibbāna* within seven lifetimes). The incident draws the notice of the king, who adopts her as a daughter and marries her to a nobleman. Thereafter, she gives alms generously to all monks and nuns.

Bystander monks take up her case and discuss it among themselves, noting how she first hated monks but after her encounter with the Buddha now enjoys a change of heart and is renowned for her almsgiving. The Buddha finds them in this discussion and says, "Monks, this is not the first time those monks offended Kāṇā; the same thing happened in a previous existence also." And at their request, he gives a brief summary of the Babbu Jātaka, which recounts her previous existence, and then connects the whole matter to the *Dhammapada* stanza on which the story is commenting: "even as a deep and calm lake is serene, so too wise people, listening to the Dhamma, become serene."[16] The story thus ends on the point of the Buddha's ability to calm and transform minds.

---

15. Dhp-a.ii.148–52 (Burlingame, *Buddhist Legends*, vol. 2, 190–92); Jātaka 137, Ja.i.477–80 (Cowell, *The Jātaka*, vol. 2, 294–96). There is yet a third intertextual reference to the story mentioned by the Dhp-a, which directs us to the Vinaya, in the context of the rules of expiation, where Kāṇā's story of her loss of husband is related and the Buddha comes to be concerned about monks overly taxing lay alms donors and seeks to limit their demands (Vin. iv.78–79; Horner, *Book of the Discipline*, vol. 2, 321).

16. Dhp 82.

The Babbu Jātaka to which this story directs us offers a rather truncated account of this story of the present and omits the part about Kāṇā abusing monks; instead, she simply weeps from the loss of her marriage. The bulk of the *Jātaka* account is given over to the story of the past, and the framing of the story suggests that it is the four alms-seeking monks who are responsible for the sorrow befalling this young woman. In the story of the past, Kāṇā is a miserly woman born as a mouse who comes to guard a treasure of gold coins left behind by a family who has since perished. As a mouse, Kāṇā befriends the Bodhisatta, a worker in a nearby mine, and she brings him coins daily on the proviso that he share meat with her purchased from the money. But then she is caught by a cat and is able to buy her release only by providing him a daily share of the meat. Another cat catches her, and she has to share her portion of the meat with him as well; and so with another cat, and then a fourth. Oppressed by their voraciousness, she turns to the Bodhisatta, who devises a stratagem to stop them. He puts the mouse in a block of pure crystal and instructs her to revile and abuse the cats to draw them close (here paralleling the reviling of the monks in the *Dhammapada* version of the story of the present), whereupon they attempt to spring on her and are broken and killed by striking the crystal. Thereafter, mouse and Bodhisatta live happily as friends.

It is not an easy matter to locate, much less judge, the main protagonist's agency or culpability in any of these accounts. In the *Dhammapada* version, Kāṇā is urged by her mother to stay back and make cakes, and she is responding to the request of alms by the monks to whom she gives them. The only real act that seems to be her own is her reviling monks, which is regarded as blameworthy, and for which she apologizes. The four monks, for their part, are merely doing what monks do, that is, seek alms, and the Buddha establishes (at least in the *Dhammapada* version) that they are not blameworthy, even though, he admits, they have brought her great sorrow. But in the story of the past, as the hungry cats, they are clearly the aggressors and opportunists. She is here represented as a victim of their rapaciousness, but of course, they are just cats doing what cats do. This shifting of blame across the stories suggests that these five people are entangled in complicated ways through these events and have collectively created a situation that is sorrowful. Though the story ends happily (and most tales do), the sadness evident in these futile entanglements with others is salient.[17]

---

17. Martin Wickramasinghe (*The Buddhist Jātaka Stories and the Russian Novel*) suggests that the *Jātaka* tales inspire in particular the feeling of sadness, as they comment on and make vivid what life in *saṃsāra* entails.

Particularly important for our purposes is noticing how the story of the past is deployed to deepen our understanding of Kāṇā's actions in the present. In both accounts, when monks try to analyze the events and understand Kāṇā, the Buddha offers the cat-and-mouse story to reframe her action. It is not just that she lost her husband in this life because of these four monks; she was tormented by them in a previous life as well. The emotion that drove her action is not something located just in her head, but is in a complicated way tangled up with these particular monks; it exists *between* them. Her moral condition cannot be understood apart from the complicated relationship with these monks in which she has been a victim of their rapacious hunger for a long time. What we learn is that people have histories with others that stretch over time, residual traces that construct action and disposition in the present, and that the real moral work here is properly framing the action to see this. We develop sympathy and understanding for her not so much by getting inside her head as by stepping back and getting a larger sense of time and personal narrative.

There are many stories of cycles of revenge and hatred where the story deliberately obscures the primacy of individual intentions. As helpfully analyzed by Ranjini and Gananath Obeyesekere in its Sinhala version, a well-known *Dhammapada* tale describes a barren cowife who, out of jealousy, brings about repeated miscarriages in her fellow wife, setting in motion a long chain of revenge between them in which they take turns at killing each other's babies across lives until we lose sight of the original perpetrator and victim and can see only the endless cycles of vengeance.[18] The cycle ceases only when one of the women seeks refuge from the Buddha, who then brings the whole thing to a stop. Stories like this suggest that people are prey to their own deepest and ugliest motivations that, once fueled by others' actions, run on with their own impetus. Moreover, these motivations are inextricably wrapped up in our dealings with particular others as we respond and react to them: we get tangled up with certain people. These narratives sketch out the idea of intersubjectivity introduced by Buddhaghosa in our first chapter, where, as we saw, Buddhaghosa acknowledges how our intentions are shaped by others in his exegesis on *cetanā*. He argues that other people's intentions can affect our fate. An example is jealousy and anger, which are contagious: as he

18. Dhp-a i.45–53. Burlingame, *Buddhist Legends*, vol. 2, 170–75. Obeyesekere and Obeyesekere, "The Tale of the Demoness Kālī."

puts it, "the anger of one is the condition of anger in another, and they both fall."[19]

These stories depict a porousness of our moral condition and how others' emotions and actions shape our responses, intentions, and emotions; they suggest that in our interactions with others, there is often little autonomy in our emotional or intentional lives. This vision of the intersubjectivity of moral intention may capture quite accurately much of our ordinary workaday moral lives in which, in fact, we rarely do seem to step back from distinct options and make, cool and gimlet-eyed, clear moral choices. Actions are reactions in a vast narrative scaffolding of intersubjective relations with others unfolding in the large stretches of time the stories construct.

The Intentionality of Arhats and Other Highly Realized Persons

We are presented with a very different kind of agency in the following stories, which feature arhats or other highly realized people. Unlike the case of Kāṇā, the intentions of these characters are much less intersubjective, and their actions are interpreted as held apart from previous conditioning and the actions of others in important ways. Our first tale is the opening story of the *Dhammapada Commentary*, which is the narrative exegesis of the root text's very first stanza that "mind is forerunner of all things."[20] This story traces the development of a monk who, through meditation practice, attains arhatship and in his old age becomes blind. His blindness is the result of exacting austerities that led him to neglect his eye disease. (The story of the past attributes the cause of his blindness to an earlier life in which as a physician he caused a woman to become blind because she refused to become his slave to pay him for his medical services.) Despite his blindness, he is a keen observer of people and knows what they are up to. He discerns that a nephew sent to bring him to a monastery has been up to no good, and he is able to tell when the king of the gods, Sakka, has come to test his extraordinary qualities. But the part of the tale interesting to us occurs right at the story's end. One day the blind arhat, fond of strolling, roams around the monastic grounds after a rain shower and steps on

19. Mp.iii.147.

20. Dhp-a i.3–21; Burlingame, *Buddhist Legends*, vol. 2, 146–58.

and destroys many insects (the grounds had not been swept by the monastic attendant). Other monks see the carnage left behind on the footpath and, offended, approach the Buddha to report on the arhat's deeds. The Buddha asks them if they saw him do it, which they deny, and then asserts that just as they did not see him tread on the bugs, the blind arhat did not see the bugs as he walked: "monks, those whose depravities are destroyed (i.e., arhats) have no intention (*cetanā*) to kill."[21]

The Buddha's reasoning here is that the arhat is not culpable because he is blind so he simply did not see the bugs he killed, but more important, he is an arhat, and so, by definition, is incapable of such intentions. The nature of this man's intentions is determined not by the actual action or its effects, but by his religious status. His blindness just reinforces that he is incapable of seeing or constructing the world in such a manner that he would be destructive. In this story, a quite different logic than the story about Kāṇā is at work. Where Kāṇā's action can be understood only through the long arc of time and entanglement with others, this action is to be understood principally by reference to the protagonist's religious status.

This suggests a rhetorical sealing off of the blind arhat's subjectivity as a way of establishing or reinforcing his high moral and religious status. Arhats, as we have seen in the more systematic treatments of their intentions, are never going to have wrong intentions no matter what actions they commit; important work is being done here to separate this monk's intentions, which must be pure, from his bodily actions, which appear problematic. Stan Royal Mumford, an anthropologist working with Gurung shamans in Nepal, suggests that intention can function as a metaphor. Mumford argues that "virtuous intent, as a metaphor that seals off subjectivity, may be viewed as historically emergent"; it arises in religious and moral systems like Buddhism that emphasize purity of mind and is not found universally.[22] Buddhist discourses that promote an ideal inner intent erect boundaries around certain minds: "within a bounded self-image, the subject can deny its complicity in the world

21. Dhp-a. i.20. "Those whose depravities are destroyed" is an epithet for arhats.

22. Mumford, *Himalayan Dialogue*, 26. Mumford is describing ritual practices among Tibetan Buddhists in Nepal that allow their participants to claim and signify, at least temporarily, a status of pure and virtuous intentions. The ritual context allows them to extricate their "inner life from its relational entanglements," in keeping with the logic of renunciation espoused by Buddhism (but quite foreign to the shamanistic elements of the Gurung context to which he contrasts these practices).

of intersubjectivity that would otherwise make the idea of pure motives inconceivable." According to Mumford, this "tight imagined boundary" or extrication of pure intention from relational entanglements is a denial; it is not that it is false, but that it is a metaphorical truth that operates to deny another truth.[23]

When and why do some stories and not others seek to extract, construct, and isolate an agent's pure intentions, denying intersubjectivity rather than invoking it? When arhats are protagonists, the purity of their intentions is known in advance of any action they may commit, and their high religious attainment is emblematic of their pure intentions. Unlike the rest of us who are, like Kāṇā, still embroiled in entanglements with others in *saṃsāra* in ways that shape what we think and do across time, arhats are, rhetorically, removed and sealed off from acting and reacting with intentions shaped by such processes; we might say their intentions are constructed as a repudiation of the intersubjective and collaborative world of acting and reacting that inflect others' intentions. Arhats' actions are not framed within a larger relational psychology that might otherwise be invoked to give them meaning.

Another example of an arhat's pure and "sealed off" intention is apparent in the sad story of Uppalavaṇṇā, a nun who was raped in her forest hut.[24] Monks discuss the incident and wonder if Uppalavaṇṇā was in some sense culpable for this rape since, they conjecture, it might have been possible for her, even as an arhat, to consent (*sādiyati*) to the pleasures of sex. Arhats are not Kolapa trees or anthills, they suggest, but living creatures who have bodies with moist flesh, so why should they not consent to and experience sexual pleasure? The Buddha shuts down this possibility quickly: "just as a drop of water fallen on a lotus petal rolls off" without staining it, so, too, "arhats do not consent to or pursue sexual pleasure." In addition to ruling out the possibility of her consent and intentional

23. Ibid., 25.

24. Dhp.-a.ii.48–52; Burlingame, *Buddhist Legends*, vol. 2, 48–52. Uppalavaṇṇā is one of the Buddha's closest female disciples, and this tragedy results in nuns being prohibited from staying alone in their own retreats (the rapist himself is swallowed up by the earth and plunged into Avīci Hell). The Vinaya and its commentary discuss this rape, as we have seen, also arguing that because she did not consent, she is not culpable of a sexual transgression. There are fascinating stories about Uppalavaṇṇā's previous lives in the *Therīgāthā* commentary (see Pruitt, *The Commentary on the Verses of the Therīs*, 232–51; and Murcott, *The First Buddhist Women*, 80–85) but no backstory about what in her past might have precipitated this rape: the rape is *not* configured karmically as the consequence of some previous misdeed on her part.

involvement in the rape, this simile has the pleasing and compassionate effect of referring directly and particularly to Uppalavaṇṇā, whose name means "Lotus Complexion" and who has a long association with lotuses in her past existences. The Buddha speaks quite pointedly to her: what has happened to her has not really touched her.

Arhats also act from *reasons* that elude bystanders. The *Milindapañho* considers the actions of a band of 500 arhats who scatter to the four winds when a rogue elephant, goaded by Devadatta, charges the Buddha.[25] Ānanda, who is not yet spiritually awakened, alone tries to protect the Buddha by putting himself between the elephant and the Buddha. Surely, King Milinda asks, we can say that the fleeing arhats had fear, despite the fact that the scriptures say they are supposedly free of such emotions. No, Nāgasena counters, they needed to flee for Ānanda's good qualities to be demonstrated and so that the Buddha can approach and tame the elephant. Here what might seem obvious in how one could infer intentions from actions is wrong—the merely apparent is dubious, and there must be a different logic to arhats' actions than meets the eye.

Given what we know about arhats' intentions from the more systematic genres—that is, that they are *kiriyacetanās* and thus are not conditioned or conditioning—pure intention is constitutive and emblematic of arhatship. They are thus sealed off from the entanglements with others and over time that constitute intentional action in stories like that of Kāṇā. But this rhetorical move is not just made for arhats. The Buddha also sometimes wants to seal off an agent's subjectivity for certain others as a way to signal their religious potential or advanced status. A favorite motif in the story collections concerns the travails of young beautiful women of high social standing who boldly defy parental authority and social convention and run off with men of low degree. These women are usually quite plucky and are treated with surprising sympathy and complexity in the stories.[26] In one such account, a young woman from a wealthy and well-placed family is hidden away by her parents on the top floor of their seven-story palace, guarded by slaves.[27] Despite this enforced isolation, she happens to see a

25. Mil 207–8. Horner, *Milinda's Questions*, vol. 1, 300–2. Milinda is referring to the Cullahaṁsa Jātaka, #533; Ja v.333–54.

26. See Wickramasinghe, *The Buddhist Jātaka Stories and the Russian Novel*, 5–9. The stories of Pāṭācara (Burlingame, *Buddhist Legends*, vol. 2, 250ff.) and Kuṇḍalakesī (227ff.), also involving young women fleeing seven-story mansions with inappropriate men, belong to this motif.

27. Dhp-a. iii.24–30; Burlingame, *Buddhist Legends*, vol. 2, 276–80.

hunter walk by, falls in love with him, and manages to sneak out and run off with him, leaving her parents bereft from their loss. They marry and have seven sons who become hunters too, and they arrange their marriages. One day the entire family comes to the Buddha's notice. He perceives their ripeness for spiritual attainment and intervenes to bring about their conversion. His intervention involves staying the hunters' traps until they are poised to shoot him with their bows. But when the wife sees this, she cries out, "Do not kill my father." Her husband and sons stop in their tracks, thinking she means her actual father (rather than her spiritual father, whom she has instantly recognized) who has now found them, and they then become friendly. With their hearts softened, they become open to the Buddha's teaching them the Dhamma, and soon attain stream-entry.

When the story ends, monks debate among themselves the woman's intentions. In their account, she was actually already a stream-enterer as a young girl in her parents' house! How then could she have married a hunter, and beyond this, whenever he asked her to bring him his weapons, she did so, becoming an accessory, as it were, to his violence? The Buddha arrives at this point to clarify the matter: of course, stream-enterers cannot be involved in taking life; when she helped her husband in this way, she was actuated only by the thought "I will obey my husband," and it never occurred to her to think "He will take what I give him and go out and kill." She did not have a bad intention (*akusalacetanā*), nor did she commit evil. Since stream-enterers cannot be involved in taking life, her intentions are quite narrowly construed. This tidy move is meant to serve the larger moral of the stanza that this story in the *Dhammapada Commentary* is meant to expand, which asserts that people who are morally upright are not sullied by what occurs around them, just as a hand with no open wound can safely carry poison. The stanza spells it out: highly spiritually advanced people are those whose intentions are in large part extricated from the compromises of life lived with others.

The story of the past explains that these people—the hunter, his wife, and their seven sons and daughters-in-law—had in a past birth been a family who gave their fortune and dedicated their lives to the construction and maintenance of a relic shrine of the Buddha Kassapa. Because of this meritorious act, they went to the realm of the gods after death and then were born in the story of the present, where the woman had, as a mere child, attained stream-entry. As a stream-enterer, she seeks to bring the others to the Dhamma, and so when she spots her former husband, she immediately falls in love and elopes with him.

As in the story of Kāṇā, the past is invoked to explain the intentions of the present. The opacity of present actions—how could a rich young woman run off with this hunter and seemingly support him in his violence?—is made clear. Events that seem problematic can be seen, in the fullness of time, as having causes from a distant life propelling them. But though the hunter's wife is involved in previous relationships with others that account for some of the plot here, in the end her intentions are largely not forged through these relationships. We instead have a quite different kind of framing than the story of Kāṇā, which depicts moral agents and their intentions as inseparably bound up with others. But in this tale, a person is created who, no matter what form her involvement with others takes, remains uncompromised by it. When the stories speak with this voice, they seek to deny interrelationality, the ways actions and the meanings of actions of certain people are constructed through involvement with others. The Buddha sees her, as a stream-enterer, as above reproach. One of the fascinating aspects of this story is that the sealing off of intention here is not reserved solely for an obvious class of religious elites. One never knows, at first glance, who among us acts from pure motive: stream-enterers number among their ranks young women who elope with inappropriate men. And again, the conjectures of bystanders concerning such people are likely to be wrong.

A final example of a story that constructs and sequesters its protagonist's pure intentions concerns a child prodigy. In this story, we get the tale of the past first, which involves a poor man unable to afford alms for the beloved elder monk Sāriputta and is thus reduced to hiding when Sāriputta comes for alms.[28] But when he finally does receive some milk-rice and a cloth, he rushes to give them to Sāriputta, for whom he has much affection. Due to this devotion, he is reborn in the womb of a wealthy supporter of Sāriputta.

This new rebirth is shaped profoundly by his devotional gift in the last birth. From the start, his mother's pregnancy is marked by great longings to give milk-rice to Sāriputta and his monks constantly. When the child is born, he is brought before Sāriputta. The baby recognizes his former teacher, and, wrapping his expensive blanket around his finger, he flings it upon him. Then the story notes the following:

> Instead of saying, "this young child did not know what he was doing," his relatives said this: "our son has given and presented this

28. Dhp-a. ii.84–103; Burlingame, *Buddhist Legends*, vol. 2, 150–62. The motif of the seven-year-old prodigy can be found also in the Atthassasdvāra Jātaka (#366), Cowell, *The Jātaka*, vol. 1, 211.

to you. Please accept his honoring you with this blanket worth a hundred thousand coins, and confer upon him the ten precepts."[29]

In this small detail, the narrator draws our notice to the construal of the event by the characters. The relatives could have taken the actions of the baby to be purely random wriggling and tossing, but instead they sought to construct them as an intentional gift. Moreover, his mother insists that hereafter she "will not interfere with the wishes of her son." The story goes on to construe the boy's intentions as single-minded religious devotion to Sāriputta. They name the child Tissa after the elder (as Sāriputta was called in his younger days). Tissa becomes a monk by age seven and, not long thereafter, an arhat. The boy is remarkable for his attractiveness to others and the ways that he inspires their automatic affection and generosity, attracting especially gifts of milk-rice and cloth.

All of these details work to construct a person with an enormous degree of moral agency and intentionality beginning even in utero. The mother stands back very deliberately from what she takes to be very forceful desires and intentions of her son, and the characters labor to construct an agency for this child that is highly purposeful.[30] On one level, this story raises questions about intentions in children. When do genuine moral agency, affections, and goodness start? Do these require higher thought processes or moral deliberation? The story works to create a moral world in which infants act generously if undeliberately: goodness is not only a matter of rational thought (many stories of animal benevolence do a similar kind of thing). But the story particularly calls into question the possibility of purely spontaneous actions, even by infants. Instead, we see intentional trajectories from past lives directing the autonomous will of a child. Like the previous stories in which a person's intentions are sealed off, there is a sense here that the child's agency is unfolding simply of its own impetus. A baby's actions are not random but purposeful, driven by a past that the characters do not know, but yet are confident is real.

29. Dhp-a. ii.86.

30. In her ethnography of Shan Buddhists in Northwest Thailand, Nancy Eberhardt describes and analyzes a similar reluctance among parents to interfere with what they take to be "an independent or autonomous will in even very young infants and babies." Babies are treated as "social agents almost immediately," not blank slates, but rather "preloaded" in significant ways. Thwarting the desires of a young child might entail going against past forces that, though mysterious, are "essential" or "emblematic" to the person that the child is (Eberhardt, *Imagining the Course of Life*, 80–82).

The story is inflected by both past and present: the boy's intentions are both rooted in a previous birth and shaped by his future attainment. The story knows what happens later—the boy grows up to be an esteemed arhat—and so its construction of events immortalizes early episodes of a baby's gestures that are taken to signal who he is. The baby's apparent autonomous and purposeful desire to give to Sāriputta is also emblematic of his future destiny. His autonomy of will in early childhood is fully realized in his later renunciation and arhatship (the stanza on which the story expands praises renunciation and solitude). Meanwhile, the whole process is shaped by others negotiating and determining who this boy is and what he intends to do; the social processes at work assigning moral agency are particularly obvious in this story, even though, ironically, they are represented as the child's own independent intentions. We must ask: why does the story grant so much agency to a baby? To ingratiate him with a senior monk and thus set his life on a certain course? To display a family's extraordinary piety and devotion, symbolized by their baby's artless giving? To account post hoc for a young prodigy? Many parents will recognize the desire and ease with which we construct who our children are from infancy. These possibilities suggest that intention is not so much something located inside the baby's head as something constructed by other people.

The stories in this section subordinate appraisal of ordinary moral actions to a soteriological status that reframes what is really occurring. Once arhats and religiously advanced people are recognized as such (by the Buddha who knows all minds), questions of their intentions are clarified. Or to put it in a different way, a certain kind of sealed-off subjectivity and intentionality is shorthand for high religious status. But there is another point of reference at work in how we come to understand these stories. As we saw in the story of the hunter's wife, the Buddha knows who she is because he can perceive the future: her family is ripe for conversion, and if handled just right, she can help the Buddha coax them into transformation. We turn now to the ways in which the Buddha's awareness of and ability to help engineer the future are just as important as his grasp of the past for interpreting minds and explaining why people do what they do.

The Offended Monk and the Remorseful Executioner

In our next story, a young granddaughter of the eminent laywoman Visākhā offends a young monk by calling him "cut head" as she serves him alms; he returns the name-calling and makes her cry.[31] Visākhā intervenes in the quarrel, asking that the young monk not be offended since in fact "cut head" is an accurate description of his shaved head. But the young monk persists in taking umbrage. A senior monk as well tries to end the quarrel by playing down the insult, to no avail.

But the Buddha sees the whole thing differently. Perceiving that the young monk possesses the capacity to attain stream-entry with just a little encouragement, he chooses to side with him. The Buddha's support causes the young monk to be quite kindly disposed to the Buddha. He feels uniquely understood: "Bhante, only you understand this matter which eludes both the laywoman and the monk." The Buddha sees that the monk is amenable to the teaching and seizes this opportunity to frame the events in such a way that will make his receptivity to the teaching grow. The final framing is simply not interested in the woman's intentions when she commits her alleged fault, or in assigning moral culpability in what is doubtless a rather trivial quarrel to begin with. Rather, this is an event that should be understood with reference to the future. The alleged insult creates a possibility, a new opportunity: we can surmise that the monk will look back on this moment not as the action by which he was offended, but as the day he developed a new relationship with the Buddha and a new spiritual conversion.

A far more challenging story is the account of an extremely violent and wicked man, Tambadāṭiko ("Red Beard"), who is spurned even by a band of dacoits because they deem him too cruel, "capable of cutting out the breast of his mother and eating it, or drawing the blood from his father and drinking it."[32] One day the dacoits are rounded up and brought before the king to be sentenced for their crimes, and Red Beard willingly becomes their executioner. Since he is so good at what he does, he becomes the permanent executioner and works in this capacity for 55 years, beheading criminals on a daily basis. As he gets old and frail, he is able to kill criminals only with several blows to the neck, causing them great torture, and so he is eventually retired on a modest pension of a single final portion of milk-rice.

At that particular moment, the great elder Sāriputta comes out of meditation, perceiving that he might be received kindly for alms by the former

---

31. Dhp-a.iii.161–63; Burlingame, *Buddhist Legends*, vol. 3, 1–2.

32. Dhp-a. ii.203–9; Burlingame, *Buddhist Legends*, vol. 2, 218–221.

executioner, which would bring the man great merit. And indeed, when Red Beard sees Sāriputta, he is filled with joy and wishes to give him the milk-rice. But Sāriputta can tell that even though he has received him with great hospitality, his host longs for the milk-rice, and so he in turn offers Red Beard the meal. Then Sāriputta attempts to give him a blessing of thanks but notices that his mind is distracted. Upon questioning, he learns that Red Beard is anxious about his past murderous deeds, whereupon Sāriputta decides to deceive him to stop his anxious mind. He asks him if his deeds were done by his own inclination or due to another's. The executioner replies that he was ordered by the king. If that is so, continues Sāriputta, then he should be assured that he did nothing bad. His mind now at ease, the former executioner is able to listen to Sāriputta's blessing and teaching, and he approaches the path of stream-entry. He later dies and is born in Tusita heaven.

Will it surprise us to learn that nattering monks discuss this affair, astonished that a murderer so cruel would achieve such a spiritual attainment and such a fabulous rebirth? "How," they ask, "could a mere blessing of thanks be so transformative of so great an evildoer?" The Buddha replies that his teachings are not to be measured as small or great and that their power works only if a person can hear them.

The story ends here without providing a story of the past to set the executioner into a larger framework of time. We are left only with the story of the present and its trajectory into the future. What is striking (in addition to the extraordinary fact that Red Beard seems to get off so easily for his crimes) is that the story emphasizes not the executioner's actual intentions but rather the opportunity for religious conversion made possible by the encounter with Sāriputta. Sāriputta's deceiving this man about his own intentions is a skillful device to calm his mind. What is not important to the story is determining the executioner's culpability in his intentions: the fact that Sāriputta has to deceive him into believing that the old standby "I was just following orders" frees him of culpability suggests that such a plea does not let him off the hook. But the point of the story is not culpability, but conversion, and Sāriputta's account of his intentions is subordinated to this aim.

Like the story of the offended shaved-headed monk, this story emphasizes the fact that the Buddha (and sometimes his disciples, like Sāriputta) can perceive in events seeds of the future, potentialities that if successfully managed can reframe the meaning of the events and shift our focus away from ordinary moral culpability. The site of debate about people's intentions is sometimes, for the Buddha, a place for a major intervention that makes possible a future that transcends ordinary considerations about moral accountability. In fact, a key message of the executioner's story counters the usual theme of the inexorability of karmic causality; the Buddha's teachings can bring karmic causality to an abrupt halt and effect radical transformation. This transformation, in effect, seals off the agent's intentions from *saṃsāra*.

The stories in this section and the previous two explore the work different perspectives of time can do in the hands of an omniscient narrator to constitute or to make sense of intentions. This works differently with the past than the future. Stories that appeal to past lives such as Kāṇā's can illustrate long-developing entanglements with others that repudiate the notion of an autonomous or present-bound intention. In sharp contrast to this, stories of the pasts of arhats are invoked to explain the religious status they enjoy as a way to deflect any possibility of an intersubjectivity or conditionality of their intentions (a perspective supported by what we know of the intentions of arhats in the more systematic genres). Finally, the setting of a story in relationship to a future conversion or transformation changes everything about a present intention, averting attention from moral considerations of accountability and culpability and toward the realization of a soteriological aim.

The final two sections in this chapter explore stories where intention and agency are opaque to others and, perhaps more importantly, to self. Set against the sort of timescapes we have been considering, where past and future inflect present moral experience and its interpretation, narratives in which past lives and future trajectories are inaccessible to ordinary people portray present intention as mysterious. We find characters who find their own intentions, actions, and moral character obscure (though to others they are often transparent). Such timescapes take us into terrain that psychoanalytic theory would treat as subconscious processes underlying conscious thought and action. The gaps in self-knowledge about intention produce at least two kinds of subjectivity. Explored in the next section is the moral (and often comic) subjectivity of the confused, and the last section depicts the anxious subjectivity of the scrupulous. In both, we find a prominent theme in the narratives (which is at odds in many ways with certain impulses in the other three genres) that suggests that moral knowledge, especially in the particular circumstances in which life is lived, can be elusive.

Knowing Minds

If mind is the forerunner of all things, how do we access it? How do we know our own thoughts and intentions, much less those of others? The stories depict a fascination with knowledge of minds, even while a common motif is the opacity of one's own mind to oneself. How might I know what my thoughts really are? If, as we have seen, the unawakened mind is a product of a karmic past, without knowing that past, the full range of our deepest dispositions and motivations is inaccessible to us. We do not know the claims the past might have on our present and what our minds are capable of thinking. Fortunately, the stories are populated with other people who can know one's thoughts and expose them in sometimes quite humorous but always psychologically illuminating ways.

In one story of the past from the *Dhammapada* collection, a king of Benares is said to make a careful examination of his thoughts, words, and deeds to discover if he had been guilty of any fault. He sees nothing problematic but reflects that "a person never sees his own faults; it takes other persons to see them," and so he roams his kingdom in disguise to learn what people say about him.[33] One's own thoughts and deeds are opaque to oneself, and the king perceives that his subjects will know things about him that he cannot.

What follows is a comedy of errors involving a previous life of the monk Little Wayman, who in this tale is a devoted but simpleminded young man incapable of learning anything but a single stanza: "you're rubbing, you're rubbing, why are you rubbing? I know too!" which his teacher gives him to make his way in the world. Quite by accident, this young man thwarts a band of thieves who are trying to enter a house through burrowing a tunnel and who hear him reciting his stanza. Thinking that "you're rubbing" refers to their digging the tunnel, the thieves fear they are found out and flee. The disguised king happens to witness this incident and makes this impressive stanza his own. And he just happens to be repeating it himself when a barber in league with the king's military commander to have him assassinated is sharpening his barber's tool (with which he had planned to sever the king's windpipe). When the barber hears the king utter "you're rubbing, you're rubbing, why are you rubbing? I know too!" he thinks the king has found him out and he confesses the assassination plot. The king then exiles the treacherous commander and replaces him with the young

33. Dhp-a.i.249–54; Burlingame, *Buddhist Legends*, vol. 1, 306–10.

simpleton who gave him the stanza. The story celebrates the idea that even a dullard can rise to the top through sheer devotion to the advice of a teacher, but along the way, the reversals and cases of mistaken identity are quite hilarious. No one who recites the silly stanza (which is quite meaningless in itself) *intends* to thwart thieves or stop assassination plots—they have no idea that they are even afoot—but no matter, sometimes people do things effectively without having any notion of what they are doing. Though the story begins with an earnest king wishing to discover the true nature of his thoughts and deeds, it ends with an ironic tale of no one knowing the true intentions of anyone!

Another funny story concerns a young man who enters the monkhood as a junior monk to his uncle.[34] He feels affronted by this senior monk when the senior monk refuses to accept a robe from him, and so he considers returning to the household life. He then wonders how he might earn a living and drifts off in his imagination to fancy himself selling his robe to buy a goat, whose offspring he can then sell to acquire some capital, whereupon he will marry and have a son, whom he will name after the uncle. He imagines that he and his family will go to visit that uncle, but that his wife will be careless and allow the child to be run over by their cart, whereupon he will beat her with a stick. He is awoken from this reverie to find to his horror that he beating the senior monk with his palm leaf fan! And he becomes even more mortified as he realizes that the senior monk knows every thought that passed through his mind as he daydreamed. He runs off to hide but is found by the Buddha and brought back from his discontent and taught a stanza about controlling wandering thoughts. The possibilities here are playful: he meant to strike his imaginary wife, but did he mean to strike his uncle, the senior monk? Since the whole daydream was precipitated by his annoyance at him, it is hard to rule out entirely a certain sublimated hostility aimed at the uncle. Humor and displacement allow for other truths to be entertained.

Another tale recounts a group of monks supported lavishly by a female lay disciple.[35] She attends to them closely and even adopts their meditation practices, which make her capable of knowing their thoughts. This ability to read their minds allows her to anticipate all of their needs. A young monk hearing of her great hospitality travels to be in her presence and

34. Dhp-a.i.300–5; Burlingame, *Buddhist Legends*, vol. 2, 10–12.

35. Dhp-a.i.290–97; Burlingame, *Buddhist Legends*, vol. 2, 1–7.

observes that she meets his every need and desire without his asking. But then he is filled with anxiety, knowing that she can also become aware of his bad thoughts: "This is serious," he frets; "ordinary folks [like me] think both good and bad thoughts, but were I to think something improper, she would discover my transgression and seize me by the topknot like a thief seizing goods." So he tries to flee the area, but the Buddha prevents him: "This is the very place you should stay." As the Buddha foresees, her knowing his thoughts stimulates the young man to purify his mind, and he becomes an arhat. He then wonders about his previous life experiences with this woman and learns that in 99 previous existences they had been married and she had conspired to have him murdered. This insight into their history she reads in his mind, and she mentally asks him to look further into their past lives together. He digs deeper into the past and sees that in one lifetime she, as his wife, had spared him. This memory causes him a great burst of joy, and he at once attains *parinibbāna*.

This story, like the one immediately before it, takes it for granted that others can come to know our thoughts and cause us acute embarrassment. Also intriguing are the rich psychological possibilities these characters' long pasts together suggest: she appears in this life as an all-knowing mother figure, anticipating his every need for food and nurture and reading his mind to know when he has been naughty (she calls him, according to convention, "my son," and she is referred to by the monks as "Mother of Matika"). Their past lives expose another dimension: they were previously married and she had murdered him many times over (perhaps she could read his thoughts then, too?). Here their psychological connections take on a violent edge, and his present fear of the harm she might do to him if she knew his thoughts is not unfounded. But then the bliss he experiences in recalling the single lifetime in which she spared (forgave?) him knows no bounds, and he is released to final *nibbāna*.

Martin Wickramasinghe is perhaps not far off to claim that these tales reveal with great subtlety the workings of the subconscious mind. He suggests that karma theory allowed Buddhist storytellers to become "instinctive psychoanalysts" able to probe human feelings and desires as the accumulated inheritance from previous lives.[36] Intriguing also is the way that other characters make self-discovery possible in these last two stories. Characters gain access to others' interiority more readily than their own,

---

36. Wickramasinghe, *The Buddhist Jātaka Stories and the Russian Novel*, 5, 26–27.

and it is their mirroring back one's mind that allows one to determine who one really is.

A Righteous Kingdom

One of the most fascinating stories from the standpoint of both investigating how intentions are ascribed and the limitations of self-knowledge is the Kurudhamma Jātaka.[37] This *jātaka* is particularly useful for us as one of the few instances where we encounter characters speaking in first-person voice about their own intentions. The plot is this: a certain kingdom plagued with drought and famine seeks the counsel of the neighboring kingdom of the Kurus whose righteousness (*dhamma*) keeps the realm in peace and prosperity. A delegation of brahmans sets out to inquire of the Kurus their principles of statecraft and morality. They learn that the Kurus' righteousness is rather straightforward—following the five precepts—but that the Kurus, from the king on down through the social hierarchy, are skeptical of their own capacity to follow it.

The brahmans begin by interviewing the king (that is, the Bodhisatta), seeking to record his advice on a golden tablet. In the king's case, the crux of his doubt about his intentions concerns a particular action he committed during a ceremonial occasion in which he, according to custom, is required to shoot arrows in each of the four directions. On this occasion, everyone saw where three of the four arrows landed, but they never found the fourth arrow. The king is anxious that the stray arrow might have impaled a fish (thus violating the first precept not to kill). He says, "Friends, I have worries about my following the Kuru Dhamma, but my mother protects it well, and you should seek [knowledge of it] from her." But the delegation protests: "Your Majesty, you did not have the intention (*cetanā*) 'let me take life,' and so did not kill anyone." They request that he tell them what he knows, and so he gives them the first precept, "do not kill," to write on their tablet. The king remains anxious, however, and insists that they seek out his mother for advice.

They find the queen mother to be equally scrupulous. She is filled with grave doubts about the propriety of a certain gift she gave. She had received fine sandalwood and a necklace as a gift but chose to give them to her daughters-in-law. She gave the elder daughter-in-law the less

37. Ja. ii.365ff. Cowell, *The Jātaka*, vol. 2, 251 (Jātaka #276).

expensive necklace since she was already quite well off and gave the much more expensive sandalwood to her younger daughter-in-law, who was not as well-to-do. But she worries that she has not treated them equally and suspects that this action has called into question her virtue (*sīla*). The delegation is again aghast that she is anxious over such a trifle, and they assure her that giving a gift as she pleases does not violate virtue. Her anxieties do not subside, however, and she urges them to seek out her virtuous daughter-in-law. This young woman confesses that on one occasion she happened to see the handsome viceroy passing in procession from her balcony and she fell in love with him and briefly fantasized about him. But she quickly chastened herself for such thoughts and never acted on them. But this flaw in her virtue weighs heavily upon her and she confesses her remorse to the delegation. The brahmans, increasingly finding themselves not so much suppliants for moral knowledge but rather judges of these people's conduct, protest that mere thoughts and fancies are not cause for moral disgrace and that her scruples are unwarranted.

The story continues in this vein: the daughter-in-law sends the delegation to the viceroy, who is himself anxious over his own trifling misdeed, and so the brahmans are passed from person to person down the royal hierarchy through 11 different people until they arrive finally at a courtesan who is anxious about her own commitment to honoring contracts. In her case, she had been contracted for her services by a client who paid her but did not come to her for three years, during which time she waited loyally for him. She eventually fell into penury and sought legal advice about whether she might resume her trade with others. She is pronounced to be in the clear legally and is urged to go about her business, but she remains troubled. She is about to contract to another person when the original client reappears and she hastens to honor her contract to him. Again the delegation protests her doubt and regards her behavior as impeccable. The story ends with the delegation bringing the principles of the Kurus back to their own kingdom, where they are put into effect and bring prosperity.

There are different frameworks for reading this story. Andrew Huxley parses the legal and ethical reasoning the cases show as they negotiate questions of intention, negligence, recklessness, and conflicts of interest. He sees in it a nascent political and legal philosophy that develops in a much later textual tradition in Southeast Asia around this story.[38] From

38. Huxley, "The Kurudhamma." He also discusses an elaborated version of the tale, the *Kurudhammakaṇḍapañho*, which may be as late as the 18th century and composed in the Middle Mekhong region.

a "management" point of view, the tale can be read for its various "job descriptions" and their attending responsibilities from the top to the bottom of the social scale. Huxley points out, too, that this is perhaps the first account we have of rulings on the five precepts, and it provides a glimpse of "the transition from uninteresting generalised ethics to semi-professional case-specific ethics."[39] His article illuminates both the ethical casuistry and the legal criteria at work in each of the cases.

For our purposes, the story is most interesting for the fastidious sense of self-doubt revealed in the interviews with the Kurus. Each has a clear sense of moral propriety but is exacting and doubtful about how his or her particular actions may fall short of it. The Kurus are anguished about their intentions—whether they intended an action that yields unintended consequences, whether they have truly honorable and virtuous intentions, whether intentions not acted upon count in some morally important way. The story raises, but never decisively answers, the following question: do the Kurus owe their righteousness to their actions or to their scrupulousness?

A Weberian reading would suggest that a certain cultivation of anxieties about intention is at work here. The text intimates that the protection of a kingdom lies not so much in following the five precepts per se as in this peculiar quality of self-doubt and anxiety evinced in the king on down. The story promotes an idealized social and political order by inscribing an overweening preoccupation with one's social duties. Each person knows his or her responsibilities and is exacting about fulfilling them, above and beyond the letter of the law: even the prostitute knows the importance of loyalty. We also see the delegation of brahmans from a neighboring kingdom playing a curious role. They speak with authority about these cases, despite being from a land where no one is even aware of the five basic moral precepts. They offer appealing and reasonable advice about how intentions ought to work, and yet since it is their kingdom that suffers natural calamity from their failure to know morality, their readings of moral intention are suspect, and the Kurus are not easily convinced. Could it be that the success of the Kuru kingdom lies in its people never presuming their moral intentions are adequate?

Although we will not acquire a grand theory of goodness, virtue, or intention from this story, the questions and possibilities it raises are

39. Ibid., 193.

suggestive. The story offers some of the few first-person narratives of people describing their own intentions and the reactions of others to their intentions. When good people offer a reflexive account of their intentions, we encounter an anxious and doubtful subjectivity.[40] Even so, the delegation's interviews with the Kurus entail negotiating the meaning and significance of their intentions. The delegation's protests attempt to determine what each person's intentions really were ("but sir, you did not have the intention 'let me take life,' and so did not kill anyone"), and they plead that the Kurus are overanxious. Nevertheless, each of the Kurus remains skeptical of these attempts to absolve them and can readily point to a worthier model of behavior. Their skepticism points to not only a certain valued self-doubt and humility but also the difficulty of genuine self-knowledge about one's own intentions and motivations. At least in this story, the more virtuous one is, it seems, the less sure one is of the virtue of one's intentions.

Conclusions

It may be useful to review, by way of concluding, the work intention does in these stories. In most of the stories considered here, the business of determining a character's intentions—asking, "Why did she do that?"—becomes a chief preoccupation of bystanding monks and the Buddha and thus for readers and listeners. Answering this question provides access first to the limited perspective of the present and then to a larger framework of time that reveals the inadequacy of the present for rendering actions intelligible. History and personal biography, selected and construed ultimately by an omniscient narrator, come to constitute the action itself.

Within such accounts, intentions come to signify who a person is and their level of religious attainment. For many characters, a given intentional action represents the culmination of a long entanglement with others in a complex and dynamic *saṃsāric* timescape. Their intentions are collaborations with or reactions to others in which the possibility of an autonomous agency or personhood is denied. Their intentions stand in

40. Consider the monk in Dhp-a.iv.115–17 who regularly goes to the root of a tree to admonish himself for his discontent with the religious life: "you shameless, immodest fellow! So you have actually decided that you wish to put on these rags, return to the world, and work for hire." He in short order becomes an arhat, and his story illustrates (even as it in another sense defies) the maxim of the stanza: "rebuke yourself by yourself; examine yourself by yourself. Protecting oneself by mindfulness, a monk lives happily" (Burlingame, *Buddhist Legends*, vol. 3, 260–62).

for the intersubjective relationship itself. However, for other characters, most notably arhats but also those approaching their spiritual attainment, pure intentions are emblematic of an autonomous agency they alone possess. Arhats act in the world and have intentions (we recall that the more systematic discourses call these *kiriya* intentions) that are extricated from the relationality of life enmeshed in *saṃsāra*. Their intentions represent and signify this fundamental feature of what it is to be awakened and truly free of *saṃsāric* conditioning.

If arhats alone are entirely free of an intentionality constituted by others, we may discern more clearly the constraints on freedom within *saṃsāra* and the ordinary human condition. MacIntyre suggests that agents "are never more (and sometimes less) than the co-authors of our own narratives." We enjoy agency in our creative capacities for action, even while that agency is shaped by the actions and narratives of others. As he puts it, "we enter a stage which we did not design and we find ourselves part of an action that was not of our making."[41] Kāṇā, our foremost example of a person represented as acting and reacting in a world she only partially created, is acted on as much as she acts, and her actions themselves are not intelligible or even identifiable without recognizing her simultaneous agency and patiency. Not so the arhat, whose freedom from contingency is operative at the level of intention. The religious program these texts advance holds out the possibility of free autonomous agency but only for these extraordinary persons. They are people with pure motives no matter what they actually do, and their intentions are scrupulously carved out and separated from the intersubjective incursions that give shape to moral agency for those still muddling through *saṃsāra*.

Intentions are also sometimes deployed as a tool for self-scrutiny (at least among nonarhats). The Kuru story suggests that the more virtuous a person is, the more anxiety and scrupulousness she brings to self-examination. Does true virtue lie in following moral norms or in anxious fretting over one's incapacity to genuinely observe them? Moreover, sometimes we are more transparent to others than to ourselves and can surmise others' intentions more easily than gain access to our own. A kind of psychoanalysis is at work in these stories, although instead of lying on the analyst's couch and talking, the characters are probed by others' forays into their minds forged through meditative insight. These stories portray and enact a religious program aimed at penetrating deeply into one's

41. MacIntyre, *After Virtue*, 213.

psyche and fomenting an anxious awareness of other minds observing one's own. There are no private interior spaces with the Buddha and other advanced meditators around.

The narratives provide a different rubric of self-work than the more systematic literatures do and have to be read differently, even as they are complementary modes of knowledge and were developed in the same contexts that produced the three *piṭakas* and their exegeses. Stories reflect on action in particular ways and value a particularism that does not necessarily lead to universals or to grand theory. They are open in important ways to multiple interpretations, and they place value on the *process* of puzzling through the opacity of human action. The bystander monks are always trying to figure out why people do what they do; the world is a diverse and mysterious place with people acting from past histories and entanglements with others that are not apparent on the surface. But, the stories seem to urge, be like these monks and get together with friends to try to understand the forces at work on people's actions. Unlike them, we do not have the fortunate presence of the Buddha, the omniscient narrator, to supply the missing pieces of biography that render action fully intelligible, but we have seen how his knowledge works and the ways that evoking an agent's biography, past and future experience, and religious status make sense of present action.

Stories also work affectively. We have mentioned the affective experiences prompted by the stories—the sadness at Kāṇā's situation (though it shifts to joy at her conversion), the embarrassment and horror of minds being exposed, the relief and bliss at being exposed yet forgiven, the laughter at folly being ridiculed. The emotional experience of the characters themselves and the way the stories make us respond to them are a large part of the work they do. The reader's subjectivity and autonomy are compromised by these tales in ways that are, we might say, potentially ethically productive.[42] To be open to these tales of others' travails and successes is to begin to allow one's own subjectivity to be penetrated and shaped by them in a manner that can generate moral sensitivity and sensibility.

A story can demonstrate explicitly how this works. The *Dhammapada Commentary* recounts the tale of ungrateful sons who neglect their aging father. The story then shifts to offering and then explicating the

---

42. On the ways that literature works to shape moral sensitivity and awareness in Buddhist sources, see Hallisey and Hansen, "Narrative, Sub-ethics, and the Moral Life"; Hansen, "Story and World" and *How to Behave*; Heim, "The Aesthetics of Excess" and "Buddhism."

following stanza: "the elephant Dhanapāla, wild and rutting, when bound, refuses to eat even a morsel: the elephant remembers the elephant grove."[43] The commentarial gloss fills in the background story here. It seems a wild elephant was captured and caged but, though offered even choice delicacies, refused to eat because he could not stop thinking of his mother left alone and uncared for back in the jungle. His anguish in imagining her without him makes him go on a hunger strike. Then the text says this:

> As the Teacher told this story of the past, relating it in detail, he caused floods of tears to fall in all present, softened their hearts and opened their ears. Then he, knowing what was beneficial for them, made known the truths and taught the Dhamma.[44]

Stories soften hearts and open ears, making possible the teaching of the Dhamma. This story is beneficial because it sensitizes the reader to general truths by experiencing the sorrow of the particular loss and grief of this elephant and his mother. The elephant remembers (or imagines) his mother in her distress, and we, too, "remember" with the Buddha as he tells this story of the past. These imaginative acts—and the very act of becoming a person who can so imagine (here, as elsewhere, animals show the way)—make us sensitive and alive to others' distress and sorrow. It may be, too, that sadness opens observers and makes them vulnerable to the experiences of others, which is here an intersubjectivity that is regarded as a valuable part of the path (at least in its initial stages). The stanza and the commentary on it then have an immediate effect on the characters in the frame story, the unfilial sons, and lead to their dramatic conversion. But the stanza alone could not do this without the narrative commentary providing the particulars of context and history.

Thus narrative commentaries ripen or mature our knowledge of the general truths we have explored in the other genres. They do so not so much by exemplifying them as by inhabiting them. The Bodhisatta may have begun to glimpse the entire architecture of the Dhamma upon his aspiration of buddhahood, but only through the eons of living, feeling,

---

43. Dhp 324.

44. Dhp-a. iv.14. Burlingame, *Buddhist Legends*, vol.3, 205.

and inhabiting these truths of life in *saṃsāra* did they became truly developed in the affective spaces that comprise knowledge and experience. It is the tacking back and forth between general and particular truth (whether between the general stanza and the particular story within a narrative, or between the more systematic genres and the narrative genres) that brings knowledge to maturity.

Conclusion

INTENTION HAS BEEN a moving target as we have traced its meaning and significance through the different domains of Theravādin thought. This is as it should be. If we abandon the idea that there is an essential core meaning to the constructs of psychological and social life (and there are very good reasons for doing so within both Buddhist thought and modern psychology),[1] we can attend more closely to the ways that meaning is a product of the explanatory systems used to explore it. By way of summing up, we might briefly recap the key insights about intentional agency in the Pāli sources and then explore a few of the broader implications these insights suggest.

The technical discussions on *cetanā* in the Suttas link it to the constructing and constructed processes of *saṅkhāra*. *Cetanā* is arranging the other factors of mental life to put together and "accumulate" experience. It involves subjective experience but need not be deliberate, and it can be shaped by others. Most importantly, *cetanā* has moral valence, depending upon the other factors it marshals in the performance of action, and the texts are chiefly concerned with its morally good and bad expressions. The most concrete treatment of intentional action is offered by discussions of the 20 full courses of action, where Buddhaghosa provides careful parsing of an action's main components and the criteria for determining its moral quality. Full courses of good actions are, intriguingly, nonactions or abstentions from the bad actions, a matter that presents challenges for how we understand the nature of intentional action. We also come to see that good intentions per se are not part of the *nibbānic* experience and to

1. Kagan, "The Meaning of Psychological Predicates."

appreciate the necessity for carving out a special kind of intention specific to the activity and experience of arhats.

As but one factor in the Abhidhamma matrices of factors, *cetanā* is defined and constituted according to the larger relational system of which it is a part. In any given thought, its moral valence is open to what else is present in that moment of conscious awareness. But it can be defined by its particular characteristic, function, mode of expression, and immediate conditions. *Cetanā* so defined is a quite rudimentary and prerational operation of the mind that arranges and galvanizes other factors toward realizing an aim or, more precisely, "producing its object." It is thus highly constructive in the making of experience; its identification with karma indicates that karma is the constructive function of mind that with and through its other factors creates an agent's present and future experience. Karma is what the mind does to craft experience, a process that is conditioned by what is present in the mind even as it is a highly creative and constructive activity.

There are both moral and soteriological dimensions to these processes. The mind can create healthy, blameless, skillful, and happy experience, depending on the whole array of other factors—feelings, motivations, dispositional tendencies, and various moral sentiments—present to it as it generates experience. But from a strictly soteriological perspective, the constructed and constructing functions of *cetanā* and karma make them problematic from a standpoint of seeking absolute freedom. This led the early Theravāda thinkers in several directions. First, much of the religious life is conceived not as *accumulating* constructed experience but as *ceasing* the constructive and acquisitive activity of mind that grasps and perpetuates existence in the restless and conditioned reality of *saṃsāra*. In this context, it became useful to talk of the many ways the mind can relinquish, abandon, and abstain from its habitual constructions and to identify the "presence of absences" as a key feature of religiously and morally advanced experience. Second, Buddhaghosa posited the idea of a kind of *cetanā*/karma that is not constructed or constructing but rather consists of a free and spontaneous kind of intention that arhats alone experience.

The Vinaya texts construct *cetanā* and, more generally, "mind" to their own purposes. Concerned with issues of culpability in interpreting the rules of monastic life, the texts construe intention as a central criterion for establishing whether a rule has been breached and for exploring the different ways one can be said to "know" what one is doing. Intention in this genre is the deliberate doing of an action (at least with regard to morally significant action) but is not to be confused with motivation. Nevertheless, the Vinaya texts provide a moral and legal education that is highly sensitive to motivation and how it works in the situated particulars of human life. This literature depicts a disciplinary culture that shapes an idealized subjectivity and intentional agency through ritual and communal practices of admonishment, confession, and other techniques.

The narrative sources have focused our attention on how context and setting identify intentional actions and render them intelligible. We come to see the social and dialogic processes at work in attributing intentions. Stories cultivate interest in why people do what they do and how various first- and third-party perspectives interpret intentions. They also provide a final and decisive interpretation by an omniscient narrator. The omniscient view always perceives the operations of time, both past and future, as crucial for interpreting present intentional action (at least for the actions of nonarhats). Finally, the intersubjectivity of intention becomes concrete in the stories: intentional action is often *reaction* shaped by entanglements with those others who comprise and constrain the possibilities of experience.

What are some of the implications of these ideas for the study of Buddhist ethics? The foregoing pages have not managed to locate the free, autonomous, and rational agent who is the subject of moral action in certain modern Western ethical systems and who is the chief protagonist in one strand of current work in Buddhist ethics. For this agent, moral thinking is a matter of determining moral obligations, weighing options, and making deliberative choices. He enjoys an autonomous will, and his moral activity consists in making decisions. Such an agent, though often presumed, is seldom argued for, and he belongs to a historical tradition peculiar, most likely, to the modern West.

Iris Murdoch has likened this conception of moral agency to visiting a shop. Enjoying total and responsible freedom, the agent surveys the value of the goods and selects among them, commanding the full resources of reason and objectivity. Murdoch criticizes this image of moral agency as "behaviorist, existentialist, and utilitarian."

> It is behaviorist in its connection of the meaning and being of action with the publicly observable, it is existential in its elimination of the substantial self and its emphasis on the solitary omnipotent will, and it is utilitarian in its assumption that morality is and can only be concerned with public acts. It is also incidentally what may be

> called a democratic view, in that it suggests that morality is not an esoteric achievement but a natural function of any normal man.[2]

This conception of human nature may be traced to or represented by Kant but is assumed in many other quarters as well.[3] In these conceptions, we encounter an "inflated yet empty conception of the will," where choice is considered paramount in moral agency yet we are never told what prepares agents for their choices, nor are we directed inward to the "empirical self" to learn of the psychic energies, desires, frailties, and capacities undergirding choice and action.[4] The idealized moral agent—"thin as a needle"—is seen as a "privileged centre of will (forever capable of 'stepping back')," though all complexities of his empirical nature have been stripped away.[5]

Murdoch calls instead for an investigation of moral agency that requires recognizing how energies, emotions, qualities of consciousness, states of mind, and most importantly, forms of attention matter.

> Neither the inspiring ideas of freedom, sincerity and fiats of will, nor the plain wholesome concept of a rational discernment of duty, seem complex enough to do justice to what we really are. What we really are seems much more like an obscure system of energy out of which choices and visible acts of will emerge at intervals in ways which are often unclear and often dependent on the condition of the system in between the moments of choice.[6]

Many of these energies, in Murdoch's view, are of a dark and depraved sort, and selfishness, ego, and illusion often carry the day. For her, ethics thus involves positing and exploring a notion of the "Good" and

---

2. Murdoch, *The Sovereignty of Good*, 8–9. Dreyfus ("Meditation as Ethical Activity") also discusses Murdoch in light of Buddhist ethics.

3. While the Kantian subject is often held up as an ideal rational, free, and autonomous agent—and indeed, for most of Kant's philosophical project, such an agent is required—Kant himself was in fact also interested in the empirical ethical subject; he wrote and taught on the topic of "pragmatic" or "practical" anthropology, what he called "the second part of morals" that would consist of an empirical science of what human beings are actually like. See Kant, *Anthropology from a Pragmatic Point of View*; and Louden, *Kant's Impure Ethics*.

4. Murdoch, *The Sovereignty of Good*, 74, 98.

5. Ibid., 52.

6. Ibid., 53.

investigating possible techniques for reorienting our attention and purifying our energies.

Theravāda Buddhist moral psychology reveals a rather precise account of that "obscure system of energy" Murdoch gestures toward, rendered much less obscure than the glimpses provided by Murdoch's own immediate resources for exploring it (she mentions psychoanalysis and Christian dogmas of original sin). We observe in the Pāli sources a close study of the empirical self of the sort that Murdoch is calling for, as well as a practical interest in technologies for reorienting it. For these thinkers, like Murdoch, moral agency must be explored through examining human psychological complexity and the particular ways that action is connected to emotions, energies, and motivations. It is not that humans do not make choices and decisions, but rather that the focus of much Buddhist ethical thought lies elsewhere than the rational processes of justifying choice and decision.

In identifying karma with intention, the Buddha was not signaling autonomous and free agency but something more like the opposite. Karma is a matter of creative world making and entails agency in this important sense: intentional action is the active construing and constructing of experience. But this is a process that is also highly conditioned—shaped (though not definitively determined) by past experience, by deep-seated motivations and dispositions, by the demands of custom and normative social life, and by intricate entanglements with others. Genuine freedom lies outside these processes, found not in ordinary human experience, but aspired to in the rarefied and extraordinary experience of arhats. Their freedom is not the natural moral condition assumed by many modern Western ethicists, but rather the highest soteriological achievement. This achievement is described not solely to gesture to the final goal of Buddhist teachings but also to illuminate ordinary unawakened human experience, to teach us how conditioned, contingent, and compromised life in *saṃsāra* is. In contrast to the arhat's freedom, the freedom of ordinary people lies in smaller movements and negotiations of the mind, rooting out problematic motivations, shaping disposition and behavior through disciplinary techniques, and pursuing the company and habits of good and wise people. Freedom is a progressive process, not an either-or proposition.

Murdoch, too, has observed that "our exercise of freedom is a small piecemeal business," a practice that advances slowly as one learns to *attend* and to *see* the world in a manner less overlaid with ego and illusion.[7] Her emphasis on attention as a tool for counteracting delusion and realizing freedom leads to a decentering of choice in ways that might also be compatible with Buddhaghosa's ideas. For him also, genuine moral freedom lies in peeling away the layers of greed, hatred, and delusion by reorienting mind. Murdoch's analysis suggests why the arhat's freedom is expressed not through choices, but through a spontaneous and fully awakened awareness of the world. Murdoch says, "If I attend properly I will have no choices and this is the ultimate condition to be aimed at."[8] Freedom is acting with a kind of spontaneity (Murdoch prefers "necessity" or even "obedience") in response to the way the world really is, where one is not poised between choices that can only arise (that is, are constructed) from a deluded and conflicted nature.

In addition to offering a thicker conception of moral agency and depictions of freedom as both gradual process and ultimate attainment, Buddhaghosa has also led me to a different methodological approach than is practiced in many styles of Buddhist scholarship current today. Scholars of Buddhist ethics have sometimes hesitated over the fact that most Buddhist texts identified as offering moral thought do not typically proceed by analyzing, arguing for, and justifying reasons for moral choices and actions. This omission or oversight in their sources has not prevented many scholars from forging ahead to uncover various rationalities alleged to be implicit in Buddhist texts (which would then provide the basis for how choices are to be made and justified). Some argue for a deep structure based on virtue; others see consequentialist or deontological rationalities underlying Buddhist moral thinking. These excavations unearth structures apparent to modern scholars but that have somehow managed to elude even the most systematic of Buddhist thinkers. Moreover, such archaeological projects are offered as comprehensive across Buddhist thinkers and traditions, revealing something called "Buddhist ethics" as a whole that is larger than any particular thinker or system (though it is thought to encompass all of them).

Buddhaghosa points to another way to encounter Buddhist moral thought, one that takes seriously how Buddhist thinkers systematized their own ideas and how they teach us to read them. With Buddhaghosa as our guide, we have grown more sensitive to how knowledge occurs and how

7. Ibid., 36.

8. Ibid., 38.

genre and context provide and constrain meaning. If context and genre are essential to meaning, then it becomes harder for us to pull passages out of context and reify concepts independently of the relational systems that help constitute their meaning. Learning to think "abhidhammically" keeps us from straying too far from the dynamic relational whole in which concepts and processes of mind are embedded. When the Buddha identified karma and *cetanā*, he was, on the readings Buddhaghosa has suggested in the Suttanta and Abhidhamma, pointing to *cetanā* as a function of mind that accumulates experience, but this task cannot be understood apart from the myriad other factors of conscious awareness it gathers and animates in producing and directing experience. In addition, a key feature in Buddhaghosa's treatment of *cetanā* in this technical sense is that it is not the site or location where one does moral work. One does not endeavor to change or improve one's *cetanās*; rather, one works on many other fronts with many factors—motivations, dispositions, ways of seeing—in an arduous process of moral cultivation.

The attention to genre and the strategies Buddhaghosa has provided for reading different kinds of Buddhist texts should not obscure the patterns and the degree of consistency in the overall system. The shift from *cetanā* as a technical term to "mind" or "thought" in the more practical and conventional usages of Vinaya and narrative is appropriate since *cetanā* indicates a vital function in the larger relational system we call, more vaguely, "mind." In such genres, employing the somewhat coarser folk category of mind is actually more useful than the fine-grained set of relational processes offered by Suttanta and Abhidhamma. Either way, what is salient in karmic agency is the mind's work of putting together experience out of the stock of present factors (themselves products of past factors) in a future-oriented direction. The Vinaya offers disciplinary practices of developing and altering the empirical self, technologies for reorienting and fundamentally changing how the mind operates (again in a manner that does not work directly on *cetanā* but on motivation, attention, habit, and culture). The stories render actions intelligible by situating them in the very particular contexts and narratives that, in fact, constitute them.

Important patterns of intersubjectivity are woven throughout these tapestries. The mind of ordinary human experience is not somehow sealed off from the past or independent of life lived with others. The arc of the four genres we have explored has gradually shifted from a phenomenological, first-person, and internal conception of mind to a highly social one (though recognition of intersubjectivity has been in evidence throughout).

Humans are porous in nature; quick to anger from others' incursions on us; shaped by culture, family life, and habit; and implicated in complicated histories and relationships with particular others. As long as we are not yet arhats, our minds and actions do not stand apart from these relationships, but are made up of them. It is in exposing the fiction of autonomy that the Buddhist sources can do some of their most important work on modern conceptions of ethics and their accompanying anachronistic readings of ancient Buddhist ideas.

Bibliography

All material from the Pāli Canon is from the editions of the Chaṭṭha Saṅgāyana CD-ROM, published by the Vipassana Research Institute, Dhammagiri, Igatpuri, India, 1995. All translations are my own unless otherwise indicated.

Adam, Martin. "Groundwork for a Metaphysic of Buddhist Morals." *Journal of Buddhist Ethics*. 12 (2005): 62–85.

Anscombe, G. E. M. *Intention*. Cambridge, MA: Harvard University Press, 2000 (1957).

Asad, Talal. *Genealogies of Religion: Discipline and Reasons of Power in Christianity and Islam*. Baltimore, MD: Johns Hopkins University Press, 1993.

Astington, Janet Wilde. "The Paradox of Intention: Assessing Children's Metarepresentational Understanding." In *Intentions and Intentionality: Foundations of Social Cognition*, edited by Bertram Malle et al., 85–103. Cambridge, MA: MIT Press, 2001.

Aung, Shwe Zan, and C. A. F. Rhys Davids, trans. *Compendium of Philosophy (Abhidhammatthasaṅgaha)*. London: Pali Text Society, 1979.

Aung, Shwe Zan, and C. A. F. Rhys Davids, trans. *Points of Controversy (Kathāvatthu)*. London: Pali Text Society, 1979.

Baier, Annette. *Death and Character: Further Reflections on Hume*. Cambridge, MA: Harvard University Press, 2008.

Bapat, P. V., and A. Hirakawa, trans. *Shan-Chien-P'i-P'o-Sha: A Chinese Version by Saṅghabhadra of Samantapāsādikā*. Poona, India: Bhandarkar Oriental Research Institute, 1970.

Bodhi, Bhikkhu, trans. *The Connected Discourses of the Buddha: A Translation of the Saṃyutta Nikāya*. Boston: Wisdom, 2000.

Bodhi, Bhikkhu, ed. *The Discourse on Right View: The Sammādiṭṭhi Sutta and Its Commentary*. Translated by Bhikkhu Ñāṇamoli. Kandy, Sri Lanka: Buddhist Publication Society, 1991.

Bodhi, Bhikkhu. *The Noble Eightfold Path: Way to the End of Suffering*. Onalaska, WA: Pariyatti, 1994.

Bodhi, Bhikkhu. *Nourishing the Roots*. Kandy, Sri Lanka: Buddhist Publication Society, 1990.

Bodhi, Bhikkhu, and Nārada Mahāthera, trans. *A Comprehensive Manual of Abhidhamma (Abhidhammatthasaṅgaha)*. Kandy, Sri Lanka: Buddhist Publication Society, 1993.

Boisvert, Mathieu. *The Five Aggregates: Understanding Theravāda Psychology and Soteriology*. Waterloo, Ontario: Wilfrid Laurier University Press, 1995.

Bond, George. *The Word of the Buddha: The Tipiṭaka and Its Interpretation in Theravada Buddhism*. Colombo, Sri Lanka: M. D. Gunasena, 1982.

Bratman, Michael. *Intentions, Plans and Practical Reason*. Cambridge, MA: Harvard University Press, 1987.

Bultmann, Rudolf. "Is Exegesis without Presuppositions Possible?" In *The Hermeneutics Reader: Texts of the German Tradition from the Enlightenment to the Present*, edited by Kurt Mueller-Vollmer, 242–47. New York: Continuum, 2006.

Burlingame, Eugene Watson, trans. *Buddhist Legends (Dhammapada Commentary)*, 3 volumes. London: Routledge & Kegan Paul, 1979.

Buswell, Robert. "The Path to Perdition: The Wholesome Roots and Their Eradication." In *Paths to Liberation: The Mārga and Its Transformations in Buddhist Thought*, edited by Robert Buswell and Robert Gimello, 107–34. Honolulu: University of Hawai'i Press, 1992.

Carrithers, Michael. *The Buddha*. Oxford: Oxford University Press, 1983.

Carter, John. "Beyond 'Beyond Good and Evil.'" *Buddhist Studies in Honour of Hammalava Saddhātissa*, ed. Dhammapala et al., 41–51. Nugegoda, Sri Lanka: University of Sri Jayewardenepura, 1984.

Clayton, Barbra. *Moral Theory in Śāntideva's Śikṣāsamuccaya: Cultivating the Fruits of Virtue*. New York: Routledge, 2006.

Collins, Steven. "The Body in Theravāda Buddhist Monasticism." In *Religion and the Body*, edited by Sarah Coakley, 185–204. Cambridge: Cambridge University Press, 1997.

Collins, Steven. Introduction to M. Wijayaratna, *Buddhist Monastic Life*. Cambridge: Cambridge University Press, 1990.

Collins, Steven. "On the Very Idea of the Pali Canon." *Journal of the Pali Text Society* 15 (1990): 89–126.

Collins, Steven. "Remarks on the Third Precept: Adultery and Prostitution in Pāli Texts." *Journal of the Pali Text Society*. 29 (2007): 263–84.

Collins, Steven. "Remarks on the *Visuddhimagga*, and Its Treatment of the Memory of Former Dwelling(s) (*pubbenivāsānussatiñāṇa*)." *Journal of Indian Philosophy* 37 (2009): 499–532.

Collins, Steven. *Selfless Persons: Imagery and Thought in Theravāda Buddhism*. Cambridge: Cambridge University Press, 1982.

Cone, Margaret. *A Dictionary of Pāli, Part I: a–kh*. Oxford: Pali Text Society, 2001.

Cone, Margaret. *A Dictionary of Pāli, Part II: g–n 2*. Oxford: Pali Text Society, 2010.

Cousins, L. S. "Good or Skilful? *Kusala* in Canon and Commentary." *Journal of Buddhist Ethics* 3 (1996): 136–64.

Cousins, L. S. "The *Paṭṭhāna* and the Development of the Theravādin Abhidhamma." *Journal of the Pali Text Society*. 9 (1981): 22–46.

Cowell, E. B., ed. *The Jātaka (Stories of the Buddha's Former Births)*, 6 volumes. Translated by various hands. New Delhi: Munshiram Manoharlal, 1990.

Cox, Collett. "Attainment through Abandonment: The Sarvāstivādin Path of Removing Defilements." In *Paths to Liberation: The Mārga and Its Transformations in Buddhist Thought*, edited by Robert Buswell and Robert Gimello, 63–105. Honolulu: University of Hawai'i Press, 1992.

Davidson, Donald. "Actions, Reasons and Causes." *Journal of Philosophy* 60 (1963): 685–700.

Davidson, Donald. *Essays on Actions and Events*. Oxford: Clarendon, 1980.

De Silva, Padmasiri. *An Introduction to Buddhist Psychology*. Lanham, MD: Rowman & Littlefield, 2000.

De Silva, Padmasiri. "Theoretical Perspectives on Emotions in Early Buddhism." In *Emotions in Asian Thought*, edited by Joel Marks and Roger T. Ames, 109–20. Albany: State University of New York Press, 1995.

Derrett, J. Duncan M. "*Musāvāda-virati* and 'Privileged Lies.'" *Journal of Buddhist Ethics*. 13 (2006): 1–18.

Desjarlais, Robert. *Body and Emotion: The Aesthetics of Illness and Healing in the Nepal Himalayas*. Philadelphia: University of Pennsylvania Press, 1992.

Desjarlais, Robert. *Sensory Biograpies: Lives and Deaths among Nepal's Yolmo Buddhists*. Berkeley: University of California Press, 2003.

Devdas, Nalini. *Cetanā and the Dynamics of Volition in Theravāda Buddhism*. Delhi: Motital Banarsidass, 2008.

Dhirasekera, Jotiya. *Buddhist Monastic Discipline*. Colombo, Sri Lanka: M. D. Gunasena, 1982.

Dihle, Albrecht. *The Theory of Will in Classical Antiquity*. Berkeley: University of California Press, 1982.

Dreyfus, Georges. "Meditation as Ethical Activity." *Journal of Buddhist Ethics* 2 (1995): 28–54.

Duff, R. A. *Intention, Agency and Criminal Liability: Philosophy of Action and the Criminal Law*. Oxford: Basil Blackwell, 1990.

Eberhardt, Nancy. *Imagining the Course of Life: Self Transformation in a Shan Buddhist Community*. Honolulu: University of Hawai'i Press, 2006.

Eilberg-Schwartz, Howard. *The Human Will in Judaism: The Mishnah's Philosophy of Intention*. Atlanta, GA: Scholars Press, 1986.

Ekman, Paul. *Emotions Revealed: Recognizing Faces and Feelings to Improve Communication and Emotional Life*. New York: Times Books, 2003.

Endo, Toshiichi. "Buddhaghosa's Role as a Commentator: Faithful Translator or Critical Editor?" *Buddhist Studies* 36 (2008): 1–37.

Endo, Toshiichi. "Some Observations on the 'Introductory Sections' of the Pāli Commentaries." *Journal of the Centre for Buddhist Studies, Sri Lanka* 7 (2009): 196–207.

Federman, Asaf. "What Kind of Free Will Did the Buddha Teach? *Philosophy East and West*. 60, no. 1 (2010): 1–19.

Fiering, Norman. *Jonathan Edwards's Moral Thought and Its British Context*. Chapel Hill: University of North Carolina Press, 1981.

Fiering, Norman. *Moral Psychology at Seventeenth-Century Harvard: A Discipline in Transition*. Chapel Hill: University of North Carolina Press, 1981.

Finot, M. Louis. "The Legend of Buddhaghosa." *Journal of the Department of Letters*, University of Calcutta. 2 (1924): 65–86.

Foucault, Michel. "About the Beginning of the Hermeneutics of the Self." In *Religion and Culture*, edited by Jeremy Carrette, 158–81. New York: Routledge, 1999.

Foucault, Michel. "The Ethics of the Concern of the Self as a Practice of Freedom." In *Ethics: Subjectivity and Truth*, edited by Paul Rabinow, 281–301. New York: New Press, 1994.

Foucault, Michel. "On the Genealogy of Ethics: An Overview of Work in Progress." In *The Foucault Reader*, edited by Paul Rabinow, 340–72. London: Penguin, 1984.

Foucault, Michel. "Technologies of the Self." In *Technologies of the Self*, edited by Luther Martin, Huck Gutman, and Patrick Hutton, 16–49. Amherst: University of Massachusetts Press, 1988.

Foucault, Michel. "What Is an Author?" In *The Foucault Reader*, edited by Paul Rabinow, 101–20. New York: Penguin, 1984.

Frankfurt, Henry. "Freedom of the Will and the Concept of a Person." In *The Importance of What We Care About: Philosophical Essays*, edited by Henry Frankfurt, 11–25. Cambridge: Cambridge University Press, 1988.

Frauwallner, Erich. *Studies in Abhidharma Literature and the Origins of Buddhist Philosophical Systems*. Translated from the German by Sophie Francis Kidd. Albany: State University of New York Press, 1995.

French, Rebecca Redwood. *The Golden Yoke: The Legal Cosmology of Buddhist Tibet*. Ithaca, NY: Cornell University Press, 1995.

Fuller, Paul. *The Notion of Diṭṭhi in Theravāda Buddhism*. New York: Routledge, 2005.

Gadamer, Hans-Georg. *Truth and Method*. Translated by Joel Weinsheimer and Donald Marshall. London: Continuum, 1989.

Garfield, Jay. "What Is It Like to Be a Bodhisattva? Moral Phenomenology in Śāntideva's *Bodhicaryāvatāra*." *JIABS*. 33, nos. 1–2 (2010–11): 333–57.

Geiger, Wilhelm. *Pali Language and Literature*. Translated from the German by Batakrishna Ghosh. New Delhi: Munshiram Manoharlal, 1978.

Gethin, Rupert. *The Buddhist Path to Awakening: A Study of the Bodhi-Pakkhiyā Dhammā*. Leiden: E. J. Brill, 1992.

Gethin, Rupert. "Can Killing a Living Being Ever Be an Act of Compassion? The Analysis of the Act of Killing in the Abhidhamma and Pali Commentaries." *Journal of Buddhist Ethics.* 11 (2004): 168–202.

Gethin, Rupert. *The Foundations of Buddhism.* Oxford: Oxford University Press, 1998.

Gethin, Rupert. "He Who Sees Me Sees Dhammas: Dhamma in Early Buddhism." *Journal of Indian Philosophy* 32 (2004): 513–42.

Gethin, Rupert. "The *Mātikās*: Memorization, Mindfulness, and the List." In *In the Mirror of Memory: Reflections on Mindfulness and Remembrance in Indian and Tibetan Buddhism,* edited by Janet Gyatso, 149–72. Albany: State University of New York Press, 1992.

Gethin, Rupert. "On the Nature of *Dhammas*: A Review Article." *Buddhist Studies Review* 22 (2005): 175–94.

Gibbs, Raymond. "Intentions as Emergent Products of Social Interactions." In *Intentions and Intentionality: Foundations of Social Cognition,* edited by Bertram Malle et al., 105–22. Cambridge,MA: MIT Press, 2001.

Glendinning, Simon. *In the Name of Phenomenology.* New York: Routledge, 2007.

Gombrich, Richard. *How Buddhism Began: The Conditioned Genesis of the Early Teachings.* New Delhi: Munshiram Manoharlal, 1997.

Gombrich, Richard. "Merit Detached from Volition: How a Buddhist Doctrine Came to Wear a Jain Aspect." In *Jainism and Early Buddhism: Essays in Honor of Padmanabh S. Jaini,* edited by Olle Qvarnström, 427–40. Fremont, CA: Asian Humanities Press, 2003.

Gombrich, Richard. *Precept and Practice.* Oxford: Oxford University Press, 1971.

Gombrich, Richard. *Theravāda Buddhism: A Social History from Ancient Banaras to Modern Colombo.* London: Routledge, 1988.

Gombrich, Richard. *What the Buddha Thought.* London: Equinox, 2009.

Gómez, Luis O. "Some Aspects of the Free-Will Question in the Nikāyas." *Philosophy East and West.* 25, no. 1 (1975): 81–90.

Goodman, Charles. *Consequences of Compassion: An Interpretation and Defense of Buddhist Ethics.* Oxford: Oxford University Press, 2009.

Gray, James, trans. *Buddhaghosuppatti, or the Historical Romance of the Rise and Career of Buddhaghosa.* Oxford: Pali Text Society, 2001.

Griffiths, Paul. "Denaturalizing Discourse: Ābhidhārmikas, Propositionalists, and the Comparative Philosophy of Religion." In *Myth and Philosophy,* edited by Frank Reynolds and David Tracy, 57–91. Albany: State University of New York Press, 1990.

Guenther, Herbert. *Philosophy and Psychology in the Abhidharma.* Berkeley, CA: Shambhala, 1976.

Gyatso, Janet. "One Plus One Makes Three: Buddhist Gender, Monasticism, and the Law of the Excluded Middle." *History of Religions* 43, no. 2 (2003): 89–115.

Gyatso, Janet. "Sex." In *Critical Terms for the Study of Buddhism,* edited by Donald S. Lopez, 271–90. Chicago: University of Chicago Press, 2005.

Hadot, Pierre. *Philosophy as a Way of Life*. Malden, MA: Blackwell, 1995.

Hadot, Pierre. *The Present Alone Is Our Happiness: Conversations with Jeannie Carlier and Arnold I. Davidson*. Translated by Marc Djaballah. Stanford, CA: Stanford University Press, 2009.

Hallisey, Charles. "Ethical Particularism in Theravāda Buddhism." *Journal of Buddhist Ethics* 3 (1996): 32–43.

Hallisey, Charles. "In Defense of Rather Fragile and Local Achievement: Reflections on the Work of Gurulugomi." In *Religion and Practical Reason*, edited by Frank Reynolds and David Tracy, 121–60. Albany: State University of New York Press, 1994.

Hallisey, Charles. "A Response to Kevin Schilbrack." *Journal of Buddhist Ethics*. 4 (1997): 184–88.

Hallisey, Charles, and Anne Hansen. "Narrative, Sub-Ethics, and the Moral Life: Some Evidence from Theravāda Buddhism." *Journal of Religious Ethics* 24, no. 2 (1996): 305–27.

Hansen, Anne. *How to Behave: Buddhism and Modernity in Colonial Cambodia, 1860–1930*. Honolulu: University of Hawai'i Press, 2007.

Hansen, Anne. "Story and World: The Ethics of Moral Vision in the Gatilok of Ukna Suttanta Prija Ind." *Udaya* 3 (2002): 45–64.

Hara, Minoru. "A Note on Vinaya." *Journal of the Pali Text Society*. 29 (2007): 285–311.

Harrison, Simon. *Augustine's Way into the Will*. Oxford: Oxford University Press, 2006.

Harvey, Peter. "Avoiding Unintended Harm to the Environment and the Buddhist Ethic of Intention." *Journal of Buddhist Ethics*. 14 (2007): 1–34.

Harvey, Peter. "Criteria for Judging the Unwholesomeness of Actions in the Texts of Theravāda Buddhism." *Journal of Buddhist Ethics*. 2 (1995): 140–51.

Harvey, Peter. "Freedom of the Will in Light of Theravāda Buddhist Teachings." *Journal of Buddhist Ethics*. 14 (2007): 35–98.

Harvey, Peter. *An Introduction to Buddhist Ethics*. Cambridge: University of Cambridge, 2000.

Harvey, Peter. "Review of *The Five Aggregates: Understanding Theravada Psychology and Soteriology*." *Journal of Buddhist Ethics*. 3 (1996): 91–97.

Harvey, Peter. "Vinaya Principles for Assigning Degrees of Culpability." *Journal of Buddhist Ethics*. 6 (1999): 271–91.

Hayes, Richard. "The Analysis of Karma in Vasubandhu's *Abhidharmakośa-bhāṣya*." In *Hermeneutical Paths to the Sacred Worlds of India*, edited by Katherine K. Young, 16–39. Atlanta, GA: Scholars Press, 1994.

Heim, Maria. "The Aesthetics of Excess." *Journal of the American Academy of Religion* 71, no. 3 (2003): 531–54.

Heim, Maria. "Buddhism." In *The Oxford Handbook of Religion and Emotion*, edited by John Corrigan, 17–34. Oxford: Oxford University Press, 2007.

Heim, Maria. "The Conceit of Self-Loathing." *Journal of Indian Philosophy* 37 (2009): 61–74.

Heim, Maria. "Shame and Apprehension: Notes on the Moral Value of *Hiri* and *Ottappa*." In *Embedded Languages: Studies in the Religion, Culture, and History of Sri Lanka*, edited by Carol Anderson, Susanne Mrozik, W. M. Wijeratna, and R. M. W. Rajapaksha, 237–60. Colombo, Sri Lanka: Godage, 2012.

Heim, Maria. *Theories of the Gift in South Asia*. New York: Routledge, 2004.

Heim, Maria. "Toward a 'Wider and Juster Initiative': Recent Comparative Work in Buddhist Ethics." *Religion Compass*. 1 (2006): 1–13.

Hobbes, Thomas. *Leviathan*, edited by Richard Tuck. Cambridge: Cambridge University Press, 1994 (1651).

Holt, John. *Discipline: The Canonical Buddhism of the Vinayapiṭaka*. Delhi: Motilal Bandarsidass, 1983.

Horner, I. B., trans. *The Book of the Discipline*, 6 volumes. London: Pali Text Society, 1949–1966.

Horner, I. B., trans. *Milinda's Questions (Milindapañho)*, 2 volumes. London: Pali Text Society, 1963.

Horner, I. B. *Women under Primitive Buddhism: Laywomen and Almswomen*. New York: Dutton, 1930.

Hüsken, Ute. "The Application of the Vinaya Term *nāsanā*." *Journal of the International Association of Buddhist Studies* 20, no. 2 (1997): 93–111.

Hutto, Daniel. *Folk Psychological Narratives: The Sociocultural Basis of Understanding Reasons*. Cambridge,MA: MIT Press, 2008.

Huxley, Andrew. "Buddhism and Law—The View from Mandalay." *Journal of the International Association of Buddhist Studies* 18, no. 1 (1995): 47–95.

Huxley, Andrew. "Buddhist Case Law on Theft: The *Vinītivatthu* on the Second *Pārājika*." *Journal of Buddhist Ethics* 6 (1999): 313–30.

Huxley, Andrew. "The Kurudhamma: From Ethics to Statecraft." *Journal of Buddhist Ethics* 2 (1995): 191–203.

Huxley, Andrew. "The Vinaya—Legal System or Performance-Enhancing Drug?" *The Buddhist Forum*, vol. 4. London: SOAS, 1996.

Izmirlieva, Valentina. *All the Names of the Lord*. Chicago: University of Chicago Press, 2008.

Jaini, Padmanabh, "Indian Perspectives on the Spirituality of Animals." In *Collected Papers on Jaina Studies*, edited by Padmanabh Jaini, 253–66. New Delhi: Motilal Banarsidass, 2000.

Jaini, Padmanabh. *"The Sautrāntika Theory of Bīja."* In *Collected Papers on Buddhist Studies*, edited by Padmanabh S. Jaini, 219–37. Delhi: Motilal Banarsidass, 2001.

James, Susan. *Passion and Action: The Emotions in Seventeenth-Century Philosophy*. Oxford: Clarendon, 1997.

Jayasuriya, W. F. *The Psychology and Philosophy of Buddhism*. Kuala Lumpur, Malaysia: Buddhist Missionary Society, 1976.

Jayatillake, K. N. "Some Problems of Translation and Interpretation." *University of Ceylon Review*. 7 (1949): 208–24.

Jayawickrama, N. A., trans. *The Inception of Discipline and the Vinaya Nidāna*. London: Pali Text Society, 1986.

Jayawickrama, N. A., trans. *The Story of Gotama Buddha (Jātaka-nidāna)*. Oxford: Pali Text Society, 2002.

Jonsen, Albert, and Stephen Toulmin. *The Abuse of Casuistry: A History of Moral Reasoning*. Berkeley: University of California Press, 1988.

Kagan, Jerome. "The Meaning of Psychological Predicates." *American Psychologist* 43, no. 8 (1988): 614–20.

Kahn, Charles H. "Discovering the Will: From Aristotle to Augustine." In *The Question of "Eclecticism": Studies in Later Greek Philosophy*, edited by John M. Dillon and A. A. Long, 234–59. Berkeley: University of California Press, 1988.

Kant, Immanuel. *Anthropology from a Pragmatic Point of View*. Edited by Robert B. Louden. Cambridge: Cambridge University Press, 2006.

Kapstein, Matthew. *Reason's Traces: Identity and Interpretation in Indian and Tibetan Buddhist Thought*. Somerville, MA: Wisdom, 2001.

Karunadasa, Y. *The Dhamma Theory: Philosophical Cornerstone of the Abhidhamma*. Kandy, Sri Lanka: Buddhist Publication Society, 1996.

Karunaratna, W. S. "*Cetanā*." In *The Encyclopedia of Buddhism*, edited by Jotiya Dhirasekera et al., 86–97. Government of Sri Lanka: Government Press, 1979.

Keith, Arthur Berriedale. *Buddhist Philosophy in India and Ceylon*. Oxford: Clarendon, 1923.

Kenny, Anthony. *Action, Emotion, and Will*. London: Routledge & Kegan Paul, 1963.

Keown, Damien. *Buddhism and Bioethics*. Basingstoke, England: Palgrave, 2001.

Keown, Damien. *The Nature of Buddhist Ethics*. New York: St. Martins Press, 1992.

Keyes, Charles, and Daniel E. Valentine, eds. *Karma: An Anthropological Inquiry*. Berkeley: University of California Press, 1983.

La Vallée Poussin, Louis de, trans. *Abhidharmakośabhāṣyam*, 6 volumes. Translated from the French by Leo Pruden. Berkeley: Asian Humanities Press, 1988.

Lang, Karen. *Four Illusions: Candrakīrti's Advice for Travelers on the Bodhisattva Path*. New York: Oxford University Press, 2003.

Law, Bimala Churn, trans. *The Debates Commentary (Kathāvatthuppakaraṇa-aṭṭhakathā)*. London: Pali Text Society, 1969.

Law, Bimala Churn. *A History of Pali Literature*. Delhi: Indological Book House, 1983.

Law, Bimala Churn. *The Life and Work of Buddhaghosa*. Calcutta: Thacker, Spink, 1923.

Locke, John. *An Essay Concerning Human Understanding*. Edited by Peter Nidditch. Oxford: Clarendon, 1975 (1690).

Louden, Robert. *Kant's Impure Ethics: From Rational Beings to Human Beings*. New York: Oxford, 2000.

MacIntyre, Alasdair. *After Virtue*. Notre Dame, IN: University of Notre Dame Press, 1984.

Mahmood, Saba. *Politics of Piety: The Islamic Revival and the Feminist Subject*. Princeton, NJ: Princeton University Press, 2005.

Malalasekera, G. P. *The Pāli Literature of Ceylon*. Kandy,Ceylon: Buddhist Publication Society, 1994.

Malle, Bertram. "Folk Explanations of Intentional Action." In *Intentions and Intentionality: Foundations of Social Cognition*, edited by Bertram Malle et al., 265–86. Cambridge, MA: MIT Press, 2001.

Malle, Bertram, and Joshua Knobe. "The Distinction between Desire and Intention: A Folk-Conceptual Analysis." In *Intentions and Intentionality: Foundations of Social Cognition*, edited by Bertram Malle et al., 45–67. Cambridge, MA: MIT Press, 2001.

Malle, Bertram, Louis Moses, and Dare Baldwin, eds. *Intentions and Intentionality: Foundations of Social Cognition*. Cambridge,MA: MIT Press, 2001.

Marshall, James. *Intention in Law and Society*. New York: Funk and Wagnalls, 1968.

Matthews, Bruce. *Craving and Salvation: A Study in Buddhist Soteriology*. Waterloo, Ontario: Wilfrid Laurier University Press, 1983.

Matthews, Bruce. "Notes on the Concept of the Will in Early Buddhism." *Sri Lanka Journal of the Humanities* (1975): 152–60.

Maung Tin, Pe, and C. A. F. Rhys Davids, trans. *The Expositor (Atthasālinī)*. London: Pali Text Society, 1969.

McDermott, James. *Development in the Early Buddhist Concept of Kamma/Karma*. New Delhi: Munshiram Manoharlal, 1984.

McDermott, James. "Kamma in the *Milindapañha*." *Journal of the American Oriental Society* 97, no. 4 (1977): 460–68.

McDermott, James. "The *Kathāvatthu* Kamma Debates." *Journal of the American Oriental Society* 95, no. 3 (1975): 424–33.

McDermott, James. "Scripture as the Word of the Buddha." *Numen* 31 (1984): 22–38.

McMahan, David. *The Making of Buddhist Modernism*. New York: Oxford University Press, 2008.

McReynolds, Paul. *Four Early Works on Motivation*. Gainesville, FL: Scholars Facsimiles and Reprints, 1969.

Meyers, Karin. *Freedom and Self Control: Free Will in South Asian Buddhism*. Chicago: University of Chicago, Ph.D. dissertation, 2010.

Mills, Lawrence C. R. "The Case of the Murdered Monks." *Journal of the Pali Text Society*. 16 (1992): 171–75.

Mishra, Pankaj. *An End of Suffering: The Buddha in the World*. New York: Picador, 2004.

Mori, Sodo. "Recent Japanese Studies in the Pāli Commentarial Literature: Since 1984." *Journal of the Pali Text Society*. 29 (2007): 175–90.

Mumford, Stan Royal. *Himalayan Dialogue: Tibetan Lamas and Gurung Shamans in Nepal*. Madison: University of Wisconsin Press, 1989.

Murcott, Susan. *The First Buddhist Women: Translations and Commentary on the Therigatha*. Berkeley, CA: Parallax, 1991.

Murdoch, Iris. *The Sovereignty of Good*. London: Routledge and Kegan Paul, 2009 (1971).

Ñāṇamoli, Bhikkhu, trans. *The Discourse on Right View: The Sammādiṭṭhi Sutta and Its Commentary*. Kandy, Sri Lanka: Buddhist Publication Society, 1981.

Ñāṇamoli, Bhikkhu, trans. *The Dispeller of Delusion (Sammohavinodanī)*, 2 volumes. London: Pali Text Society, 1996.

Ñāṇamoli, Bhikkhu, trans. *The Minor Readings (Khuddakapāṭha)*. London: Pali Text Society, 1978.

Ñāṇamoli, Bhikkhu, trans. *The Path of Purification* (*Visuddhimagga*), 5th ed. Kandy, Sri Lanka: Buddhist Publication Society, 1991.

Ñāṇamoli, Bhikkhu, and Bhikkhu Bodhi, trans. *The Middle Length Discourses of the Buddha: A Translation of the Majjhima Nikāya*. Somerville,MA: Wisdom, 2001.

Nārada, Mahāthera, and Bhikkhu Bodhi, trans. *A Comprehensive Manual of Abhidhamma: The Abhidhamma Sangaha of Ācarya Anuruddha*. Kandy, Sri Lanka: Buddhist Publication Society, 1993.

Norman, K. R. *Pāli Literature*. Wiesbaden: Otto Harrassowitz, 1983.

Nussbaum, Martha. *Love's Knowledge: Essays on Philosophy and Literature*. New York: Oxford University Press, 1992.

Nussbaum, Martha. *Upheavals of Thought: The Intelligence of Emotions*. Cambridge: Cambridge University Press, 2001.

Nyanaponika, Thera. *Abhidhamma Studies: Buddhist Explorations of Consciousness and Time*. Somerville, MA: Wisdom, 1998.

Nyanatiloka, Mahathera. *Guide through the Abhidhamma-Piṭaka*. Kandy, Ceylon: Buddhist Publication Society, 1983.

Obeyesekere, Ranjini, and Gananath Obeyesekere. "The Tale of the Demoness Kāḷī: A Discourse on Evil." *History of Religions* 24, no. 4 (1990): 318–34.

O'Flaherty, Wendy Doniger, ed. *Karma and Rebirth in Classical Indian Tradition*. New Delhi: Motilal Banarsidass, 1983.

Palihawadana, Mahinda. "Dhammapada 1 and 2 and Their Commentaries." In *Buddhist Studies in Honour of Hammalava Saddhātissa*, edited by Dhammapala et al., 189–202. Nugegoda, Sri Lanka: University of Sri Jayewardenepura, 1984.

Payutto, Phra. *Buddhadhamma: Natural Laws and Values for Life*. Translated by Grant Olson. Albany: State University of New York, 1995.

Payutto, Phra. *Good, Evil, and Beyond*. Translated by Bruce Evans. Buddha Dhamma Education Association (www.buddhanet.net/pdf_file/good_evil_beyond.pdf).

Peters, R. S. *The Concept of Motivation*. New York: Humanities Press, 1960.

Pettit, Philip. "Desire." In *Routledge Encyclopedia of Philosophy*, edited by E. Craig. London: Routledge, 1998.

Pocket, Susan, William Banks, and Shaun Gallagher, eds. *Does Consciousness Cause Behavior?* Cambridge, MA: MIT Press, 2006.

Pollock, Sheldon. "Future Philology? The Fate of a Soft Science in a Hard World." *Critical Inquiry*. 35 (2009): 931–61.

Premasiri, P. D. "Early Buddhist Concept of Ethical Knowledge: A Philosophical Analysis." In *Buddhist Philosophy and Culture: Essays in Honor of N. A. Jayawickrema*, edited by D. Kalupahana and W. G. Weeraratne. Colombo,Sri Lanka: N. A. Jayawickrema Felicitation Volume Committee, 1987.

Premasiri, P. D. "Interpretation of Two Principal Ethical Terms in Early Buddhism." *Sri Lanka Journal of the Humanities*. 2, no. 1 (1976): 63–74.

Pruitt, William, trans. *The Commentary on the Verses of the Therīs*. Oxford: Pali Text Society, 1999.

Rahula, Walpola, and Sara Boin-Webb, trans. *Abhidharmasamuccaya: The Compendium of Higher Teaching*. Fremont, CA: Asian Humanities Press, 2001.

Rhys Davids, C. A. F. *The Birth of Indian Psychology and Its Development on Buddhism*. London: Luzac, 1936.

Rhys Davids, C. A. F., trans. *A Buddhist Manual of Psychological Ethics (Dhamma-saṅgani)*. London: Royal Asiatic Society, 1923.

Rhys Davids, C. A. F. "On the Will in Buddhism." *Journal of the Royal Asiatic Society of Great Britain and Ireland* (1898): 47–59.

Rhys Davids, T. W. "Translators Introduction." In V. Fausböll, trans. *Buddhist Birth Stories*. London: Trübner, 1880.

Rhys Davids, T. W., and William Stede. *The Pali Text Society's Pali-English Dictionary*. Oxford: Pali Text Society, 1992.

Ricoeur, Paul. *Interpretation Theory: Discourse and the Surplus of Meaning*. Fort Worth, TX: Texas Christian University Press, 1976.

Ronkin, Noa. *Early Buddhist Metaphysics: The Making of a Philosophical Tradition*. New York: Routledge Curzon, 2005.

Rosen, Lawrence, ed. *Other Intentions: Cultural Contexts and the Attribution of Inner States*. Santa Fe, NM: School of American Research Press, 1995.

Rosenthal, Edward. *The Era of Choice: The Ability to Choose and Its Transformation of Contemporary Life*. Cambridge, MA: MIT Press, 2006.

Ryle, Gilbert. *The Concept of Mind*. New York: Barnes and Noble, 1949.

Sadaw, Ledi. "Some Points in Buddhist Doctrine." *Journal of the Pali Text Society*. 14 (1913–14): 115–69.

Saddhānanda, Nedimāle, ed. "Saddhammasangaha." *Journal of the Pali Text Society*. 4 (1890).

Scheer, Richard. "Intentions, Motives, and Causation." *Philosophy* 76, no. 3 (2001): 397–413.

Scheer, Richard. "The 'Mental State' Theory of Intentions." *Philosophy* 79, no. 1 (2004): 121–31.

Scheer, Richard. "The Origin of Intentions." *Philosophical Investigations* 29, no. 4 (2006): 358–68.

Schneewind, J. B. *The Invention of Autonomy: A History of Modern Moral Philosophy*. Cambridge: Cambridge University Press, 1998.

Schofer, Jonathan Wyn. *The Making of a Sage: A Study in Rabbinic Ethics*. Madison: University of Wisconsin Press, 2005.

Schopen, Gregory. "The Buddhist Bhikṣu's Obligaton to Support His Parents in Two Vinaya Traditions." *Journal of the Pali Text Society*. 29 (2007): 107–36.

Schopen, Gregory. "Ritual Rites and Bones of Contention: More on Monastic Funerals and Relics in the *Mūlasarvāstivāda-vinaya*." In *Buddhist Monks and Business Matters, edited by Gregory Schopen*, 285–328. Honolulu: University of Hawai'i Press, 2004.

Searle, J. R. "Collective Intentions and Actions." In *Intentions in Communication*, edited by J. M. P. R. Cohen, M. Pollack, and E. Pollack, 401–16. Cambridge, MA: MIT Press, 1990.

Searle, J. R. *Intentionality: An Essay in the Philosophy of Mind*. Cambridge: Cambridge University Press, 1983.

Shih Juo-Hsüeh, Bhikkhunī. *Controversies over Buddhist Nuns*. Oxford: Pali Text Society, 2000.

Shweder, Richard. *Thinking through Cultures: Expeditions in Cultural Psychology*. Cambridge, MA: Harvard University Press, 1991.

Sinnott-Armstrong, Walter. "Keynote." *Contemporary Perspectives on Buddhist Ethics*, conference at Columbia University, October 6–7, 2011 (www.cbs.columbia.edu/buddhist_ethics/keynote-two.html).

Skilling, Peter. "Scriptural Authenticity and the Śrāvaka Schools: An Essay towards an Indian Perspective." *Eastern Buddhist* 41, no. 2 (2010): 1–47.

Skilling, Peter. "Theravāda in History." *Pacific World*. 11 (2009): 61–93.

Sorabji, Richard. *Emotion and Peace of Mind: From Stoic Agitation to Christian Temptation*. Oxford: Oxford University Press, 2000.

Stalnaker, Aaron. *Overcoming Our Evil: Human Nature and Spiritual Exercises in Xunxi and Augustine*. Washington, DC: Georgetown University Press, 2006.

Streng, Frederick. "Reflections on the Attention Given to Mental Construction in the Indian Buddhist Analysis of Causality." *Philosophy East and West*. 25, no. 1 (1975): 71–80.

Thanissaro Bhikkhu. *The Buddhist Monastic Code*. Valley Center, CA: Thanissaro Bhikkhu. 1994.

Thittila, Ashin, trans. *The Book of Analysis (Vibhaṅga)*. London: Pali Text Society, 1969.

U Narada, trans. *Conditional Relations (Paṭṭhāna)*. London: Pali Text Society, 1969.

U Thiṭṭila, trans. *The Book of Analysis (Vibhaṅga)*. London: Pali Text Society, 1969.

Velez de Cea, Abraham "The Criteria of Goodness in the Pāli Nikāyas and the Nature of Buddhist Ethics." *Journal of Buddhist Ethics* 11 (2004): 123–42.

von Hinüber, Oskar. "The Arising of an Offense: *āpattisamuṭṭhāna*." *Journal of the Pali Text Society*. 16 (1992): 55–69.

von Hinüber, Oskar. "Buddhist Law According to the Theravāda Vinaya: A Survey of Theory and Practice." *Journal of the International Association of Buddhist Studies* 18, no. 1 (1995): 7–45.

von Hinüber, Oskar. "Buddhist Law According to the Theravāda Vinaya II: Some Additions and Corrections." *Journal of the International Association of Buddhist Studies* 20, no. 2 (1997): 87–92.

von Hinüber, Oskar. *A Handbook of Pāli Literature*. New Delhi: Munshiram Manoharlal, 1997.

Wagner, Roy. "Hazarding Intent: Why Sogo Left Hweabi." In *Other Intentions: Cultural Contexts and the Attribution of Inner States*, edited by Lawrence Rosen, 161–75. Santa Fe, NM: School of American Research Press, 1995.

Walshe, Maurice, trans. *The Long Discourses of the Buddha: A Translation of the Dīgha Nikāya*. Boston: Wisdom, 1995.

Wayman, Alex. "Discussion of Frederick Streng's 'Reflections on the Attention Given to Mental Construction in the Indian Buddhist Analysis of Causality' and Luis O. Gomez's 'Some Aspects of the Free-Will Question in the Nikāyas.'" *Philosophy East and West*. 25, no. 1 (1975): 91–93.

Wickramasinghe, Martin. *The Buddhist Jataka Stories and the Russian Novel*. Colombo: Associated Newspapers of Ceylon, 1956.

Wijayaratna, Mohan. *Buddhist Monastic Life According to the Texts of the Theravāda Tradition*. Translated by Claude Grangier and Steven Collins. Cambridge: Cambridge University Press, 1990.

Wijeratne, R. P., and Rupert Gethin, trans. *Summary of the Topics of Abhidhamma and Exposition of the Topics of Abhidhamma* (*Abhidhammatthasaṅgaha* and *Abhidhammatthavibhāvinī*). Oxford: Pali Text Society, 2002.

Index